Power, Policy and Profit

Corporate Engagement in Politics and Governance

Edited by

Christina Garsten

Professor of Social Anthropology, Department of Social Anthropology and Stockholm Centre for Organizational Research (SCORE), Stockholm University, Sweden

Adrienne Sörbom

Associate Professor of Sociology, Stockholm Centre for Organizational Research (SCORE), Stockholm University, Sweden

Cheltenham, UK • Northampton, MA, USA

Published by
Edward Elgar Publishing Limited
The Lypiatts
15 Lansdown Road
Cheltenham
Glos GL50 2JA
UK

Edward Elgar Publishing, Inc.
William Pratt House
9 Dewey Court
Northampton
Massachusetts 01060
USA

A catalogue record for this book
is available from the British Library

Library of Congress Control Number: 2017939801

This book is available electronically in the **Elgar**online
Business subject collection
DOI 10.4337/9781784711214

ISBN 978 1 78471 120 7 (cased)
ISBN 978 1 78471 121 4 (eBook)

Typeset by Servis Filmsetting Ltd, Stockport, Cheshire
Printed and bound in Great Britain by TJ International Ltd, Padstow

Contents

Contributors

Franck Aggeri, Professor of Management Science, CGS, MINES ParisTech, France.

Eva Boxenbaum, Professor, Centre de Gestion Scientifique, PSL – MINES ParisTech, France.

Jean-Yves Caneill, PhD, Head of Climate Policy at Électricité de France (EDF), France.

Mélodie Cartel, Assistant Professor, Department Management & Technology, Grenoble School of Management, France.

Marie-Laure Salles-Djelic, Sciences Po, Centre de Sociologie des Organisations (CSO), Paris, France.

Hervé Dumez, Professor, École polytechnique, Director of Research at I3/CRG, Centre National de la Recherche Scientifique (CNRS), France.

Mikkel Flyverbom, Associate Professor, Department of Management, Society and Communication, Copenhagen Business School, Denmark.

Christina Garsten, Professor, Department of Social Anthropology, Stockholm University, Sweden.

Alain Jeunemaître, Professor, École polytechnique, Director of Research at I3/CRG, Centre National de la Recherche Scientifique (CNRS), France.

Anette Nyqvist, Associate Professor, Department of Social Anthropology, Stockholm University, Sweden.

Mar Pérezts, Associate Professor in Management, Law and Human Resources, emlyon business school, MDRH Department & OCE Research Center, France.

Xavier Philippe, Associate Professor in Human Resources Management and Sociology of Work, EM Normandie & Métis Lab, France.

Sébastien Picard, Professor of Corporate Political Behavior, SCUNIV – Singapore Corporate University, Singapore.

Bo Rothstein, Professor, Blavatnik School of Government, University of Oxford, UK.

Adrienne Sörbom, Associate Professor, Stockholm Centre for Organizational Research (SCORE), Stockholm University, Sweden.

Véronique Steyer, Assistant Professor in Management, i3-CRG, École polytechnique, CNRS, Université Paris Saclay, France.

Renita Thedvall, Associate Professor, Stockholm Centre for Organizational Research (SCORE), Stockholm University, Sweden.

Anna Tyllström, PhD, Institute for Futures Studies Stockholm, Sweden.

David A. Westbrook, Professor, School of Law, University of Buffalo, USA.

Acknowledgements

This book has materialized as the result of long-term and dynamic network connections between researchers in the social sciences sharing an interest in corporate influence on politics. Much experimentation, probing and analysis have taken place over the five years of exchange in the Govemark (Governance of Markets) network. We wish to thank all those who participated with ideas and papers in the Govemark network, first of all the contributors to this book, and also, in alphabetical order: Oana Brindusa Albu, Jonathan Alensky, Michael Barnett, Christoph Brumann, Steve Coleman, Jana Costas, Matilda Dahl, Colette Depeyre, Pauline Garvey, Malin Gawell, Patty Gray, Chris Grey, Martin Gustavsson, Melissa Fisher, Staffan Furusten, Hans Krause Hansen, Axel Haunschild, Frank den Hond, Dan Kärreman, Anna Leander, Monica Lindh de Montoya, Mark Maguire, Kathleen McNamara, Afshin Mehrpouya, Gwen Mikell, Peter Miller, Miguel Montoya, Fiona Murphy, Horacio Ortiz, Josef Pallas, Gustav Peebles, Ian Richardson, Jamie Saris, Mattias Schlögl, Ola Segnestam Larsson, JP Singh, Jens Stilhoff Sörensen, Tom Strong, Emma Svensson, Xavier C Tanghuy, Scott D Taylor, Steen Vallentin and Janine Wedel. We are grateful to the Swedish Foundation for Humanities and Social Sciences for funding the network activities of Govemark, and to the Stockholm Centre for Organizational Research (SCORE) at Stockholm University and Stockholm School of Economics for support.

To our contributing authors – it has been inspirational to work with you all! Thank you for sharing your research and your findings with us, for constructive conversations and for moving the field ahead. A large portion of the work for this book has blended in various ways with spheres other than academia, corporations or politics –with life itself. To our near and dear – our loving thanks.

Christina Garsten and Adrienne Sörbom
Stockholm, February 2017

Introduction: political affairs in the global domain

Christina Garsten and Adrienne Sörbom

INTRODUCTION: THE POLITICAL TURN OF BUSINESS

This book sets out to investigate the manifold ways in which corporate actors attempt to influence political activities in the broad sense, in other words activities aimed at influencing the development of society. It brings together scholars from different fields in the study of global governance, to address the rising influence and power of corporate actors on the political scene, at national and transnational levels. These questions are addressed throughout the book by way of illustrative cases demonstrating the various ways in which corporations pursue political activities in the broad sense and how they aim to influence policy. One by one and taken together the chapters present an understanding of how corporate governance is pursued and with what types of consequences.

Corporate ascendancy has emerged as a universal organizing principle in the contemporary world. Corporations, and their funded offsprings, appear as both heroes and villains in tales of political and policy change. Proponents often present them as the 'new', responsible kind of corporate actors that global politics need, building networks across national borders and contributing to multi-stakeholders' solutions to complex issues. Sceptics view them as cunning organizations, barely masking their financial interests behind a thin layer of social and political concern. Both camps, however, would not deny the fact that corporate influence in what was usually seen as a nation-state domain of political affairs, have gained tremendous leverage over the last few decades. Through vast ideological shifts in the late twentieth century, markets rather than governments came to be seen as the more effective governance and the road to prosperity. Governments came to seek out the managerial expertise, technology and investment resources that corporations can bring. The corporate social responsibility movement (CSR) expresses this contemporary and double image of the corporation, as both a potentially accountable 'corporate citizen', capable of regulating and overseeing its own activities and as a profit-seeking, expansionist exploiter of human and natural resources. On both accounts, the political dimension of the corporation and of CSR is highlighted (Scherer and Palazzo 2011; Vallentin and Murillo 2012).

We are witnessing what we may term the political turn of corporations. Whilst corporations have always aimed to exert a degree of influence on the political infrastructures in which they operate and on decisions pertaining to regulatory frameworks, this trend has lately been intensified. With the restructuring of the provision of welfare services, and the accumulation of private capital, opportunities for corporations to influence political affairs have multiplied (Barley 2010; Sklair 2001). In recent decades we have seen an increase in corporate activities aiming to influence policymakers' perceptions of a particular problem, as well as the institutional arrangements in which they conduct their business (Lawton et al. 2012). Corporations have gained increased influence in certain policy areas and broadened their influence onto other policy areas usually under public control. A wide variety of firms are now involved in political activities in industries as varied as oil and gas, air transport, information technology, tobacco and pharmaceuticals. There are as well high levels of corporate participation in political fields such as energy and environmental policy, transportation, education and health care at national levels (see for example, Braithwaite and Drahos 2000). Influence is exercised by a variety of means, such as political campaign contributions, lobbying with policymakers, interlocking of board memberships, setting up political action committees (PACs), by providing analyses and research, creating standards for social responsibility and transparency and, at times, even by way of bribery (see for instance Austen-Smith and Wright 1996; Delmas and Montes-Sancho 2010; Hansen and Mitchell 2000; Okhmatovskiy 2010; Ring et al. 1990; Spiller 1990; Yoffie and Bergenstein 1985). Corporations have been able to amplify their influence as not merely implementers of public policy, but as agenda-setters and co-authors of policy. Furthermore, the resources at the command of corporations to do so are more powerful than ever. Yet, this development has hitherto not gained the attention it deserves.

Relations between what is commonly perceived as the spheres of politics and business are dynamic and complex, and corporations stand in a dynamic and complex relation to politics and policy. Oftentimes, corporations are analysed as separate from political institutions, practices and visions; as dependent on them; as creatively responsive to them; or, as is often the case, as antagonistic to them. As Neil Fligstein (2001, p. 6) maintains, however, '[t]he frequently invoked opposition between governments and market actors, in which governments are simply viewed as intrusive and inefficient, and firms as efficient wealth producers, is simply wrong. Firms rely on governments and citizens for making markets.' In other words, to 'make markets' and to pursue their interests, corporations rely on appropriate political and regulatory structures, for which they need to organize accordingly. The scope of corporate influence in politics and policymaking varies with time and space. Irrespective of scope, corporate political activity is central for the organization of markets (Ahrne et al. 2015).

Globalization processes have made it both possible and necessary for corporations and corporate-funded organizations to act politically outside the nation-state arena. The extensive movement in favour of market-driven approaches to stimulate growth and improve living and working conditions put in place since the late 1970s has leveraged transnational corporations as legitimate actors with a part to play in an emerging system of global governance. Some of the big global questions, such as climate, forced migration, unemployment and threats to security, are now conceptualized as demanding transnational forms of collaboration into which corporations are often invited. A case in point is the G20 meetings, at which the role of business leadership in promoting and strengthening an open global market economy is now recognized to be central. Thus, large transnational corporations, such as The Evian Group, are invited to be part of deliberations. Another kind of arena for the fostering of interactions of state and non-state actors is the Club of Rome, a global think tank that deals with a variety of international political issues. Founded in 1968 at Accademia dei Lincei in Rome, Italy, the Club of Rome describes itself as 'a group of world citizens, sharing a common concern for the future of humanity'. It consists of current and former heads of state, UN bureaucrats, high-level politicians and government officials, diplomats, scientists, economists and business leaders from around the globe, convening to sort out issues of the contemporary state of affairs. One of its projects, to only give one example of the intersection of politics and corporations it constructs, regards 'circular economy', looking at the impact of a circular economy on jobs, carbon emissions and the trade balance in five different European economies, namely Finland, Sweden, France, the Netherlands and Spain. The results from the project were presented in front of the European Commission in October 2015 as an input to for the European Commission's package on Circular Economy, arguing that in all five countries, an economy based on circular resource flows would create jobs, reduce carbon emissions and improve the trade balance (http://www.clubofrome.org/project/circular_economy_and_societal_benefit/, accessed 3 July 2016). Another pertinent example is Microsoft Corporation, an organization whose financial assets override those of many nation-states. Some of the wealth accumulated by its founder, Bill Gates, has been channelled into the Bill and Melinda Gates Foundation, which is now one of the most resourceful foundations in the world. The foundation is in itself active globally in shaping policy agendas, for instance by being present at the meetings of the World Economic Forum, where it is given ample space to present its views and propositions before other world leaders, but it also sponsors think-tank based research and analysis which is drawn upon in wider political settings. Finally, the Foundation is commonly credited for eradicating malaria in Africa. In this way, Microsoft influences not only markets but also political institutions and organizations.

Corporate influence on the political arena is thus taking on new and powerful forms. Due to their financial and organizational resources and their structural importance to employment, economic growth and technological innovation, corporations are in a privileged position on the global arena compared to other actors. Corporate actors also benefit from a host of international regimes that prioritize policy objectives such as free trade and free investment flows over others such as sustainability. This is not to say, however, that corporate actors will always dominate policy processes or dictate outcomes. Other types of actors, mainly from civil society, are invited to the arenas. The standing of corporations in these settings are, however, a reflection of the varying sources of power available to different types of non-state actors and the relative strength of corporations. We may concur that the nature of global governance is shifting, and with it the balance between political actors. The articulation of transnational politics will depend on a number of aspects, such as the issue-specific circumstances and power resources brought into play, which may also benefit other non-state organizational actors rather than businesses in certain circumstances. In a globalizing world, political processes and their outcomes are likely to be more open-ended than ever before (Cerny 2010).

The amplification of globalization thus brings to the fore and highlights the multifarious ways in which governments and market actors are interdependently configured. Research into these kinds of activities is becoming all the more urgent and complex, not least because the pursuit of competitive advantage through political means may be ethically problematic and challenge established democratic procedures. What does such corporate engagement at transnational scale mean in terms of shaping policy priorities and agendas? What are the predominant ways by which corporate actors shape the way policymakers and politicians frame urgent problems? What are the means by which they contribute to defining what is the 'right way' forward?

This volume addresses the dynamic, complex and often conflictual relation of corporations to policy and power. This relation is indeed a long standing one, but one that keeps transforming along with geopolitical trends, financial fluctuations and social priorities. The relation is thus a moving target with potentially wide ramifications that calls for a close examination. Our starting point is that any investigation of emerging forms of global governance must now take into account the significance of corporate actors. A number of crucial questions call for attention: What are the mechanisms used by corporations and corporate-funded organizations to exert influence in the political sphere? What are the resources upon which such actions are based? What are the scenarios aimed for by the political activities of corporate actors? How do corporations and corporate-funded organizations achieve legitimacy as political actors? And what are the future prospects for democracy and welfare, as profit-driven actors engage in pursuing their interests in the public domain?

CORPORATE POLITICAL AFFAIRS AT LARGE

In this volume we focus our attention on corporations or corporate-funded organizations acting at national or transnational level to influence politics and policy. We take a broad perspective on politics, as relations involving authority, power, and the struggle for the allocation of resources and rights, taking place in most areas of day-to-day life as well as those commonly termed politics. Common to the authors of this book is thus the view of politics in the broad sense and taking a processual view on politics, implying that it is the continuous construction of interests and priorities, and the continuous negotiation and struggle over definitions of reality that concerns us most. In all chapters, it is the processes through which organizations attempt to gain influence and construct authority, rather than the resulting decisions and structures, which are in the limelight. Moreover, as stated by Andrew Abbott (2016, p. 41), there is no fixed 'topology of politics', no fixed location in which politics is done. Contemporary politics may take place outside of established political localities, in the interstices of political structures and with unconventional actors involved. In other words, places may be others than administrative councils, state agencies and formal legislatures and actors may be of many different kinds: corporate leaders, think tanks experts, PR-consultants, as well as elected politicians and civil servants. We also share the conviction that politics, as a social force, may be seen as productive as well as destructive (Spencer 2007). Politics allow for the mobilization of collectivities, for the articulation of shared and conflictual interests and ultimately for social change. The destructive side of politics means that collectivities may be torn by struggles over resources and access to decision-making arenas, and it may hinder social change and development. We wish, in other words, to work with an expansive notion of politics, which gives weight to the meaning-making, performative and aspirational dimensions of politics, beyond the instrumental (compare with Spencer 2007).

Policy is intimately related to politics, broadly seen as the ways in which politics is articulated and implemented. As pointed out by Wedel et al. (2005, p. 31):

> [i]n an ever-more inter-connected world, public policies, whether originating with governments, businesses, supranational entities, nongovernmental (NGOs), private actors, or some combination of these, are increasingly central to the organization of society. Policies connect disparate actors in complex power and resource relations and play a pervasive, though often indirect, role in shaping society.

Policy is not to be seen as produced by rational choice, measured by positivist models and transferred by straightforward diffusion. Such approaches tend to miss out the contestations over meaning negotiations and political struggles that are integral to policymaking. In contrast, policy processes are messy, socially produced and embedded in power hierarchies (Shore et al. 2011). A focus on policy as a 'connector' between diverse organizational actors is, we believe, a fruitful way to investigate emerging forms of governance, power and politics.

Our curiosity about corporations and their relation to politics and policy stems from an interest in the operations of power in contemporary society. We take inspiration from Nikolas Rose and Peter Miller's viewpoint (1992, p. 175) – that 'political power today is exercised through a profusion of shifting alliances between diverse authorities, to govern a multitude of facets of economic activity and social life.' The common political vocabulary, structured by differences between state and civil society, public and private, coercion and consent and the like, is no longer apt to characterize the diverse ways in which power is exercised in advanced liberal democracies at global level. To analyse these aspects of contemporary power, we need to relocate the state and the market and the concepts of politics and non-politics. Moreover, power is a complex matter, which, as stressed by Steven Lukes in the revised version of his now classic book, shall be seen as a capacity that is constructed and not something which actors have or have not. Power may or may not be exercised, and actors may or may not be powerful by satisfying others' interests (Lukes 2005, p. 12). Thus, the interesting aspect of power is not primarily over what corporations may be powerful, since that changes over time, but in what sense and by what means they create the capacity to make others follow their interests, however non-unified, conflicting and shifting these interests may be. This perspective serves as a launch pad for investigations into the operations of power across and among organizational spheres: the public, private and civil spheres – nationally and transnationally.

We conceptualize the profusion of shifting alliances between diverse authorities as part of a move towards new forms of global governance (Hall and Biersteker 2002; Scholte 2004; Rhodes 1996), more specifically as the development of new public domains in which the boundaries between spheres are not as clear (Ruggie 2004). In this transnational domain states are still highly important actors, but they are also devolving some of their authority to private actors, such as corporations, think tanks and policy institutes (Stone 2008). Characteristic for activities relating to the global domain is the relativization of the significance of national boundaries. Even if actors still have their base in a given geographical territory, their activities are not tied to that territory (compare with Scholte 1996; 2005). They are to be understood as transnational in their capacity to operate and influence beyond national borders. Compared to the political sphere of international relations, which rely on established institutional structures, actors and procedures, transnational relations are still in a state of formation, with structures still emerging, actors competing for space and influence among themselves, and procedures of often ad hoc, contingent or flexible character. This means that the boundaries of the global domain are somewhat permeable, offering opportunities for many different and capable actors to participate. Examples of such non-state organizations are the World Economic Forum, Brookings Institute, Fairtrade International Organization for Standardization, Motorola, Standard & Poor's, Transparency International and Freedom House. Conjunctly, they all testify to the fact that the regulation of social and political concerns is no longer the business of nation-states alone. The state has to share regulatory agency with other organizations, such as corporations, international governmental organizations and international non-governmental organizations. Whilst these actors may not have the 'hard' power exercised by the State by way of legal frameworks and sanctions, they work by crafting and diffusing norms, standards, codes of conduct and by putting into work political programmes for the transformation of minds and actions (Djelic and Quack 2010; Djelic and Sahlin-Andersson 2006). In Saskia Sassens's terminology (2003), new organizational 'sites of normativity' are appearing on the global scene, with power and resources to influence, shape and fashion the thoughts and actions of others.

The new global political domain that these actors are constructing is multilayered (Sassen 2006). It involves local, regional, state and transnational operations alongside and intertwined with each other. It involves a partial disaggregation of states as governments into extensive transnational networks, linking state authorities with international institutions, international non-governmental organizations and transnational corporations. Due to increasing crossover partnerships, global governance is more fragmented, decentralized and diffuse compared to nation-state based governing (Josselin and Wallace 2001; Scholte 2005). Regulation of global financial flows and social impacts of global market operations takes place through multilateral consultations and coordination. Representatives of corporations may consult, negotiate and make decisions with representatives of state departments, international organizations and so on. Corporate actors have learnt to exploit the space between state agencies, international organizations and INGOs, contributing to ever more complex multi-stakeholder constellations. Diane Stone (2008, p. 24) describes global policymaking as consisting of 'multilevel and polycentric forms of public policy in which a plethora of institutions and networks negotiate within and between international agreements and private regimes have emerged as pragmatic responses in the absence of formal governance'.

This also implies that matters of accountability, transparency and responsibility often become acute (Garsten and Lindh de Montoya 2008; Hansen 2012; Hansen and Flyverbom 2015; Hood and Heald 2006; West and Sanders 2003). Demands for transparency and accountability are raised by a variety of actors. The question is whether and to what extent corporations will take on the rights and the social obligations that accrue to them as legal entities whose activities have far-ranging implications for social lives. Furthermore, we may ask how these activities will be rendered transparency and accountability. Looking beyond accountability and transparency demands, an equally urgent question is how and to what extent corporations and corporate-funded organizations are themselves the architects of regulatory frameworks and governance structures. It is from this topical question that the authors of this book investigate corporate political activities.

Earlier research, as for instance in the impressive work of James Braithwaite and Peter Drahos (2000) regarding global economic regulation has clearly shown the importance of corporations in globalization processes, as has Leslie Sklair in his analysis of what he terms 'the new transnational capitalist class' (Sklair 2001). From the perspective of political science and economics Karin Svedberg Helgesson and Ulrika Mörth (2013) also discuss the concept of corporate citizenship and the political role of corporations in contemporary politics, arguing that transnational corporations have increasingly gained authority in global governance in later decades. Annegret Flohr and colleagues (Flohr et al. 2014) in similar terms analyse the role of business, pointing to the importance of self-regulation in for instance socio-economic and environmental fields when business corporations participate in the setting of norms. From a political economy perspective, Christopher May (2006) has explored the ways in which corporations affect the practices and structures of the global political economy, stressing the role of global governance for constraining the power of global corporations. Within anthropology, important contributions have been made by for example Catherine Dolan, who shows how corporate engagement in fair trade also turns into being a political affair (Dolan 2008; Dolan and Scott 2009). Tania Lee (2007) has demonstrated the wide-ranging impact of private interests in the domain of international development, which again points in the direction of a political influence. Significant contributions have also been made in the area of CPA, defined as the study of corporate attempts to shape government policy in ways favourable to the firm (Baysinger 1984) in disciplines such as strategic management, sociology, political science, economics and finance (see Hillman et al. 2004 for overview; Lux et al. 2011).

The current volume adds to these lines of earlier research in two main ways. First, as will be elaborated in the next section, by introducing the concept of corporate bricolage in the field of corporate political activities. The concept offers a nuanced perspective as to the ways in which policy influencing by corporations is attempted. Second, by offering a number of empirical, mainly ethnographical studies, of these activities. Even though ethnographic research regarding the relationship between business and politics do exist, there is still a great need for close up studies of how corporations mould their environments.

CORPORATE BRICOLAGE

In a general sense, and as outlined by Lawton et al. (2012), studies of corporate political activity have focused rather narrowly on how firms use their strategic political resources and capabilities to improve their profitability (McWilliams et al. 2002). However, a broader interest in how a corporation deploys its political resources in a concerted fashion to manage its political environment has attracted growing attention. The relevance of the 'endogenous context', in which the firm expects to be confronted by policy decisions, stakeholders, issues or actions within a non-market political system, has been emphasized (Kim and Prescott 2005). Facing an unpredictable exogenous context, the corporation must react to this anticipated policy context through effective use of its political resources (Capron and Chatain 2008). Corporate attempts to influence policy have long been channelled to influence state agencies and other relevant parties by direct use of its political resources.

Corporate influence may also be shielded by the creation of new organizations that more directly work to influence policy on behalf of corporations (Barley 2010). Corporations may establish political action committees (PACs), lobby firms, think tanks or other kinds of issue-focused organizations that work to establish knowledge, frame problem perceptions and shape agendas. These shielding organizations, whilst often focused on particular problem areas or policy issues, may voluntarily or involuntarily bar insight into the character and extent of corporate influence. An example of an influential North American PAC is the National Beer Wholesalers Association Political Action Committee (NBWA PAC). This is the largest PAC in the licensed beverage industry. NBWA PAC represents nearly 3,000 licensed, independent beer distributors, who have operations in every state and congressional district across the United States. The organization works to strengthen and maintain the state-based system of alcohol regulation.

Other organizations that may indirectly funnel corporate influence are think tanks funded by corporate capital and/or foundation capital. In a general sense, think tanks are organizations that undertake research and advocacy on specific and often burning topics and are most often registered as non-profit organizations. The growth of think tanks across the world over the last few decades have meant enhanced possibilities and intensified attempts of influencing policy (Ricci 1993; Rich 2004; Smith 1991; Stone 2000). As noted by Andrew Rich (2004, p. 153), 'the work of think tanks can be important to an issue beginning years before it becomes a subject of debate among policy makers.' It may also fluctuate along the timeline of a policy process. And its real impact is more often than not very difficult to trace. Think tanks may as well depend on a large and varied portfolio of funders for their operations, which makes it difficult to trace the actual influence of a particular corporate funder. The Competitive Enterprise Institute (CEI), a free-market think tank founded in the US in 1984, stands out as an example of a corporate-funded think tank. CEI takes a significant portion of its funding from private corporations. As expressed by Tom Medvetz (2012, p. 127): '. . . while CEI's directors would not likely embrace the label corporate think tank, neither do they make any secret of their ultimate purposes as advocates for corporate interests'. Another case in point, but with an entirely different structure and agenda, is the World Economic Forum, financed by 1,000 of the world's largest corporations (Pigman 2007; Garsten and Sörbom 2016). Incorporated as a non-profit foundation, the World Economic Forum aims to be 'an independent international organization committed to improving the state of the world by engaging business, political, academic and other leaders of society to shape global, regional and industry agendas' (http://www.weforum.org/content/

leadership-team, accessed 3 October 2013). At the meetings arranged by the Forum, industry leaders meet with leaders from for example the United Nations, the World Trade Organization, with prime ministers and presidents, as well as with leaders from major civil society organizations, including Bill and Melinda Gates and other characters with double roles. Discussions on core global issues with high government officials take place in meetings that are not publicly announced. The idea propelled by the Forum, as the organizer of these meetings, is that the solutions put forth at the discussions should be pursued in the local settings of the participants, which also occasionally happens.

Another example of such an endeavour in the global policy domain is the World Business Council on Sustainable Development (WBCSD). The council organizes 200 of the world's largest corporations, who, as the organization presents it, on a daily basis are in contact with 50 per cent of the entire world's population. Its aim is to put forth 'business solutions for a sustainable world' (wbcsd.org, accessed 2 September 2013). As Patricia Arnas at the council's Washington, DC office declares when we meet:

> We are a global organization, we aim to work at the global level. We do global, not national, advocacy work. Not lobbying. This dictates who we are and who we partner with. Today we target mainly UN-types of organizations as the OECD, UNEP, UNDP, OECD and Clean Energy Ministerial. The types of policies we work on are general, to fit the global level. For example: policy on carbon, where we are claiming the need for a global prize on carbon. We are not picking a type of energy source, we are just saying that there should be a cost, and it should be global, and subsidies must be abandoned. We aim to address issues at a higher level, at a high level of generalizability. (Interview 2014)

The Council does work in tandem with INGOs, but it also works directly with its own member corporations in order to inspire them to take social responsibility. The WBCSD is always invited to the WEF annual meetings in Davos, and many of its members are also members of the WEF. In turn, these members may turn up as the firm that an institutional investor with a 'responsible' profile may choose to invest in. Or, the members of WBCSD will meet with a partner from Fairtrade International at a side event for a UN climate change meeting, set up by WBCSD and the International Emissions Trading Associations (IETA). IETA has in turn visited Davos and the WEF annual meeting and are members of a WEF task force working group on accelerated investments in low-carbon technologies. The intersections between the different organizations active here are plentiful. WBCSB is an organization that is moulding its environment (see Barley 2010), and explicitly so at a global level.

Unintentionally, we find that most of the organizations explored in the volume have, in one way or another, been in contact with World Economic Forum, by being part of their partially organized network. For example, Susan C. Schwab, a member of a Global Action Council at the WEF, is also a board member of Boeing. The FLO international strategic partner HIVOS is a regular attendee at WEF-meetings. Apart from being a WEF strategic partner, Google is commonly understood to set up the best party during the Davos week, when WEF participants are entering the village for its annual meeting. Participants from Atlas Transnational of course also take part in WEF-activities.

Bringing to mind knowledge production in this manner thereby also points to the existential phenomena of global bricolage. Just like the economic entrepreneur recombines and makes creative use of existing resources, capitalizing on the capacity to mobilize practical knowledge in a way that challenges general theoretical approaches (Baker et al. 2003), corporate actors involved in global governance mobilize by combining resources, social as well as economic. Policy bricolage, then – understood as a mix of disorderly processes and institutional reassemblages – is grounded in cultural political economy and explores a cobbling together of multiple kinds of self-organization in national blocs and is only loosely meshed as a mode of informal global governance (Mittelman 2013). Further, the bricolage approach offers a grammar, a way to examine the combination of spontaneity and international groupings without one-sidedly emphasizing the former or the latter. It thus views this experimentation as glimmerings of potential modifications in ways to steer the global political economy.

Evoking the Claude Lévi-Strauss concept of 'the bricoleur' (1966) in the public policy domain we see these corporate actors as policy bricoleurs, as organizations with the capacity to act both as market actors and as political actors, putting together different resources in heterogeneous forms. In the sphere where markets and politics are brought together, the bricolage character of such organizations makes them agile enough to manoeuvre across and combine market and political interests. The organizations involved in political affairs are therefore finicky to define as either or. They can be important for markets, but they are also important for politics and they are certainly active in combining both types of activities. Depending on the context and the interest pursued, they perform as primarily market actors or political actors.

At the emic level organizations that are set up to exert political influence often describe themselves in ambiguous terms, being for instance simultaneously foundations, non-governmental organizations and think tanks. The WEF, for example, describes itself as simultaneously a foundation, a non-profit organization, an international institution and a think tank. It may shift flexibly between positions and roles in markets and in political circles, thus moving readily on the grazing grounds of both corporations and politicians, speaking freely with corporate leaders as well as with high-level politicians. In the same vein, as Tom Medvetz (2012) describes think tanks, ambiguity is a resource for policy bricoleur successes. Less bound by clearly defined roles – compared to, for example, universities and governments – think tanks, NGOs, research institutes and other organizations such as these are able to more freely draw upon the former institutions as established sources of knowledge, hereby establishing themselves as policy intellectuals, doing the 'intellectual groundwork' (Medvetz 2012, p. 5), influencing how citizens and lawmakers perceive the world. As for example the technical or architectural bricoleur turns to the tools at hand, establishing a dialogue with her/him self, the policy bricoleur draws upon existing resources, asking new questions of them, and thereby making them into something that carries further the sign of credibility but with a partly new understanding of the content. These types of ambiguous organizations are not a particularly new phenomenon. What is new is the scale and political importance of the activities of these kinds of organizations. Both nationally and transnationally governance outside and in between governments are staged to an increasing, and unprecedented, level.

PROFIT, POWER AND POLICY CLOSE UP

As Stephen Barley contends (2010), organizational researchers have not been that interested in how corporations mould their environment. They have instead focused their attention on the internal affairs of corporations, less so on their outward interests. This pattern is true also for research based in other traditions and perspectives. Economists and sociologists with an interest in corporate political activity have analysed this in order to answer questions pertaining to why corporations may have an interest in funding politics, which corporations fund the most and their role vis-à-vis governmental organizations (see for instance Boies 1989; Burris 2001; Hillman et al. 2004; Ronit 2001; Ronit and Schneider 1999; Hansen and Mitchell 2000). Political scientists, primarily interested in governmental activities, have had their prime interest in governmental politics and not corporate politics (Archer 2001; Stone 2012). The strands of research on international political economy stand out as exceptions (as seen in for example Braithwaite and Drahos 2000; Koppel 2010).

This book answers the criticism raised by Barley, and asks questions regarding corporations and their relation to politics. The relationship is old, but due to the scale and the increasing importance of these kinds of political affairs they call for a close examination. What kinds of activities do corporations pursue, in what forms, on what issues and with what solutions put forward? How do they achieve legitimacy as actors in the global political domain?

When looking for answers to these questions the policy bricolage concept invites us to look for empirical examples that reflect the flexibility and ambiguities in the organizational relations that these actors oftentimes display. Global rules for markets do emerge from intergovernmental organizations in the form of treaties and conventions. But they are also announced by non-governmental bodies, sometimes formed by corporations or in quasi-governmental forms where corporations in different forms are active together with other types of organizations, for example by issuing standards and/or recommendations (Koppel 2010, p. 8). The contribution of *Power, Policy and Profit* is to analyse some of these flex organizations in motion.

First, the volume presents a number of chapters that analyse corporate interests in shaping regulation. Mikkel Flyverbom in his chapter on advocacy by corporations, Christina Garsten and Adrienne Sörbom on the role of corporations in the World Economic Forum, Picard et al. on corporate governance and Anna Tyllström regarding lobbying consultancy, all give empirical insights as to the intermixing of corporate interests for policy, power and profit. Marie-Laure Salles-Djelic's chapter relates to this theme but from an interest for Atlas TI as the originator of neoliberal think tanks. Hervé Dumez and Alain Jeunemaître's chapter focuses on how a large corporation attempts to cross the public–private sector divide, in order to create increased rents, thereby altering regulations of markets (for instance, who has the right to run schools).

Second, the volume also presents analyses of corporate interests in 'doing good', that is to say of business as prefigurative politics (compare Leach 2013). As for social movements, the fundamental idea here is to change the world by changing the means employed, internally in the company and externally for customers. The chapters by Renita Thedvall and Anette Nyqvist respectively, show how some corporations and financial institutions attempt to make money by doing the 'right thing', that is, by politicizing their activities. In the chapter by Bo Rothstein, however, the reversed idea is presented, when arguing for corporations being in need of non-market based ideology to control their activities.

OUTLINE OF CHAPTERS

Chapter 1, by Marie-Laure Salles-Djelic presents the role of Atlas Transnational, the mother of neoliberal think tanks. Over the last 40 years or so, neoliberalism has become the 'new dominant regime of truth' (Burgin 2013; Djelic 2006) with a significant performative impact on national policymaking (Campbell and Pedersen 2001) as well as in regards to dynamics of transnational governance (Lee and McBride 2007). Of particular interest here is the carrier and boundary-spanning role of the dense ecology of neoliberal think tanks and research institutes that has come to be structured over the past four decades. These think tanks espouse a market- and business-friendly ideology and have made it their mission to champion, spread, defend and entrench, as widely and deeply as possible and in a multiplicity of contexts, this ideology and its associated politics. In the chapter, Salles-Djelic presents the historical dynamics of emergence of this dense ecology of neoliberal think tanks. Salles-Djelic explores the role of Atlas, that was created to 'litter the world' with free-market think tanks (Blundell 2001) with a particular interest for the process through which the organizational form of the 'neoliberal think tank' came to be constructed, diffused and progressively institutionalized during that period. Unpacking potent – albeit subtle and indirect – mechanisms of influence that have largely been neglected in the literature Salles-Djelic contributes to the understanding of the relationship between business and politics. As the chapter shows, neoliberal think tanks were constructed to shape and spread ideological, political and practice templates and to help crystallize and stabilize them across the world both in the corporate and in the political world.

Departing from an interest in the involvement of business leaders in the sphere of politics, in the broad sense, Christina Garsten and Adrienne Sörbom analyse the role of business within the World Economic Forum (WEF). Many global business leaders today do much more than engage narrowly in their own corporation and its search for profit, and the WEF is one such arena through which firms act through to advance their interests, financial as well as political. The organization has built its position and reputation on providing an arena for large-scale business corporations and top-level political elites, and the influence of corporations on the structure and content of activities should not be underestimated. The chapter indicates a number of conduits through which business may draw upon the WEF and its platforms as a strategically positioned amplifier for their non-market interests. However, the WEF cannot only be conceived as the extended voice of corporations. The WEF also makes use of the corporations to organize and expand its own agency, which doesn't necessarily coincide with the interests of multinational corporations. Garsten and Sörbom introduce the notion of policy bricolage in the chapter as a way to capture the ambiguous, creative and agile role of the WEF and its relation to corporations. By way of corporate financial resources, the tapping of knowledge and expertise and access to vast networks of business relations, the WEF is also able to amplify its own voice. On top, it is through the support and engagement of business, as well as that of political leaders and non-governmental high profiles, that the organization gets its spin. The global policy bricolage of the WEF is thus not just a complex form of global governance, but also an intricate system of interweaving market and political interests, and one that both amplifies and blurs the choir of voices.

Drawing the case of construction of the European carbon market (EU-ETS) Mélodie Cartel, Eva Boxenbaum, Franck Aggeri and Jean-Yves Caneill, in Chapter 3, address the question how public policies can be designed and implemented when facing strong reluctance from both politicians and private corporations? The EU-ETS was adopted in 2003 as the corner stone of the European climate policy. The authors analyse the collective dynamics of the making of the European carbon market. Based on a rich set of archival data and interviews, the analysis reconstitutes the original strategy deployed by the electricity sector to implement a carbon market in Europe. Empirically, the chapter shows that during the Kyoto Protocol, the European Commission opposed emissions trading, and the industrial companies pleaded against any measure involving a price on carbon. In spite of this reluctance, a handful of actors in the electricity sector believed that a carbon market could be an effective solution to manage carbon emissions at the company level. From 1999 to 2001, these actors organized two successive experiments where they invited industrial companies to build and test various carbon market prototypes. The chapter indicates that these experiments triggered an intellectual shift among participants and considerably fuelled the policymaking process that led to the EU-ETS.

The point of departure for Tyllström, in Chapter 4, is an interest in giving ethnographic evidence to lobbying, something that, in spite of the plethora of organizations devoted to political influence that has emerged globally since the 1970s, has been conspicuous by their absence (Barley 2010). Drawing on ethnographic fieldwork from the realm of public affairs consultancy, the chapter provides insights into the practical nature of corporate lobbying, as well as a discussion of how these consultants practice lobbying, and the role of lobbying may have in politics and markets. The case describes how a powerful industry player wishes to influence policy, hires a consultant who uses classical tools to gain political influence such as identifying key players and enemies, good arguments and counter-arguments. As such, the case gives a rare account of how these tools are used by public affairs consultants. In generalized terms, the chapter shows the lobbying of public affairs consultants to revolve around five practices; information-gathering, contact management, visibility management, role-switching and ideological proactivity. These five types of practice are distinctly observable aspects of lobbying work, but they also feed into and amplify each other. Tyllström shows how the switching roles facilitates the establishment of contacts, which in turn enables the gathering of better, more valuable information. Furthermore, the constant management of boundaries between invisibility and visibility, the rich contact networks and the constant adjustment of identities together makes it possible for consultants to launch their own political ideas into the opinion landscape. Understanding these qualities of practice and how they interact is crucial to understanding the resurgent critique against lobbyism concerning its hidden nature and role confusion. As Tyllström concludes, fuzziness is not external to lobbying practices; it is at the heart of it.

In Chapter 5 Dumez and Jeunemaître analyse political strategies of firms, based on the case of Boeing from the late 1990s and early 2000s. The traditional view of firms' political strategies is that, by acting on the state, they will protect and expand firms' interests. But whereas in the classic game (to prevent the vote of an adverse law for example) corporate interests from the outset were seen as clearly defined, in the new game companies frequently are seen as identifying their interest in the course of actions and interactions with politicians (Woll 2008). The context of political action is often deeply uncertain. Therefore, the traditional opposition between market and non-market strategies, and between relational and transactional political activities should be questioned, especially in a period marked by globalization. Boeing's strategy in the late 1990s and early 2000s serves as an illustrating case of these tendencies. Boeing had been accustomed to traditional strategies of lobbying (for example in the context of its rivalry with Airbus) and financing political life. But in the late 1990s, it developed ambitious strategies aimed at building up influence rents. These strategies failed for Boeing, but analytically Dumez and Jeunmaître are able to draw on the case for identifying new types of relationships between firms and the state.

Mikkel Flyverbom, in Chapter 6, sets out to expand the conception of corporate advocacy by pointing to the growing importance of knowledge, data and visualizations. Drawing on insights from the literature on the politics of knowledge (Rubio and Baert 2012) and the importance of knowledge in governance (Foucault 1980; Stone 2002) Flyverbom develops a conceptual entry point for enhancing the understanding of how Internet companies engage multiple forms of knowledge and visualizations as resources in their efforts to shape public perceptions, politics and regulation. To this end, the chapter uses illustrations from a study of Google and Facebook. Based on interviews with policy directors, participant observations in multi-stakeholder dialogues initiated by the UN, as well as documentary research, the chapter discusses the various forms of corporate advocacy that play out in this field. These prove to be: relationship building, message crafting and data provision. While the first two are well established, the focus on the provision of data, algorithms and technological platforms adds a new dimension to our understanding of corporate advocacy. This typology and the empirical illustrations serve as the basis for a conceptual and contextual embedding of visual numbers- and data-based forms of knowledge production and advocacy in relation to prevalent forms and understandings of corporate political activities.

Contrary to the earlier chapters, where focus has been on how firms and corporations attempt to diffuse their specific views and interests to other actors, the chapter 'Talking like an institutional investor: on the gentle voices of financial giants' (Chapter 7) by Anette Nyqvist, analyses how corporate actors attempt to relate to norms and scripts for taking social responsibility. Through analysing the talk of institutional investors Nyqvist describes and discusses some of the ways in which organizations with the primary goal of 'making money' increasingly also embark on projects of 'doing good'. Institutional investors, such as mutual funds, insurance companies and pension funds, are large shareholder organizations commissioned to manage other people's money. These have in later decades emerged as influential front figures of the responsible investment industry, claiming to make money and make a difference and positioning themselves as the 'active' and 'responsible' do-gooders of finance. Nyqvist sees them as intermediary organizations that in a relatively short time have grown in size and scope and now dominate corporate ownership globally. They are normative and fostering financial actors that aim to, in their view, better the way companies conduct their businesses. Nyqvist shows how institutional investors use 'voice', 'dialogue' and 'small talk' with the intent to (1) define and position themselves as a particular type of financial market actor, (2) foster and try to change companies that they own shares in and (3) set new standards for the investment industry.

In Chapter 8, Sébastien Picard, Véronique Steyer, Xavier Philippe and Mar Pérezts offer a broad vision of corporate political activities, highlighting its institutional reach, and describing its concrete institutionalizing effects. Drawing on Michel Lallement (2008) the authors attempt to open the black box of the institutionalization processes of corporate political activity and the institutional dynamics associated with this type of activity. Using data from an in-depth ethnography in VaxCorp, a leading corporation in the vaccine industry, the authors analyse how the company shapes its institutional field by imposing the dominant 'vaccinology' imaginary. In practice this takes shape in a modus operandi that goes beyond the mere maximization of VaxCorp's interests to organize actions and behaviours of other institutional actors (for example, State, WHO). The analysis indicates that this imaginary emerges from but also intertwines institutionalizing processes into a larger and coherent pattern, which eventually legitimizes corporations' dominance in an institutional field.

Renita Thedvall demonstrates in Chapter 9 the dynamics of standardization (Brunsson et al. 2012) when implementing fairtrade standards in a chocolate factory. What worldviews and ideals are embedded in Fairtrade International's standards? How are these worldviews and ideals negotiated and navigated in relation to economic issues of marketability as well as other political ideals present in the factory? The chapter gives ethnographic insights of the attempts of the long-established chocolate factory to develop a product in line with the fairtrade standard. Interestingly, the production process of conventional chocolate would be identical to the one following the standard. However, the purchase and storage of fairtrade raw material proved to be a challenge bringing attention to political concerns within the chocolate factory. In fact, the factory's choice to use an ethical label on one of its products brought a whole set of political discussions, as well as new priorities within the factory. The political in this context was not primarily the words and values in the fairtrade standards documents and certification criteria being implemented as part of the CSR strategy of the chocolate factory. Instead it was the fact that the fairtrade label, and its standards and compliance criteria, opened a space for politics in the chocolate factory. In this way, the words and the values in the standards documents and compliance criteria were translated and adjusted turning the fairtrade labelled products into a political affair matching the chocolate factory's political ideals. Still, the negotiated fairtrade ideals did not carve out a space for them in the milk chocolate segment. Thus, making a business out of being fairtrade opened a space for politics within the factory but not for business and the carefully chosen chocolate bar wrapping including the fairtrade label was discarded and wrapping papers without labels were put in the flowpack machine.

In the chapter authored by Bo Rothstein (Chapter 10), the focus is set on corporations, corruption and power, thus stressing the intersection between policy and markets. The analysis starts from the term 'legal corruption', coined by former leading World Bank economist Daniel Kaufmann. The term is to be understood as a problem of collective action, leading to a social trap, in which it makes no sense of acting legally when one does not know if other actors do too. As Rothstein argues, corruption is one important factor in explaining the financial crisis in 2008, and the main aim of the chapter is to present four interrelated arguments that sum up to a theory about the relation between the logic of markets, regulation and social efficiency. The first argument is that competitive markets are, hitherto, the most efficient organizational form of creating a utilitarian-based economic efficiency for the production of most goods and services. Second, Rothstein maintains that in order to reach this utilitarian-based efficiency, markets need a large and quite complicated set of institutions, formal as well as informal. The third argument, however, is that we have little reason to expect that such institutions will be created endogenously by agents acting from the standard self-interested utility-maximization template. This is because such efficient institutions are genuine public goods and therefore are prone to the well-known problem of collective action. Thus, as argued by Rothstein, contrary to what has been taken for granted by most policymakers in the area of financial regulation the implication is that we should expect market agents to act in a way that either will prevent efficient institutions to be established, or if they are established, will try to destroy them by various forms of 'free riding'. The fourth argument is, therefore, that markets can only reach social efficiency if the agents that have the responsibility to produce and reproduce the necessary institutions act according to a logic that is different from the logic that market agents use when operating in the market.

David Westbrook concludes the volume stressing the points of departure for the volume as a whole, the need for 'leaving flatland' in the analysis of relationships between markets and politics. In *Flatland*, the Victorian author Edwin Abbott told the story of a square, prosperously living in a society located (and understood) in a two dimensional plane, but challenged by a visitor in form of a sphere (Abbott 1884[1998]). Analogous to Flatland, we, the social scientists, tend to commonly address a complex fabric of relations with a very simple normative vocabulary: liberalism. Along the same lines as Abbott, Westbrook asks how we, from within the liberal plane, might conceive of the social, so that we might imagine politics in at least three dimensions? As Westbrook argues, the impoverishment of political discourse as it is commonly portrayed in social sciences may be unwise, even dangerous. Instead, Westbrook suggests that the social sciences, and anthropology in particular, can help to foster a more institutional, and more responsible, political imagination. While social science may still find itself constrained to present itself as a science, the inquiry at issue here is into collective subjectivity, and thus inherently interpretive, rather than objective. If the new science distinguished itself from its ancestors by abandoning teleology, it is precisely the reengagement with teleology that is urged here, not for the study of nature, but for the study of communities, with their constitutive norms.

REFERENCES

Abbott, A. (2016), *Processual Sociology*, Chicago: Chicago University Press.
Abbott, E.A. (1884), *Flatland: A Romance of Many Dimensions*, in [1998], Penguin Classics.
Archer, C. (2001), *International Organizations*, New York: Routledge.
Ahrne, G., P. Aspers and N. Brunsson (2015), 'The organization of markets', *Organization Studies*, **36** (1), 7–27.
Austen-Smith, D. and J.R. Wright (1999), 'Theory and evidence for counteractive lobbying', *American Journal of Political Science*, **40**, 543–64.
Baker, T., A.S. Miner and D.T. Eesly (2003), 'Improvising firms: Bricolage, account giving and improvisational competencies in the founding process', *Research Policy*, **32**, 255–76.
Barley, S. (2010), 'Building an institutional field to corral a government: A case to set an agenda for organization studies', *Organization Studies*, **31** (6), 777–805.
Baysinger, B.D. (1984), 'Domain maintenance as an objective of business political activity: An expanded typology', *Academy of Management Review*, **9** (2), 248–58.
Blundell, J. (2001), 'Waging the War of Ideas, London: IEA', at http://www.iea.org.uk/sites/default/files/publications/files/upldbook226pdf.pdf. Accessed 3 July 2016.
Boies, J.L. (1989), 'Money, business and the state: Material interests, Fortune 500 corporations, and the size of political action committees', *American Sociological Review*, **54** (5), 821–33.
Braithwaite, J. and P. Drahos (2000), *Global Business Regulation*, Cambridge: Cambridge University Press.
Brunsson, N., A. Rasche and D. Seidl (2012), 'The dynamics of standardization. Three perspectives on standards in organization studies', *Organization Studies* **33** (5–6), 613–32.
Burgin, A. (2013), *The Great Persuasion*, Cambridge, MA: Harvard University Press.
Burris, V. (2001), 'The two faces of capital: Corporations and individualists as political actors', *American Sociological Review*, **66** (3), 361–81.
Campbell, J. and O. Pedersen (eds) (2001), *The Rise of Neoliberalism and Institutional Analysis*, Princeton, NJ: Princeton University Press.
Capron, L. and O. Chatain (2008), 'Competitors' resource-oriented strategies: Acting on competitors' resources through interventions in factor markets and political markets', *Academy of Management Review*, **33**, 97–121.
Cerny, P.G. (2010), *Rethinking World Politics: A Theory of Transnational Neo-Pluralism*, Oxford: Oxford University Press.
Courpasson, D. and S. Clegg (2006), 'Dissolving the iron cages? Tocqueville, Michels, bureaucracy and the perpetuation of elite power', *Organization* **13**, 319–43.
Delmas, M.A. and M.J. Montes-Sancho (2010), 'Voluntary agreements to improve environmental quality: Symbolic and substantive cooperation', *Strategic Management Journal*, **31**, 575–601.
Djelic, M.L. and K. Sahlin-Andersson (eds) (2006), *Transnational Governance, Institutional Dynamics of Regulation*, Cambridge: Cambridge University Press.
Djelic, M.L. and S. Quack (2010), *Transnational Communities: Shaping Global Governance*, Cambridge: Cambridge University Press.

Dolan, C. (2008), 'In the mist of development: Fair trade in Kenyan tea fields', *Globalizations*, **5** (2), 305–18.
Dolan, C. and L. Scott (2009), 'Lipstick evangelism: Avon trading circles and gender empowerment in South Africa', *Gender and Development*, **17** (2), 203–18.
Fligstein, N. (1996), 'Markets as politics: A political-cultural approach to market institutions', *American Sociological Review* **61**, 656–73.
Fligstein, N. (2001), *The Architecture of Markets: An Economic Sociology of Twenty-First Century Capitalist Societies*, Princeton: Princeton University Press.
Flohr, A., L. Rieth, S. Schwindenhammer and K. Wolf (2014), *The Role of Business in Global Governance, Corporations as Norm Entrepreneurs*, Basingstoke: Palgrave Macmillan.
Foucault, M. (1980), *Power/Knowledge: Selected Interviews and Writings 1972–1977*, New York: Pantheon Books.
Garsten, C. and M. Lindh de Montoya (eds) (2008), *Transparency in a New Global Order: Unveiling Organizational Visions*, Cheltenham: Edward Elgar.
Garsten, C. and A. Sörbom (2014), 'Values aligned: The organization of conflicting values within the World Economic Forum', in S. Alexius and K. Tamm Hallström (eds) *Configuring Value Conflicts in Markets*, Cheltenham: Edward Elgar.
Garsten, C. and A. Sörbom (2016), 'Magical formulae for market futures: Tales from the World Economic Forum meeting in Davos', *Anthropology Today*, **32** (6), 18–26.
Hall, R.B. and T.J. Biersteker (2002), *The Emergence of Private Authority in the International System*, New York: Cambridge University Press.
Hansen, H.K. (2012), 'The power of performance indices in the global politics of anticorruption', *Journal of International Relations and Development*, **15** (4), 506–31.
Hansen, H.K. and M. Flyverbom (2015), 'The politics of transparency and the calibration of knowledge in the digital age', *Organization*, **22** (6), 872–89.
Hansen, W. and N. Mitchell (2000), 'Disaggregating and explaining corporate political activity: Domestic and foreign corporations in national politics', *American Political Science Review*, **94**, 891–903.
Hillman, A.J., G.D. Keim and D. Schuler (2004), 'Corporate political activity: A review and research agenda', *Journal of Management*, **30** (6), 837–57.
Hood, C. and D. Heald (eds) (2006), *Transparency: The Key to Better Governance?* Oxford: Oxford University Press, pp. 3–23.
Josselin, D. and W. Wallace (eds) (2001), *Non-State Actors in World Politics*, Basingstoke: Palgrave.
Kim, B. and J.E. Prescott (2005), 'Deregulatory forms, variations in the speed of governance adaptation, and firm performance', *Academy of Management Review*, **30**, 414–25.
Koppel, J.G.S. (2010), *World Rule, Accountability, Legitimacy, and the Design of Global Governance*, Chicago: University of Chicago Press.
Lallement, M. (2008), 'L'entreprise est-elle une institution? Le cas du Familistère de Guise', *Revue Française de Socio-Economie*, **1**, 67–87.
Lawton, T., S. McGuire and T. Rajwani (2012), 'Corporate political activity: A literature review and research agenda', *International Journal of Management Reviews*, **15**, 86–105.
Leach, D.K. (2013), 'Prefigurative Politics', *The Wiley-Blackwell Encyclopedia of Social and Political Movements*. DOI: 10.1002/9780470674871.wbespm167.

Lee, S. and S. McBride (eds) (2007), *Neo-Liberalism, State Power and Governance*, Dordrecht: Springer.
Lee, T. (2007), *The Will to Improve: Governmentality, Development, and the Practice of Politics*, Durham: Duke University Press.
Lévi-Strauss, C. (1966), *The Savage Mind*, Chicago: Chicago University Press.
Lukes, S. (2005), *Power: A Radical View*, 2nd Edition, Basingstoke: Palgrave Macmillan.
Lux, S., T.R. Croock and D.J. Woehr (2011), 'Mixing business with politics: A meta-analysis of the antecedents and outcomes of corporate political activity', *Journal of Management*, **37** (1), 223–47.
Mandel, R. and C. Humphrey (eds) (2002), *Markets and Moralities: Ethnographies of Post-socialism*, Oxford/New York: Berg.
May, C. (2006), *Global Corporate Power*, International Political Economy Yearbook 15, Lynne Riener Publishers.
McGann, J.G. (2007), *Think Tanks and Policy Advice in the United States. Academics, Advisors and Advocates*, Oxon: Routledge.
McWilliams, A., D. Van Fleet and K. Cory (2002), 'Raising rivals' costs through political strategy: An extension of resource-based theory', *Journal of Management Studies*, **39**, 707–23.
Medvetz, T. (2012), *Think Tanks in America*, Chicago: Chicago University Press.
Mittelman, J.H. (2013), 'Global bricolage: Emerging market powers and polycentric governance', *Third World Quarterly*, **34** (1), 23–37.
Okhmatovskiy, I. (2010), 'Performance implications of ties to the government and SOEs: A political embeddedness perspective', *Journal of Management Studies* **47**, 1020–47.
Pattberg, P. (2005), 'The institutionalization of private governance: How business and nonprofit organizations agree on transnational rules', *Governance* **18** (4), 22.
Pigman, G.A. (2007), *The World Economic Forum: A Multi-Stakeholder Approach to Global Governance*, Abingdon: Routledge.
Rhodes, R.A.W. (1996). 'The new governance: Governing without government', *Political Studies*, **44** (4), 652–67.
Ricci, D. (1993), *The Transformation of American Politics, The New Washington and the Rise of Think Tanks*, Yale: New Haven University Press.
Rich, A. (2004), *Think Tanks, Public Policy, and the Politics of Expertise*, Cambridge: Cambridge University Press.
Ring, P.S., S.A. Lenway and M. Govekar (1990), 'Management of the political imperative in international business', *Strategic Management Journal* **11**, 141–51.
Ronit, K. (2001), 'Institutions of private authority in global governance: Linking territorial forms of self-regulation', *Administration & Society*, **33**, 555.
Ronit, K. and V. Schneider (1999), 'Global governance through private organizations', *Governance: An International Journal of Policy and Administration*, **12** (3), 243–66.
Rose, N. and P. Miller (1992), 'Political power beyond the state: Problematics of government', *The British Journal of Sociology*, **43** (2), 173–205.
Rubio, F.D. and P. Baert (eds) (2012), *The Politics of Knowledge*, London: Routledge.
Ruggie, J. (2004), 'Reconstituting the global public domain: Issues, actors and practices', *European Journal of International Relations*, **10**, 449.
Sassen, S. (2006), *Territory, Authority, Rights: From Medieval to Global Assemblages*, Princeton: Princeton University Press.

Scherer, A.G. and G. Palazzo (2011), 'The new political role of business in a globalised world: A review of a new perspective on CSR and its implications for the firm, governance and democracy', *Journal of Management Studies*, **48**, 899–931.
Sassen, S. (2003), 'Globalization or denationalization?' *Review of International Political Economy*, **10**, 1–22.
Scholte, J.A. (2005), 'Civil society and democracy', in R. Wilkinson (ed) *The Global Governance Reader*, London: Routledge, pp. 322–40.
Scholte, J.A. (2004), *Globalization and Governance: From Statism to Poly-Centrism*, CSGR Working Paper No.130/04.
Scholte, J.A. (2000), *Globalization: A Critical Introduction*, Basingstoke: Palgrave Macmillan.
Scholte, J.A. (1996), 'Beyond the buzzword: Towards a critical theory of globalization', *Globalization: Theory and Practice*, 43–57.
Shore, C., S. Wright and D. Però (eds) (2011), *Policy Worlds: Anthropology and the Analysis of Contemporary Power*, New York & Oxford: Berghahn Books.
Sklair, L. (2001), *The Transnational Capitalist Class*, Oxford: Blackwell.
Smith, J.A. (1991), *The Idea Brokers: Think Tanks And The Rise Of The New Policy Elite*, New York, NY: The Free Press.
Spencer, J. (2007), *Anthropology, Politics and the State: Democracy and Violence in South Asia*, Edinburgh: University of Edinburgh.
Spiller, P.T. (1990), 'Politicians, interest groups, and regulators: A multiple-principals agency theory of regulation, or "let them be bribed"', *Journal of Law and Economics*, **33**, 65–101.
Stone, D. (2012), 'Transfer and translation of policy', *Policy Studies*, **33** (6), 483–99.
Stone, D. (2008), 'Global public policy, transnational policy communities and their networks', *Policy Studies Journal*, **36** (1), 19–38.
Stone, Diane (2002), 'Global knowledge and advocacy networks', *Global Networks*, **2** (1), 1–11.
Stone, D. (2000), 'Introduction: The changing think tank landscape', *Global Society*, **14** (2), 149–52.
Svedberg Helgesson, K. and U. Mörth (2013), 'Introduction: The political role of corporate citizens', in K. Svedberg Helgesson and U. Mörth (eds), *The Political Role of Corporate Citizens: An Interdisciplinary Approach*, Basingstoke: Palgrave Macmillan.
Vallentin, S. and D. Murillo (2012), 'Governmentality and the politics of CSR', *Organization*, **19** (6), 825–43.
Wedel, J. et al. (2005), 'Towards an anthropology of public policy', *Annals of the American Academy of Political and Social Science*, **600** (1), 30–51.
West, H.G. and T. Sanders (2003), 'Introduction: Power revealed and concealed in the new world order', in Harry G. West and Todd Sanders (eds), *Transparency and Conspiracy: Ethnographies of Suspicion in the New World Order*, Durham: Duke University Press, pp. 1–37.
Woll, C. (2008), *Firm Interests: How Governments Shape Business Lobbying on Global Trade*, Cornell: Cornell University Studies.
Yoffie, D. and S. Bergenstein (1985), 'Creating political advantage: The rise of the political entrepreneur', *California Management Review*, **28**, 124–39.

1. Building an architecture for political influence: Atlas and the transnational institutionalization of the neoliberal think tank

Marie-Laure Salles-Djelic

INTRODUCTION

In a famous 1970 *New York Times* article, Milton Friedman argued for the principled separation and strict division of labor between political and economic spheres (Friedman 1970). Political elites should set and monitor basic (and limited) rules of the game in independence. Meanwhile, economic elites should be left to maximize utility within the bounds of these rules. Such principled and strict separation, however, is difficult to reconcile with empirical observation. Historically, politics and economic affairs have always been connected one way or another (Goldthwaite 1987; Mills 1956). The nature, the extent and the mechanisms of this interplay, however, evolve through time and with changing contexts. In particular, the dynamics of power and influence between economic and power elites vary significantly (Martin and Swank 2012; Mills 1956; Pearson 1997). In non-market and state-run economies, political elites tend to have the upper hand. In market societies, the situation may be more complex.

In market societies, politics and politicians can still steer and orient the conduct of economic affairs through the formalization and monitoring of regulations and rules of the game. In parallel, however, economic actors can deploy various strategies to influence politics and politicians. The game then becomes a complex circular one where political actors may have the capacity to impose rules and structures on economic actors but those rules and structures might be strongly influenced, if not shaped ultimately, by economic actors themselves. Globalization and corporate capitalism's progress across the world have made that circular interplay all the more striking. Today, more than 50 of the largest hundred economic entities in the world are corporations – the others are nation states. Those large transnational corporations are not only major economic players. Their size and transnational reach also makes them powerful political actors (Bakan 2004; Perrow 1991).

Corporations are powerful political actors in different ways. First, they have an intense direct impact on politics and politicians – and hence rule-making and rule monitoring – through large-scale lobbying and/or political or campaign financing (Bebchuk and Jackson 2013; Borisov et al. 2014; Igan et al. 2009; Smith 2000; Woll 2008). They have this kind of impact at the local, national or even transnational – for example European – level. Second, the exercise of corporate social responsibility can be reinterpreted as one more expression of the political role and impact of business (Scherer and Palazzo 2007). Corporations are making consequential political decisions as they compensate for 'failed states' (Chomsky 2006), act through delegation from disengaging states (Singer 2008) or become increasingly involved in transnational multi-stakeholder rule making (Djelic 2011). Third, there is an even more subtle way in which politics and the corporate world interact. Corporations are themselves infused with certain ideologies and hence politics that frame and shape their strategies, structures, processes and behaviors. These ideologies and politics that infuse corporations also have a tendency to influence and impact the world outside and beyond corporate boundaries. In particular, they find their way to politicians and to the political sphere. Different kinds of actors contribute actively to this infusion of particular political programs both within corporations and in the political sphere – consulting firms, lobby and advocacy groups, academics (from business schools and economics departments mostly), as well as a dense ecology of think tanks and research institutes.

Over the last 40 years or so, neoliberalism has become the 'new dominant regime of truth' (Burgin 2012; Mirowski and Plehwe 2009; Djelic 2006; Foucault [1978] 2004; Harvey 2005) with a significant performative impact, through time, on national policymaking (Campbell and Pedersen 2001) and on dynamics of transnational governance (Lee and McBride 2007). This powerful ideological program translates into concrete politics with influence both in the corporate and political worlds. Of particular interest here is the carrier and boundary-spanning role of a dense ecology of neoliberal think tanks and research institutes that has come to be structured over the past four decades (Cockett 1995; Aligica and Evans 2009; Jackson 2012; Medvetz 2012). Neoliberal think tanks espouse a market- and business-friendly ideology and have made it their mission to champion, spread, defend and entrench, as widely and deeply as possible and in a multiplicity of contexts, this ideology and its associated politics.

In this chapter, I am interested in the historical dynamics of emergence of this dense ecology of neoliberal think tanks. Starting from the setting up, in 1955, of the Institute of Economic Affairs (IEA) in Britain, I explore the role of an organization, Atlas, that was created to replicate and diffuse the success of the IEA and to 'litter the world' with free-market think tanks (Blundell 2001). As I explore the founding of Atlas and its early years of operation, I am particularly interested in the process through which the organizational form of the 'neoliberal think tank' came to be constructed, diffused and progressively institutionalized during that period. Through this historical case study, I hope to contribute to our understanding of the contemporary interplay between business and politics. I unpack potent – albeit subtle and indirect – mechanisms of influence that have largely been neglected in the literature. Neoliberal think tanks were constructed to shape and spread ideological, political and practice templates and to help crystallize and stabilize them across the world both in the corporate and in the political world. The key, as Hayek argued in 1949, was 'to shape public opinion' and orient it towards a belief in the superiority of market solutions and economic logics (Hayek 1949, p. 417). Politics and policymaking would then necessarily have to adapt, under pressure from an evolving and mobilized public opinion – and this would occur across a great diversity of institutional and cultural contexts.

METHODS AND DATA

This article builds upon an in-depth historical case study (Skocpol 1984). Historical case studies belong to the category of 'process research' (Langley 1999). They are particularly well suited to exploring processual sequences and bundles of causal patterns that lead up to an important situation (Skocpol 1984; Van de Ven and Sminia 2012). The 'situation' I am interested in is the contemporary existence of a dense ecology of neoliberal think tanks with ideological and political impact. And my focus is on the historical dynamics and causal sequences leading up to that 'situation'. As space is constrained, I focus my account on the early steps and sequences creating the conditions for such a 'situation' to emerge. I follow, hence, the early years of one particular organization, Atlas, from the context of its emergence to the role it played, during its first years of operation, in the diffusion and institutionalization across different parts of the world of a new organizational form – the neoliberal think tank. The period that is explored goes from 1955 and the creation by Antony Fisher of the first neoliberal think tank, the Institute of Economic Affairs (IEA) in London, through the creation of Atlas in 1981 and until Fisher's death in 1988.

The data presented reflect the classic combination, in historical case studies, of primary and secondary data. Primary data sources are 'forms of evidence produced during the historical period under investigation' (Witkowski and Jones 2006, p.72). Unfortunately, access to Atlas' full archives has been impossible. However, a wealth of primary documents is available from the website of Atlas as well as from a number of other sources. A number of personal archives (those of Margaret Thatcher and Friedrich Hayek in particular) as well as the websites and archives of a number of organizations connected to Atlas – some of which are available online – are all useful sources of information on the setting up and early development of Atlas. The reference section provides an exhaustive list of the websites and archives that have been consulted and exploited for the generation of this historical case study. As a complement, I have also used the documents that make up a 'history from within' the neoliberal constellation – books, memoirs and biographies. As much as possible, I have triangulated the information in those documents with available primary sources. I have also consulted and used existing secondary contributions by historians and social scientists. There is a broad secondary literature by now on the historical development of the neoliberal movement in general, a rapidly increasing production on the topic of neoliberal think tanks but nothing as yet on Atlas and its particular role in the neoliberal constellation.

CONTEXTUALIZATION – BUILDING THE INSTITUTE OF ECONOMIC AFFAIRS

In 1955, Sir Antony Fisher, a World War II British Air Force veteran turned chicken farmer, set up the Institute of Economic Affairs (IEA) in London. In the following years, Fisher himself constructed and spread the 'creation myth'. After reading a Reader's Digest version of Hayek's book, *The Road to Serfdom*, Fisher went to the London School of Economics in 1946 to meet Hayek in person and propose his services to the cause of free markets (Muller 1996). When Fisher suggested he could go into politics, Hayek countered with an alternative proposition:

> Society's course will be changed only by a change in ideas. First you must reach the intellectuals, the teachers and writers with reasoned argument. It will be their influence on society, which will prevail and the politicians will follow. (As quoted in Blundell 2003, p. 17)

The seed for the IEA and the first neoliberal think tank had thus been planted. Fisher brought it alive in 1955, after he had accumulated sufficient financial resources through his entrepreneurial success with the mass production of chicken. To run the IEA, Fisher recruited Ralph Harris, a young intellectual from the Conservative Party (Blundell 2003, p. 17). Harris then convinced Arthur Seldon – a bright liberal economist – to join as editorial director. The IEA engaged in intense intellectual activism, producing and diffusing 'papers and pamphlets for an educated audience' (Blundell 2003, p. 21; Seldon 2005). It also relayed the work of Hayek and other prominent members of the still young Mont Pèlerin Society (Mirowski and Plehwe 2009). Initially, the period and the country were not conducive to free-market ideas – quite to the contrary:

> We were a scorned, dismissed, heretical minority. There was a preordained path for the state to regulate, to plan and to direct – as in war, so in peace. If you questioned it, it was like swearing in church. At times this overwhelming consensus intimidated us, and we sometimes held back. We often felt like mischievous, naughty little boys. (Blundell 2003, p. 20)

By the beginning of the 1960s, though, the IEA had found a space and an audience in the intellectual ecology of Britain. Around the IEA and its numerous press and social events – where academics and other contributors presented and discussed papers with policy implications – the network of free-market supporters and champions became denser through time (Muller 1996; Seldon 2005). It brought together a great diversity of people from academia, the media, the professional world and business. By the mid-1970s, the Institute of Economic Affairs was in the process of asserting its intellectual influence in Britain. With the IEA, Fisher, Harris and Seldon had successfully institutionalized the prototype of a new kind of organization – the neoliberal think tank. This organization had four characteristic features. First, its mission was 'to conduct a war of ideas' and to champion 'market philosophy' (Muller 1996). Second, it would do so by attempting to influence those people Hayek called 'second hand dealers in ideas' (Hayek 1949) – the 'academic scribblers and intellectuals who shaped, promulgated and even advertised ideas, journalists, broadcasters, teachers, students and political commentators' (Muller 1996 p. 90).

Third, the organization refused allegiance to any political party and vowed not to receive any public or government funds to keep its 'independence'. Funding initially came from private individuals, and in particular from Fisher. Later on, private firms became important contributors (Muller 1996). Fourth, the IEA rapidly managed to co-opt academics into its activities and hence progressively developed academic and scientific rigor and legitimacy. All those features were striking and quite specific to the IEA then. They would soon become the defining markers of the neoliberal think tank as a new organizational form.

The concrete influence of the IEA was confirmed in May 1979, when the Conservative Party won the British parliamentary elections by a wide margin and Margaret Thatcher became prime minister (Muller 1996, 101ff). On 18 May, she sent a warm thank you note to Ralph Harris (and to the IEA as a whole):

> Let me thank you for what you have done for the cause of free enterprise over the course of so many years. It was primarily your foundation work, which enabled us to rebuild the philosophy upon which our Party succeeded in the past. The debt we owe to you is immense and I am very grateful. (Thatcher 1979)

In June 1979, Margaret Thatcher made Ralph Harris her first peer, raising him as Lord Harris of High Cross (Blundell 2008, p. 190). Harris liked to say that 'he was not a Thatcherite' but that Britain was lucky that 'Margaret Thatcher was an IEA-ite' (Wolf 2006).

DIFFUSING AND INSTITUTIONALIZING THE NEOLIBERAL THINK TANK

In the 1970s already, Fisher had in mind the idea of replicating the success of the IEA through the multiplication of parallel initiatives. As he made clear in 1977:

> To those who ask for a concentrated effort I plead with all the power at my command for proliferation. We are getting near the truth; let it be propounded from as many sources as possible. (Frost and Moller 2008, p. 20)

In 1975, a Canadian businessman, Patrick Boyle, asked Fisher to come and help him set up what would become the Fraser Institute. Things, then, started to accelerate. Fisher was being contacted, from different parts of North America, to help with the launch of organizational 'brothers' and 'sisters' to the IEA; the Manhattan Institute in 1978 in New York, the Heritage Foundation in Washington or the Pacific Research Institute in San Francisco, where he and his wife moved in 1979.

Building upon Early Success – Towards the Creation of Atlas

After the political victory of Thatcher in 1979, Antony Fisher was more eager than ever to foster the proliferation of neoliberal think tanks beyond the shores of Britain, Canada or the United States. He tested, with a few persons, his idea of an organization that would be in charge of proliferation. On 1 January 1980, Hayek wrote back, giving him his full support:

> I entirely agree with you that the time has come when it has become desirable and almost a duty to extend the network of institutes of the kind of the London Institute of Economic Affairs ... I am more convinced than ever that the method practiced by the IEA is the only one, which promises any results ... This ought to be used to create similar institutes all over the world and you have now acquired the special skill of doing it. (Hayek 1980)

The new organization Fisher had in mind would fulfill the mission of helping to set up neoliberal think tanks across the world. The Institute for Economic Affairs would serve as the prototype for the think tanks themselves and Fisher planned to build upon his recent experience as 'think tank entrepreneur' in Canada and in the United States. On 20 February 1980, he received another warm endorsement for that project, this time from Margaret Thatcher:

> I applaud your aim to build on the success of the IEA in Europe, America and further afield. I believe it deserves the most urgent and generous support of all concerned with the restoration of the market economy as the foundation of a free society. (Thatcher 1980)

After winning the Nobel Prize in 1976, Milton Friedman had retired from the University of Chicago and settled in San Francisco. There, he was a visiting scholar at the Federal Reserve Bank of San Francisco and fellow at the Hoover Institution in Stanford (Taylor 2000). The Friedmans lived in the same apartment block as Antony Fisher and his wife (Friedman 2002). So, not only did Milton Friedman endorse Fisher's idea right away; he was also closely associated with the early development of the project.

The Atlas Economic Research Foundation (Atlas) was incorporated in the State of Delaware on 14 July 1981. The offices of Atlas were initially located in San Francisco, in the Mills Building at 220 Montgomery Street. In the summer of 1988, just after Antony Fisher died, Atlas moved its offices to George Mason University in Fairfax, Virginia – a few miles from Capitol Hill and the Washington power center. John Blundell then became the new president and stayed in that position until 1991 when he moved to the Institute of Economic Affairs (Frost and Moller 2008, p. 38).

The name Atlas has two possible origins. It can obviously refer to the Greek Titan who held up the world on his shoulder. In Greek mythology, though, Atlas is strong but not very smart, easily deceived by Ulysses. Archimedes, the Greek astronomer, proposed a rational reinterpretation of the Atlas myth that was, apparently, the source of inspiration for Antony

Fisher (Frost and Moller 2008, p. 27). Archimedes purportedly said: 'Give me a place to stand and a lever long enough and I will move the world.' The lever, in our story, was the Institute for Economic Affairs prototype to be diffused across the world. In the neoliberal thought collective, however, Atlas is also easily associated with the work of Ayn Rand, in particular her best-selling book *Atlas Shrugged*. The official position of the Atlas Economic Research Foundation on the origin of its name is relatively non-committal:

> The name was not derived from the book, in fact the word 'Atlas' in our name has to do with the global nature of our work. And although we share many of the free market values found in *Atlas Shrugged* and held by the Atlas Society and Ayn Rand Institute, we are quite separate organizations. (Atlas 2013b)

Atlas' beginnings were small. Pamela Lentz joined Atlas as full-time secretary/office manager on 1 January 1982. In 1985, Alejandro Chafuen, a young Argentinian with a PhD in economics from California (and a member of the Mont Pèlerin Society since 1980), joined the team (Chafuen 2011). Chafuen was president of Atlas from 1991 to 2009 and he remains a member of the board.

In the early period, Antony Fisher did most of the work with the support of his wife, Dorian (Chafuen 2011). The budget of Atlas, for the first year, was around $150,000 (Chafuen 2011). Donors included a Canadian family that to this day desires to remain anonymous. The Sarah (Mellon) Scaife Foundation donated 30 percent of the initial budget and is still a major donor. The Scaife Foundation is a Pittsburg-based family foundation that gives large sums of money to many members of the neoliberal thought collective, and is arguably the 'leading financial supporter of the movement that reshaped American politics in the last quarter of the twentieth century' (Kaiser 1999, p. A1). Charles Brunie, Dorian Fisher (Antony's rich wife) and a number of private philanthropists from the United States and Canada were also among the early donors (Chafuen 2011).

Fostering Proliferation – Atlas and the Early Diffusion of Neoliberal Think Tanks

The main mission of Atlas, initially, was to expand the reach of the neoliberal agenda by fostering the rapid proliferation of think tanks on the model of the London IEA in different regions of the world. The idea was that those think tanks, just like the IEA had done in Britain, would 'influence public sentiment' across the world and that this would in turn 'make legislation possible' (Fisher 1985). During its early period, Atlas fostered the proliferation of think tanks in essentially two ways. First, it provided seed money. Even though amounts were small, this role of 'think tank angel' proved extremely important as it would start the engine', as it were. As Antony Fisher was keenly aware:

> One of the difficulties in setting up an institute is to raise the money in the first place, because usually businessmen don't know what it is all about. They need to see the publications producing results by selling in universities and attracting media coverage. Without the product, fundraising is always slow. (Fisher 1981)

Second, Fisher and the small team around him played the role of coach and consultant. Building upon the experience accumulated throughout the 1970s with the first generation of neoliberal think tanks, they identified success factors and different ways to deal with obstacles. Atlas was not itself a think tank, nor did it 'run(s) or control(s) any institute' but it 'used the IEA's experience to advise an ever-growing family of independent institutes' (Atlas 1987).

The first investment ever of Atlas after 1981 was in a French institute – the Institut Economique de Paris (IEP) (Fisher 1983). Pascal Salin, an economist, and Guy Plunier, a businessman, were the local team behind the IEP (Chafuen 2011). Even though this institute did not survive, Salin has remained very active in the fight for a revival of liberalism in France (Salin 2000). Fisher also put high hopes in John Goodman, a bright young scholar with a PhD in economics from Columbia. Atlas gave Goodman a starting grant of US$20,000. This allowed him to launch in 1983 the National Center for Policy Analysis (NCPA) in Dallas, Texas. The Center would go on to become a highly influential think tank that worked extensively to diffuse 'new ideas' in the United States, particularly when it comes to the privatization and marketization of healthcare (NCPA 2013). In South America, Fisher started by helping Hernando de Soto, a Peruvian economist trained in Switzerland who went back to Peru in 1981 to found, with the help of Atlas, the Institute for Liberty and Democracy (ILD) (Chafuen 2011). The influence of Fisher and Atlas on the Institute for Liberty and Democracy was extremely significant, as de Soto later recalled:

> It was on the basis of his (Fisher's) vision that we designed the structure of the ILD. He then came to Lima and told us how to structure the statutes, how to plan our goals, how to build the foundation, what to expect in the short and long term. (As quoted in Frost 2002)

Initially, the Institute for Liberty and Democracy fought for the institutionalization of private property rights in Peru. In 1987, de Soto wrote a book outlining a liberal agenda that would have a significant impact in Peru and in other developing countries across the world. The title chosen for that book – *The Other Path* – was provocative in itself, as it clearly referred to and confronted the powerful Shining Path Maoist movement, which was at that time extremely active and powerful in Peru (Atlas 1991).

In Iceland, Fisher set his sights on Hannes Gissurarson. With a small grant from Atlas, this young man launched the Jon Thorlaksson Institute in 1983. In 1985, he defended his PhD thesis in political science at Oxford University, with the title *Hayek's Conservative Liberalism*. The Jon Thorlaksson think tank was named after an Icelandic prime minister from the 1920s who had been a fervent champion of economic freedom. This think tank disappeared in 1988 but was in fact replaced by a new organization. The Icelandic Research Center for Innovation and Economic Growth is the 'direct heir to the Jon Thorlaksson Institute' and is registered with the tax authorities under the same identification number as the old institute (RNH 2013). Gissurarson is still today the academic director of that organization. In Australia, Fisher worked with Greg Lindsay in the early 1980s, as the latter was busy creating the Center for Independent Studies (Lindsay 1996). The Center for Research in Applied Economics in Italy, launched by Antonio Martino, was another institute that Atlas and Fisher helped create. Fisher also spearheaded or assisted projects in Mexico, Venezuela, Chile, Australia and Spain (Neubauer 2012). He even encouraged Eastern European researchers based in the United Kingdom to start working on the question of communism, with a view to a pending post-communist turn (Chafuen 2011).

By 1985, there were 26 organizational members in the constellation of neoliberal 'secondhand dealers of ideas' associated with Atlas. Fisher and/or Atlas were behind the creation or development of almost all of them (Fisher 1985).

CONNECTING THE THINK TANKS TO THE NEOLIBERAL THOUGHT COLLECTIVE

Beyond its role in fostering the diffusion of neoliberal think tanks across the world, Atlas also had a significant impact during that period as a connector and mediating organization. It played a major role in facilitating the inscription of the various think tanks into what could be called the common neoliberal 'thought collective' (Mirowski and Plehwe 2009).

A first dimension of that inscription was the creation of a direct connection between the think tanks and their leaders and the intellectual core of the neoliberal movement, the Mont Pélerin Society (MPS), which Hayek had set up in 1947 (Djelic 2006; Mirowski and Plehwe 2009). A key mechanism was the co-optation of leaders of the early think tanks into the

MPS. Among the 26 think tanks associated with Atlas in 1985, 20 had a leader who was by that date already a member of the Mont Pèlerin Society. In the following years, four more would be connected to the Mont Pèlerin through membership of the leader. In general, the connection between think tank leaders and the Mont Pélerin Society started either a few years before or after the setting up of the think tank. This points to two probable trajectories. Either, Antony Fisher scouted the individual in the context of Mont Pèlerin Society meetings and identified him/her as a promising future think tank leader. Alternatively, the think tank leader was brought into the core organization of the neoliberal 'thought collective' precisely because of his/her role in the building up of a successful think tank.

This proximity with the core meant that the think tanks were regularly involved in the activities of the MPS. The Institute of Economic Affairs helped organize the Oxford meeting of the MPS in 1959, and organized two further meetings in Scotland in 1968 and 1976. The Fraser Institute organized MPS regional meetings in Vancouver in 1983 and again in 1999. In the context of MPS meetings, the members of this 'thought collective' were regularly exposed to an intellectual orthodoxy that became increasingly controlled and powerful as conflicts and contradictions within the MPS were progressively expunged (Djelic 2006; Mirowski and Plehwe 2009).

A second important dimension of the inscription in a neoliberal 'thought collective' was the embeddedness of the intellectual activity of the various think tanks in a set of structuring references that were surprisingly homogeneous. Atlas helped diffuse the ideas of the core into the swelling ranks of neoliberal second-hand dealers of ideas. Greg Lindsay, the founder and leader of the Australian Center for Independent Studies made that very clear:

> The strategy mapped out by Hayek in The Intellectuals and Socialism was one of working with people who transmit ideas to everyone else. I still think that is right . . . We (the local institutes) are the retailers and wholesalers of ideas. (Lindsay 1996, p. 20)

Atlas financed, in that early period, the translation in different languages of some of the key texts of Hayek, Friedman and of the papers initially produced by the Institute for Economic Affairs. It also facilitated the reproduction and diffusion of materials produced by some of the older neoliberal think tanks (Chafuen 2011). The texts written by Friedrich von Hayek came close, in that context, to being a common 'sacred reference'. *The Road to Serfdom* (Hayek 1944) was not far from being the 'Bible' of the neoliberal community, or, more precisely, the Reader's Digest condensed version of *The Road to Serfdom* (Frost 2002). Hayek also wrote many texts and pamphlets for the IEA that were later on broadly reprinted, translated and circulated by Atlas. Between 1968 and 1983, Hayek wrote 13 such texts; on inflation, currency, trade unions, privatization, rent restriction or unemployment among others.

A third way in which Atlas fostered the inscription of individual think tanks into the neoliberal 'thought collective' was through its active involvement in the local organization of meetings and workshops. Atlas helped finance and organize local meetings and events, even securing in a number of cases the participation of core actors. For example, Antony Fisher convinced both Hayek and Friedman to come to France and give their support to Pascal Salin and his liberal colleagues, a few months before the creation of the Institut Economique de Paris (IEP) in 1982, and a few months after the election in France of a Socialist president, François Mitterrand (Brookes 2014, p. 15ff). In the early 1980s, Hayek and/or Friedman visited more or less all the countries where Fisher was busy helping with the development of a think tank: Iceland, Peru, Chile, Venezuela, Australia, France, Italy, Spain (Ebenstein 2003; 2007). In some cases, Fisher was there first and mobilized the help of Hayek or Friedman. In other cases, Hayek created the contact with Fisher when he felt that there was an interesting opportunity; this was the case for example in Peru with Hernando de Soto (Mitchell 2009). In the quite different local contexts they explored in that early period, Fisher and the Atlas team hence played the very important role of mediators. By bringing along with them the big names of the neoliberal 'thought collective', who by then were Nobel Prize winners, and mobilizing them around local events, they imbued local think tanks and their leaders with legitimacy and visibility. In the process, they buttressed weak and fragile initiatives.

ATLAS OR THE 'MOTHER ORGANIZATION' – STUMBLING INTO THE NURTURING ROLE

As a result of these efforts, the membership base of Atlas increased rapidly. In 1981, when he was launching Atlas, Fisher had claimed:

> There are ten operating institutes using similar methods, fourteen more trying to get started, and at least sixteen other places where help would be effective. That would be a total of some forty institutes in thirty countries. (As quoted in Chafuen 2011)

By 1985, Fisher could already identify close to 30 think tanks across the world that were connected to Atlas (Fisher 1985). In the spring of 1988, a few months before Fisher died, Atlas was 'in touch with over forty institutes in twenty plus countries' – not too far from what Fisher had anticipated eight years before (Atlas 1988).

The original project of Antony Fisher, with the creation of Atlas, had been to foster and facilitate the development, around the world, of neoliberal think tanks modeled after the Institute for Economic Affairs (Fisher 1985; Friedman 2002). As this started to happen, in the early 1980s, Atlas 'bumped', as it were, into another necessary and complementary role. Atlas became a central hub for a transnational network in the making. Setting up think tanks was not enough; their founders also needed to create the conditions for them to 'sing in unison'. The Atlas team was rapidly convinced that 'in order to influence public opinion and ultimately public policy' across different countries, you needed 'choruses and not (multiple) solos' (Antony Fisher Speech May 1980, quoted in Chafuen 2013). Atlas, it turned out, would have to structure and nurture the emerging transnational community of neoliberal second-hand dealers in ideas (Djelic and Quack 2010).

In fact, this would become the principal role for Atlas starting in the 1990s. Those developments are beyond the scope of this chapter, but we identify here some of the early activities that Atlas launched in that direction in the early 1980s. The very structure of Atlas was, in reality, already a step in that direction. Sitting on the first board of Atlas, in July 1981, were leaders of some of the older Institutes: Ralph Harris (IEA), Patrick Boyle (Fraser), Charles Brunie (Manhattan) and Jim North (PRI). From the start, it seemed, Atlas was thought of as a 'common home'. Soon, Fisher launched the yearly Atlas International Workshops. The first one, in September 1983, took place in Vancouver, Canada, and was organized jointly with the Fraser Institute. Then followed Cambridge (UK), Sydney (Australia), Saint Vincent (Italy) and Indianapolis (US). In each case, the organization of the workshop was a joint effort between Atlas and the local Institute(s) inscribed in the Atlas constellation. And the Atlas meetings were systematically organized in conjunction with the meeting, that same year, of the Mont Pèlerin Society. The Atlas Workshops took place on the weekend before the start of the Mont Pèlerin Society meeting, which always began on a Sunday (Liberaal Archief 2005).

These international workshops were relatively small at the beginning and the main objective was to bring members of the emerging transnational community together, physically, at least once a year. The first workshop for which we have concrete information is the fifth Atlas Workshop, which took place in September 1986 in Indianapolis, with close to 100 participants (Atlas 1988). Three different groups of speakers presented. First, there were representatives of the 'old institutes': Harris (IEA), Michael Walker (Fraser), William Hammett (Manhattan), William Mellor (PRI),

Alejandro Chafuen and Antony Fisher (Atlas). Second, was a group of representatives from the younger 'child Institutes' of Atlas: Greg Lindsay (CIS), John Goodman (NCPA), Hernando de Soto (ILD), Antonio Martino (CREA). Finally, there were a few invited participants; for example a secretary of state from the Thatcher government, an academic from Washington University, a retired manager and board member of the Heritage Foundation (who later contributed funding to Atlas) and a journalist from the *Wall Street Journal* (Atlas Workshop 1987). Interestingly, the program and application form for the Atlas Workshop clearly indicated that attending the workshop did not imply an automatic invitation to the Mont Pèlerin meeting (ibid.). Each year, the neoliberal constellation physically came together, but the way in which it did underscored the hierarchy and partial separation between the core and the layer of second-hand dealers in ideas. Still, the proximity of the two events, in time and space, was probably a good motivating mechanism for the young up-and-coming think tank leaders, who could thus hope to be invited, one day, to the mysterious meetings of the holy core.

CONCLUSION

According to Hayek, an intellectual revolution could only happen if the framing work of a core of utopian thinkers was relayed through time by increasing numbers of intellectual 'foot soldiers' (Hayek 1949). This layer of 'secondhand dealers in ideas' was essential to the architecture of influence that Hayek was thinking about, in the mid-1940s, to revive the (economic) liberal project. It would translate and disseminate the programmatic agenda of the core. The work of this second layer was about institution-building with two main objectives: to influence cognitive maps and 'public opinion' in many different local contexts and to impact, in time, political programs in different places, to generate the new 'governing force of politics' (Hayek 1949, p. 417).

When Antony Fisher created the Institute for Economic Affairs in 1955, he had in mind this programmatic structure, which he had discussed with Hayek himself. In all likelihood, however, he did not envision that this early initiative would come to have such a consequential impact. The path was clearly not an easy one and in the first period of this story, many accidental developments hindered or facilitated the proximate diffusion of a new type of organization – the neoliberal think tank. When Fisher created Atlas in 1981 it was built on slightly more solid ground. Atlas could build upon the success of the IEA and it was born in a much more favorable political context following the political triumph of Margaret Thatcher in Britain and of Ronald Reagan in the US. The objective thus shifted to taking the next steps, accelerating the process of diffusion and the expansion of neoliberal think tanks in many different parts of the world. Milton Friedman nicely summarized those different stages:

> If Antony had done no more in the think-tank world (than creating the IEA), it would have been enough to put all believers in freedom in his debt. But after a digression to breeding green turtles, scientifically successful but commercially disastrous, he returned to breeding think tanks, at first on a retail basis, and then, with the establishment of the Atlas Economic Research Foundation, on a wholesale basis. (Friedman 2002)

When Fisher died in 1988, he had created a new organizational form – the neoliberal think tank. He had significantly contributed to both the design of that organizational form and to its diffusion and progressive institutionalization across a great variety of contexts. The neoliberal think tank, as a powerful 'secondhand dealer in ideas', was contributing considerably to the progressive emergence across a number of countries of a new institutional field – the field of neoliberal influence building. In the last years of his life, Fisher saw his vision come to fruition:

> Numerous press clippings report how the institutes in the Atlas network are redefining the boundaries of 'politically impossible' policies worldwide . . . 'This illustrates how institutes dedicated to the principles of the free market and private property are making a difference in the world,' commented Atlas Chairman Antony Fisher. (Atlas 1988)

By then, there were close to 40 neoliberal think tanks in more than 20 countries. According to DiMaggio, 'new institutions arise when organized actors with sufficient resources see in them an opportunity to realize interests that they value highly' (DiMaggio 1988, p. 14). DiMaggio calls those organized actors 'institutional entrepreneurs'. In that sense, Antony Fisher was indeed an 'institutional entrepreneur'. What this story shows, however, is that Fisher could not have accomplished what he did alone. The process described was a complex one, with ups and downs, unintended developments, the involvement of a multiplicity of other actors and resources and clearly different stages with evolving logics. The type of 'institutional entrepreneurship' at work here was not the heroic type, even though Fisher has unsurprisingly been hailed as a hero in the community he did so much to spearhead. I have shown instead that the process of institutional emergence in that context resulted 'from spatially dispersed, heterogeneous activities' (Lounsbury and Crumley 2007) and that it reflected complex collective interplays, ambiguous and unintended developments, as well as significant temporal sequencing (Djelic 2010).

As it turns out, the story told here was only the beginning. Since 1988, the network of influence spanned and nurtured by Atlas has expanded in a striking way. Today Atlas boasts a membership of more than 400 think tanks in more than 70 nations across the world (Atlas 2013). As the numbers increased, the role of keeping the network together and of structuring and nurturing a transnational community of neoliberal think tanks has become both more important and more challenging for Atlas (Djelic and Quack 2010). How Atlas has managed to deal with that challenge since the late 1980s is another interesting story. It is, however, beyond the scope of this chapter.

REFERENCES

Aligica, P.D. and A. Evans (2009), *The Neoliberal Revolution in Eastern Europe*, Cheltenham, UK and Northampton, MA, USA: Edward Elgar.
Bakan, J. (2004), *The Corporation*, London, UK: Robinson Publishing.
Bebchuk, L. and R. Jackson (2013), 'Shining light on corporate political spending', *Georgetown Law Journal*, **101**, 923–67.
Borisov, A., E. Goldman and N. Gupta (2014), 'The corporate value of (corrupt) lobbying, working paper', at European Corporate Governance Institute http://papers.ssrn.com/sol3/papers.cfm?abstract_id=2443104. Accessed 3 May 2017.
Brookes, K. (2014), 'Le rôle des clubs et des réseaux d'intellectuels libéraux dans la diffusion du néolibéralisme en France, Sciences Po Grenoble, Working Paper 16', at http://www.sciencespo-grenoble.fr/wp-content/uploads/2013/11/SPGWP16.pdf. Accessed 3 May 2017.
Burgin, A. (2012), *The Great Persuasion: Reinventing Free Markets since the Great Depression*, Cambridge, MA: Harvard University Press.
Campbell, J. and O. Pedersen (eds) (2001), *The Rise of Neoliberalism and Institutional Analysis*, Princeton, NJ: Princeton University Press.
Chomsky, N. (2006), *Failed States*, New York: Henry Holt & Co.
Cockett, R. (1995), *Thinking the Unthinkable*, London: Fontana Press.
DiMaggio, P. (1988), 'Interest and agency in institutional theory', in L. Zucker (ed.), *Institutional Patterns and Organizations*, Cambridge, MA: Ballinger, pp. 3–32.
Djelic, M.L. (2006), 'Marketization: From intellectual agenda to global policy making', in M.L. Djelic and K. Sahlin-Andersson (eds), *Transnational Governance*, Cambridge, UK: Cambridge University Press, pp. 53–73.
Djelic, M.L. (2010), 'Institutional perspectives: Working towards coherence or irreconcilable diversity?', in G.J. Morgan, J.L. Campbell, C.C. Crouch, O.K. Pedersen and R. Whitley (eds), *The Oxford Handbook of Comparative Institutional Analysis*, Oxford, UK: Oxford University Press, pp. 15–40.
Djelic, M.L. (2011), 'From the rule of law to the law of rules', *International Studies of Management and Organization*, **41**(1), 35–61.
Djelic, M.L. and S. Quack (eds) (2010), *Transnational Communities*, Cambridge, UK: Cambridge University Press.
Ebenstein, A. (2003), *Friedrich Hayek: A Biography*, Chicago: University of Chicago Press.

Ebenstein, A. (2007), *Milton Friedman: A Biography*, New York: Palgrave Macmillan.
Foucault, M. [1978] (2004), *Naissance de la Biopolitique*, Paris: Seuil.
Friedman, M. (1970), 'The social responsibility of business is to increase its profits', *The New York Times*, 13 September 1970.
Frost, G. (2002), *Anthony Fisher: Champion of Liberty*, London: Profile Books.
Goldthwaite, R. (1987) 'The Medici Bank and the world of Florentine capitalism', *Past & Present*, **114**, 3–31.
Harvey, D. (2005), *A Brief History of Neoliberalism*, Oxford, UK: Oxford University Press.
Hayek, F. (1949), 'The intellectuals and socialism', *University of Chicago Law Review*, Spring, 417–33.
Igan, D., P. Mishra and T. Tressel (2009), 'A fistful of dollars: Lobbying and the financial crisis, IMF working paper', at http://www.imf.org/external/pubs/ft/wp/2009/wp09287.pdf. Accessed 3 May 2017.
Jackson, B. (2012), 'The think tank archipelago: Thatcherism and neoliberalism', in B. Jackson and R. Saunders (eds), *Making Thatcher's Britain*, Cambridge, UK: Cambridge University Press, pp. 43–61.
Kaiser, R. (1999) 'Money, family name shaped Scaife, Washington Post, May 3', at http://www.washingtonpost.com/wp-srv/politics/special/clinton/stories/scaifemain050399.htm. Accessed 3 May 2017.
Langley, A. (1999), 'Strategies for theorizing from process data', *Academy of Management Review*, **24**, 691–710.
Lounsbury, M. and E. Crumley (2007), 'New practice creation: An institutional perspective on innovation', *Organization Studies* **28**(7), 993–1012.
Martin, C. and D. Swank (2012), *The Political Construction of Business Interests*, Cambridge, UK: Cambridge University Press.
Medvetz, T. (2012), *Think Tanks in America*, Chicago: The University of Chicago Press.
Mills, C.W. (1956), *The Power Elite*, Oxford, UK: Oxford University Press.
Mirowski, P. and D. Plehwe (eds) (2009), *The Road from Mont Pèlerin*, Cambridge, MA: Harvard University Press.
Mitchell, T. (2009), 'How neoliberalism makes its world: The urban property rights project in Peru', in P. Mirowski and D. Plehwe (eds), *The Road from Mont Pèlerin*, Cambridge, MA: Harvard University Press, pp. 386–416.
Muller, C. (1996) 'The Institute of Economic Affairs: Undermining the post-war consensus', *Contemporary British History*, **10**(1), 88–110.
Neubauer, R. (2012), 'Dialogue, monologue or something in between? Neoliberal think tanks in the Americas', *International Journal of Communications*, **6**, 2173–98.
Pearson, M. (1997), *China's New Business Elite*, Oakland, CA: University of California Press.
Perrow, C. (1991) 'A society of organizations', *Theory & Society*, **20**, 725–62.
Scherer, A.G. and G. Palazzo (2007), 'Toward a political conception of corporate social responsibility', *Academy of Management Review*, **32**, 1096–120.
Singer, P. (2008), *Corporate Warriors*, Ithaca, NY: Cornell University.
Smith, M. (2000), *American Business and Political Power*, Chicago: University of Chicago Press.
Skocpol, T. (1984), *Vision and Method in Historical Sociology*, Cambridge, UK: Cambridge University Press.

Van de Ven, A. and H. Sminia (2012), 'Aligning process questions, perspectives and explanations', in M. Schultz, S. Maguire, A. Langley and H. Tsoukas (eds), *Constructing Identity in and around Organizations*, Oxford, UK: Oxford University Press, pp. 306–19.
Witkowski, T. and B. Jones (2006), 'Qualitative historical research in marketing', in R. Belk (ed.), *Qualitative Historical Research Methods in Marketing*, Cheltenham, UK and Northampton, MA, USA: Edward Elgar, pp. 70–82.
Woll, C. (2008), *Firm Interest*, Ithaca, NY: Cornell University Press.

Atlas – History from Within

Blundell, J. (2001), 'Waging the war of ideas, London: IEA', at http://www.iea.org.uk/sites/default/files/publications/files/upldbook226pdf.pdf. Accessed 3 May 2017.
Blundell, J. (2008), *Margaret Thatcher*, New York: Algora Publishing.
Blundell, J. (2011), *Ladies for Liberty*, New York: Algora Publishing.
Chafuen, A. (2011), 'Atlas Economic Research Foundation early history', at http://www.chafuen.com/atlas-economic-research-foundation-early-history. Accessed 3 May 2017.
Chafuen, A. (2013), 'Fisher quotes', at http://www.chafuen.com/fisherquotes. Accessed 3 May 2017.
Frost, G. and D. Moller (2008), 'Antony Fisher, champion of liberty condensed version, London: IEA', at http://www.iea.org.uk/publications/research/antony-fisher-champion-of-liberty. Accessed 3 May 2017.

Think Tanks and Their Leaders

Edwards, L. (1997), *The Power of Ideas: The Heritage Foundation at 25 Years*, Jameson Books.
Fraser (1999), 'Challenging perceptions: 25 years of influential ideas', at http://www.fraserinstitute.org/uploadedFiles/fraserca/Content/About_Us/Who_We_Are/25th_Retrospective.pdf. Accessed 3 May 2017.
Fraser (2004), 'The Fraser Institute at 30: a retrospective', at http://www.fraserinstitute.org/uploadedFiles/fraserca/Content/About_Us/Who_We_Are/30th_Retrospective.pdf. Accessed 3 May 2017.
Gissurarson, H. (2013), 'Reports of capitalism's demise exaggerated. Speech at the University of Iceland, February 19', at http://www.rnh.is/?p=3492. Accessed 3 May 2017.
Lindsay, G. (1996), 'The CIS at twenty – Greg Lindsay talks to Andrew Norton, *Policy*, Winter: 16–21', at https://www.cis.org.au/images/stories/policy-magazine/1996-winter/1996-12-2-andrew-norton.pdf. Accessed 3 May 2017.
Seldon, A. (2005), *The IEA, the LSE and the Influence of Ideas*, Indianapolis, IN: Liberty Fund.
Seldon, A. and R. Harris (1977), *Not from Benevolence*, Kingston, RI: University of Rhode Island.
Wolfe, T. (2004), 'The Manhattan Institute at 25', in Manhattan Institute (ed.), *Turning Intellect into Influence*, Auckland, NZ: Reed Press, pp. 29–30.

Websites

ASI (2013), *Adam Smith Institute Website*, at http://www.adamsmith.org/. Accessed 3 May 2017.

Atlas (2013a), *Atlas Network Website*, at http://atlasnetwork.org/. Accessed 3 May 2017.

Atlas (2013b), *Frequently Asked Questions, Atlas Economic Research Foundation*, at http://atlasnetwork.org/blog/2010/11/frequently-asked-questions-2/#ref9. Accessed 3 May 2017.

DeSmogBlog (2010), *Mont Pèlerin Directory*, at http://www.desmogblog.com/sites/beta.desmogblog.com/files/Mont%20Pelerin%20Society%20Directory%202010.pdf. Accessed 3 May 2017.

Fraser (2013), *Fraser Institute Website*, at http://www.fraserinstitute.org/. Accessed 3 May 2017.

HF (2013), *Heritage Foundation Website*, at http://www.heritage.org/. Accessed 3 May 2017.

MI (2013), *Manhattan Institute Website*, at http://www.manhattan-institute.org/. Accessed 3 May 2017.

NCPA (2013), *National Center for Policy Analysis – History*, at http://www.ncpa.org/about/national-center-for-policy-analysis-history. Accessed 3 May 2017.

PRI (2013) *Pacific Research Institute*, at http://www.pacificresearch.org/about/pris-history/ Accessed 3 May 2017.

RNH (2013), *Icelandic Research Center for Innovation and Economic Growth*, at http://www.rnh.is/?page_id=346 Accessed 3 May 2017.

Personal Pages and Biographical Information

Boyle, P. (2013) at http://www.fraserinstitute.org/programs.aspx?pageid=6442451036&terms=Patrick+Boyle. Accessed 3 May 2017.

Brunie, C. (2013), at http://www.hudson.org/learn/index.cfm?fuseaction=staff_bio&eid=BrunChar. Accessed 3 May 2017.

Butler, E. (2013), at http://eamonnbutler.com/about/. Accessed 3 May 2017.

Butler, S. (2013), LinkedIn Profile.

Persico, J. (1991), *The Lives and Secrets of William Casey*, Penguin Books.

Casey, B. (2013), at http://billcasey.ca/. Accessed 3 May 2017.

Feulner, E. (2013), at http://www.heritage.org/about/staff/f/edwin-feulner. Accessed 3 May 2017.

Harris, R. (2000), 'Interview of Ralph Harris by PBS – Commanding Heights', at http://www.pbs.org/wgbh/commandingheights/shared/minitextlo/int_ralphharris.html#8. Accessed 3 May 2017.

Mellor, W. (2013), at http://www.ij.org/wmellor-2. Accessed 3 May 2017.

Murray, C. (2013), at http://www.aei.org/scholar/charles-murray/. Accessed 3 May 2017.

Pipes, S. (2013), LinkedIn Profile.

Pirie, M. (2013), at http://eamonnbutler.com/about/. Accessed 3 May 2017.

Walker, M. (2013), at http://www.fraserinstitute.org/author.aspx?id=15364&txID=3266. Accessed 3 May 2017.

Wolf, M. (2006), 'Obituary Lord Harris of High Cross, Financial Times, October 19', at http://mobi.fcpp.org/publication.php/1557. Accessed 3 May 2017.

Archives and Interviews

Atlas (1987), *Atlas Economic Research Foundation – Recent Highlights, May, Issue 6*, at http://atlasnetwork.org/blog/2010/11/highlights-archives/. Accessed 3 May 2017.

Atlas (1988), *Atlas Economic Research Foundation – Highlights, Spring*, at http://atlasnetwork.org/blog/2010/11/highlights-archives/. Accessed 3 May 2017.

Atlas Workshop (1987), *Atlas – Indianapolis Seminar*, 5–6 September: at https://docs.google.com/a/essec.edu/viewer?a=v&pid=sites&srcid=Y2hhZnVlbi5jb218d3d3fGd4OjU3NTRkZjRiNGRiMmQ1YzM. Accessed 3 May 2017.

Fisher, A. (1981), 'Letter to a businessman in Jamaica', reprinted in A. Chafuen, *Fisher Quotes*, at http://www.chafuen.com/fisherquotes. Accessed 3 May 2017.

Fisher, A. (1983), 'Pourquoi l'IEA? Conférence prononcée à l'Institut Economique de Paris le 29 septembre 1982', *Liberté économique et progrès social*, n° 46–47, Octobre.

Fisher, A. (1985) 'Atlas presentation and promotion video', at: http://www.youtube.com/watch?v=nW8ukG8WdQg. Accessed 3 May 2017.

Hayek, F. (1980), 'Letter to Antony Fisher. January 1', at http://www.margaretthatcher.org/document/117149. Accessed 3 May 2017.

Liberaal Archief (2005), *Inventory of the General Meeting Files Mont Pèlerin Society* (1947–98), at www.liberaalarchief.be. Accessed 3 May 2017.

Taylor, J. (2000), 'An interview with Milton Friedman, Conducted on May 2 in San Francisco', at http://www.stanford.edu/~johntayl/Onlinepaperscombinedbyyear/2001/An_Interview_with_Milton_Friedman.pdf. Accessed 3 May 2017.

Thatcher, M. (1979), 'Note to Ralph Harris, May 18', at http://www.margaretthatcher.org/document/117145. Accessed 3 May 2017.

Thatcher, M. (1980), 'Letter to Antony Fisher. February 20', at http://www.margaretthatcher.org/document/117154. Accessed 3 May 2017.

Thatcher, M. (1993), 'The new world order, speech at the Fraser Institute, November 8', at http://www.margaretthatcher.org/document/108325. Accessed 3 May 2017.

Van Offelen, J. (2005), 'Preface by a former Belgian minister, member of the Mont Pèlerin Society to the inventory of the general meetings files', Ghent: Liberaal Archiev, at www.liberaalarchief.be. Accessed 3 May 2017.

2. Global policy bricolage: the role of business in the World Economic Forum

Christina Garsten and Adrienne Sörbom

INTRODUCTION: BUSINESS WITH A GEOPOLITICAL EDGE

Tuesday, 13 November 2012. We are sitting in the magnificent lobby of the Mina A'Salam luxury hotel in Dubai with Dieter Weiss, executive at a leading global management firm. In the grand lobby, men and women, flawlessly dressed in official dress codes from across the world, stand small talking, exchanging news and gossip, talking on their phones, or waiting for a colleague, friend or partner. Mr Weiss, who has not yet had his breakfast, invites us to join him, ordering a cappuccino, orange juice and a sandwich. We decline, apart from the coffee. In half an hour, the Summit on the Global Agenda, organized by the World Economic Forum (WEF), will resume its second day of meetings, to share ideas and options to address the grand challenges of the twenty-first century. The Mina A'Salam hotel, cast as 'a replication of images of ancient Arabia', accommodates the majority of invited WEF strategic partners, business and government participants who have flown in from all parts of the world in take part in the summit.

Mr Weiss, a modest-looking man in his mid-fifties, is a leading member of the Global Agenda Council on the Arctic. The group is entirely new, and Mr Weiss believes it was created upon the initiative of the WEF. It took the WEF a few months to appoint members to the group, but now it has been formed. This is the first Global Agenda Council (GAC) meeting that he participates in, and his expectations are highly set. So far, Mr Weiss is content with the work of the group. He describes it as meaningful. They have decided to compose a shorter text about the Arctic. There are so many ideas about the Arctic, he says. Ideas that are not true. For example, many believe it is uninhabited, which is completely wrong. Business activities have also been ongoing for a long time.

The group wants to correct this faulty image of the Arctic and describe what the current challenges are. Mr Weiss is honest about the fact that he himself knew little about the Arctic before he joined the group. But he is well experienced in leadership, organizational developments and business opportunities. The other members of the group are business representatives, government officials and researchers, who contribute their expert knowledge to the discussions. A big problem, as he sees it, is the fact that there are parts of the Artic that no one owns, in the legal sense, and therefore it cannot be claimed for business. This issue has to be solved. The Arctic region is a new Klondike and future area of business. 'There is an unlimited amount of money to be made here,' Mr Weiss says. The chief reason for him and his company to join the WEF and the GAC group is the fact that most of their customers and competitors are also members. In this sense, the WEF works as a magnet that pulls on other business 'materials'. Everyone wants to go to Davos, to see and to be seen and ultimately to have their GAC questions appear on the agenda. 'It's all about networking and branding,' Mr Weiss claims. But there are, he admits, also a number of Big Egos, and it remains unclear what these figures can contribute.

This episode illustrates the traction power and pulling force of the World Economic Forum among global business leaders and suggests some of their motives for engaging in what is essentially an extra-market activity with a non-profit foundation, intent to secure a place for itself on the international political arena.

This chapter departs from an interest in the involvement of business leaders in the sphere of politics, in the broad sense. Many global business leaders today do much more than engage narrowly in their own corporation and its search for profit. At a general level, we are seeing a proliferation of usages of non-market corporate strategies, such as testimony, lobbying, interlocking of positions and other means to influence policymakers at all levels of government and international institutions as an adjunct to the firm's market strategies (Barley 2010; Lawton et al. 2012). Conversely, there is an enhanced interest on the part of policymakers to influence firm behaviour through multi-stakeholder involvement, public–private agreements and network forms of governance (Scherer and Palazzo 2011). The chapter brings to the fore the role of corporations in the WEF, and how firms act through the WEF to advance their interests, financial as well as political. What is the role of business in the WEF and how do business corporations advance their interests through the WEF?

From a US-based perspective, Barley (2010) has shown how corporations systematically built an institutional field during the 1970s and 1980s to exert greater influence on the US Federal government. The resulting network, he argues (2010 p. 777), 'channels and amplifies corporate political influence, while simultaneously shielding corporations from appearing to directly influence Congress and the administration'. Organization scholars, he underscores, should take up the Parsonian imperative to study not only the internal processes of organizations, but also how organizations adapt to the situations they face, and how organizations influence the larger sociocultural context in which they are embedded. Organizational theorists have largely ignored Parsons's second and third mandates, he contends (2010, p. 778). This is also true for the organizational landscapes outside of the US.

Taking inspiration from Barley, and based on our research on the WEF, we wish to contribute to a more general discussion of how corporations participate in the creation of governance propositions in the international arena and how they contribute to set some of these into motion. Empirically, the paper builds on ethnographic fieldwork at several of the meetings organized by the WEF, as well as interviews with staff at the headquarters in Cologny, Switzerland, in the period between January 2011 and September 2013.[1] Theoretically, we draw on the notion of 'bricolage' as first introduced by Lévi-Strauss (1966), but relating it to policy actors and activities at the global level.

The first part of the paper introduces the WEF (also called the Forum), presenting the Annual Meetings in Davos, the organization and activities at the headquarters in Geneva. The organization has built its reputation on being an arena for big business and political elites. But rather than simply providing a voice for corporations, the WEF also uses corporations to organize its own agency, which doesn't necessarily coincide with the interests of transnational corporations. The notion of the policy bricolage is then introduced, as a way to capture the mixed and agile role and the precarious mandate of organizations such as the WEF in the global arena. We then go on to discuss the ways corporations may work to influence the identification of problems, the shaping of agendas and the proposition of solutions through their engagement with the WEF. Finally, we discuss our findings and suggest that the engagement of corporations in the WEF allows for a variety of pathways through which corporate leaders may shape and influence the perception of political problems, frame debates and contribute to the crafting of propositions and scenarios. However, corporate engagement is not solely to be seen as a way for corporate leaders to amplify and gain leverage for their own priorities. It is also a means by which the WEF itself, as a civil society actor and a policy bricoleur, may amplify its own voice, and not just the voice of corporations.

WORLD ECONOMIC FORUM – THE ORGANIZATION

The World Economic Forum is formed as a private foundation, with headquarters in Cologny, just outside of Geneva, Switzerland. It was founded in 1971 by Professor Klaus Schwab as the European Management Forum, under the patronage of the European Commission and European industrial associations. The first forum was attended by 444 participants from a wide range of West European firms, concentrating on how European firms could catch up with US management methods (Pigman 2007 p. 9). During the first years of existence Schwab (who in 2016 is still president of the WEF) launched what he termed 'the stakeholder model', arguing that even though for example unions, NGOs, a country government and a business association differ from each other, they may be stakeholders around the same particular issues, and therefore at times need to meet. This idea has since 1974, when the first politicians were invited (as a reaction to the oil crisis), been the leading idea for the Forum as an organization.

In the 1980s the mission of the organization was expanded in two interrelated ways. First, the Forum broadened its activities to include informal gatherings in diplomatic and political matters. For example, in 1982, cabinet-level officials and leaders of multilateral organizations such as the World Bank (WB), the International Monetary Fund (IMF) and the General Agreement on Tariffs and Trade (GATT), were invited to a specific gathering outside of the Annual Meeting. Second, in 1987 the Forum changed its name, signaling a move from targeting Europe and management, to a broader focus on the world and global issues (Pigman 2007 pp. 14–15). The Forum thus took a broader outlook both in geographical terms and in terms of the matters it would actively engage in.

The expansion also meant a considerable broadening of Forum activities in terms of time and space. Although the earlier version of the Forum had included meetings and summits apart from the Davos event, it gradually expanded these kinds of activities. The Annual Meeting in January was paralleled with a number of activities all around the year, and all over the globe. Perhaps most notably, the headquarters in Cologny, Geneva, has hosted a vast number of off-protocol gatherings of political stakeholders, something that has developed into a prime interest for the Forum. The expansion did not occur without difficulties. Both managers and funders of the Forum received criticism internally for not focusing enough on the needs of the corporations (Interview, September 2004).

At present, approximately 650 employees staff the headquarters, but the figures have been constantly increasing since the widening of the Forum outlook. It is situated at the shore of Lake Geneva – right across from the UN – in a modern-looking, dark grey building that had to be rebuilt in order to not only supply office space for the expansion of staff, but also to host the many informal meetings that are set up in the building. Its geographical location opposite the white UN building metaphorically stands testimony to the WEF being something of an alternative organizational model to the established international institutions – a notion oftentimes commented upon by staff.

POLICY BRICOLAGE AND POLITICAL AFFAIRS

Historically, foundations, think tanks and policy institutes have played a significant role in producing, advancing and utilizing policy-relevant knowledge. Notable are foundations such as Ford, Nuffield, Aga Khan, the Bill and Melinda Gates Foundation, the Soros Foundations Network, and think tanks such as Brookings, Carnegie and RAND. Knowledge produced in such organizations often aims precisely at targeting political audiences and at influencing policy and political decision making. Increasingly, think tanks have come to function as funnels for corporate influence, channeling and amplifying corporate interests (Campbell and Pedersen 2014; Medvetz 2012a, 2012b; Rich 2004; Smith 1991; Stone 1996, 2013; Stone and Denham 2013). With corporate political activity having been the subject of state regulation for quite some time, corporate political activity (CPA), or corporate attempts to shape government policy in ways favorable to the firm (see for example Hillman et al. 2004) have had to seek new routes. Think tanks stand out as one of the channels through which corporate political activity may be routed (Barley 2010; Stone 1996). Business leaders with an interest in investing profits in a larger social project, of 'doing good', may achieve leverage for their ideas through think tanks. The surge of the World Economic Forum in the area of global political affairs manifests these trends. Committed to 'improving the state of the world' the Forum 'engages the foremost political, business and other leaders of society to shape global, regional and industry agendas' (www.weforum.org, accessed 26 April 2016), and invites discussions regarding the form and shape of global politics as well as the role of non-governmental actors funded by corporate capital in the leveraging of policy-relevant knowledge.

Organizations set up or used by corporations to do good often describe themselves in ambiguous terms, being simultaneously foundations, non-governmental organizations and think tanks. The WEF is a pertinent case here, describing itself as a foundation, a non-profit organization, international organization and a think tank. As mentioned earlier, its funders consist of large-scale transnational corporations, who provide the funding base for the organization. With different types of encounters, some oriented to enhancing business opportunities and some oriented towards the political aspects of business, such organizations may alternate between positions and roles in the market and in political circles. Neither pure market actors, nor entrusted political actors, but corporate-sponsored and politically minded, they move freely on the global grazing grounds for both corporations and politicians. They speak freely with corporate leaders, tapping into their knowledge and experience, but also with high-level politicians, providing a safe place for informal discussions, as well as with civil society leaders on urgent issues impacting on the global economy. In this sense, the WEF and similar organizations may be seen as constructing global policy bricolage and a form of polycentric governance mixing disorderly processes and institutional reassemblages (Mittelman 2013). Just like the economic entrepreneur recombines and makes creative use of existing resources, capitalizing on the capacity to mobilize practical knowledge in a way that challenges general theoretical approaches (Baker et al. 2003), the WEF mobilizes by combining and resources (social as well as economic) in untraditional ways, thus challenging the relations between markets and politics. This bricolage character provides the WEF with an agility to operate across the market and political spheres, cobbling together various actors in the political landscape. Moreover, its status as a foundation and non-profit organization opens up for deliberations beyond the scope of international organizations (such as the United Nations), where its non-state character makes it a useful arena for off-protocol gatherings of the political and corporate elites.

The bricolage character of WEF activities is to some degree explicable by the precarious political mandate enjoyed by such organizations. With expansionist ideas, political zeal, and often globalist visions, they aim to influence the sense-making and actions of policymakers and politicians on a global scale. The challenge stems from the fact that their status denies them such influence, in the direct sense. Unlike international organizations such as the United Nations or the OECD, they do not represent the nations in which they are situated, nor do they represent any membership contingent other than the corporations, and corporations are oftentimes not welcome as political actors. Thus, they work by mobilization and attraction (see for instance Nye 2004), relying on the power of persuasive arguments (Fischer and Forester 1993) and the social capital they can muster through funders and guests. In Lakoff's words, they prepare the seedbed of our brains with their high-level general principles (2008 p. 239).

Fligstein (1990 p. 4) contends that 'the worlds of top managers have always been highly structured and their actions shaped by social and political contexts'. Corporate managers tend to see the world in a certain way, and their points of view change along with social and political tides and how they need to act to keep their corporation afloat, as it were. Corporate leaders who are keen to look after their interests in new emerging markets, to voice their views on impeding regulations, or to prepare new markets for investments by working against corruption, have good reasons to involve themselves in the work of think tanks. From the other side, as policymakers and politicians grapple with the challenges of globalization, governance gaps and evermore complex policy issues, they seek out the advice of knowledgeable professionals in the field, thus drawing corporate managers and others into their deliberations (Campbell and Pedersen 2014).

Whilst the phenomenon of corporate political activity is by no means new, what is new is the scale and significance of corporations and corporate-funded organizations in the shaping of the global political domain. The growth of this institutional field, Barley (2010) argues, has in the US given rise to an almost impenetrable network of relations between corporations on the one hand, and policymakers and politicians, on the other. Political actions committees, think tanks and PR firms may thus shield corporate political influence in effective ways. This, he contends (2010 p. 796):

> suggests a system designed not only to amplify but to shield. Ad hoc organizations certainly shield funders and founders. More importantly, in this structure agents shield principals. Employing law and lobbying firms, ad hoc organizations, PR firms, and think tanks makes it more difficult to identify whose interests are in play. In the case of think tanks, the shield lends scholarly legitimacy to funders' agendas, whereas ad hoc organizations and PR firms reduce the risk that clients will suffer de-legitimation.

As Campbell and Pedersen (2014 p. 13) rightly contend, structures, practices and ideas may involve convergent tendencies across countries. The manner in which this occurs is, however, 'heavily mediated by the nationally specific arrangements of knowledge, policymaking and production regimes'. At the global level, we maintain, where political institutional arrangements are weak, corporations, think tanks and foundations such as the WEF are pivotal in contributing to the construction of a global domain of politics and markets (compare Braithwaite and Drahos 2000; Ruggie 2004). This global domain is multilayered, involving local, regional, state and transnational operations alongside and intertwined with each other. It is fragmented, decentralized and diffuse compared to nation-state based domains of governance (Scholte 2005). It operates through consultations, coordination and consensus seeking. In these processes, representatives of corporations and corporate-sponsored organizations may consult, negotiate and make decisions with representatives of state departments, international organizations and multilaterals (well described in Braithwaite and Drahos 2000).

At the WEF, the ways in which corporate funders of the organizations may get leverage for their ideas are manifold. We identify five general routes through which this may happen: funding, marketing and selling, testifying and informing, in- and outsourcing and 'deep lobbying'. We will describe these routes in more detail below.

FUNDING

Financially, the WEF is built on its 1,000 funders, accepted as funders since they are seen as 'companies that run the world economy forward'. The typical funding company has about $5 billion in revenues, and is rated as one of the best in the industry or the country in which the company operates. Funding is stratified, starting at its lowest at around 30,000 Euros, giving (somewhat) more influence to those who are willing to pay more for being part of the organization. A company may for example be invited to enter 'the industrial partnership', which is linked to certain privileges, and is open only to roughly 300 selected companies. These privileges then entail more exclusive access opportunities to the different networks and activities of the Forum, such as the 'Governors' meeting' and selected regional meetings. The Strategic Partnership is reserved for merely 100 selected companies. This funding category is, as the WEF describes it, at the center of the 'Forum's knowledge generation activities' (weforum.org, accessed 26 April 2016). All funders are invited to send at least one participant to the Annual Meeting in Davos, but the number of invitations varies in accordance with the ranking of the funder. At the Annual Meeting, ranking is also visible by the fact that only funders paying the largest dues may enter into the restricted sections. They are also offered a private car and a driver, something which ordinary funders and most guests are not allowed to use.

As in any think tanks, the WEF funders, the 1,000 corporations, do not know exactly what the money will be used for. Funders pay, and the Forum then continues to build and develop the organization along the lines of its statutes. Funders do not have any direct control of what the money is used for. The Strategic and Event Partners, paying most and having most to say, only provide general direction to the Forum and the Annual Meeting in Davos, but does not constitute the highest decision body. The highest rank is given to the Forum Board, which is set up by a mixture of individuals seldom representing any of the funding companies. Thus, funders may complain, but internally the Forum Board is not held accountable to the funders.

Rather than a possibility to directly influence what the Forum does by democratic procedures, the relationship between the funders and the WEF can be characterized as a business deal. Through funding the WEF, corporations are buying themselves an arena where they can do business. For a corporation with global ambitions the WEF-funding is a form of recognition that opens the door to being appreciated at a global level as among the prime actors in their area of business. To be in Davos is to be seen, and to see others. Harry Woodpecker, one of our informants, a senior manager at a global consultancy firm, describes his company's interest in WEF as tied to a chance of being given the keys to the Davos event. Being there means demonstrating to others that you are on the same playing field, and that you are someone of weight, chosen by the Forum as one of the drivers of economy in their business field.

At the other end of the deal, funding does provide the Forum with the resources needed, in the form of money and participation, to set up the Davos event. Without the funders attending, the Forum would jeopardize legitimacy for the Annual Meeting as an event. As several informants at the Geneva headquarters have described it, 'Davos is the prime Forum showcase' (quote from Mads Pedersen, managing director). They need to get attention enough for this event to attract interest in their other activities. Leaders from the world's largest corporations gathering together with political tycoons ensure the Forum has the image of an important actor in global governance. To be sure, there is an imbalance in the deal, not everyone is equally happy. The WEF needs both the financial and social capital that business brings, but additionally it needs people from other walks of life in order to be the political animal it also seeks to be. There is therefore a constant struggle and haggling going on at the headquarters about who different groups within the WEF would want to see participate in Davos. There are quotas to be filled; quotas for different groups that Forum staff wants to bring in. But the WEF has to be polite to the funders, at the same time it is not interested in having too many of them there. The funders for their part complain that they pay substantial sums of money but do not get as much as they want out of it. Peter Bond, a high-level manager in a global consultancy corporation that has been a WEF-funder for many years, told us of his disappointment that his company could only bring four participants to Davos, and after all the money and time they spent on the Forum he would still not be let into the inner circles, something that he found strange.

MARKETING AND SELLING

One important aspect of Forum events is that they function as a marketplace, and/or as arenas where selling and buying may take place. Without this function many funding corporations would have difficulties legitimizing the costs for attending WEF meetings and participating in other types of WEF activities. The Forum is therefore in need of, and sees no problem in, organizing its outward activities in such a way that its funding corporations can have a more direct business related use of the meetings, in spite of it being framed in terms of political aspirations, and a desire to improve the state of the world.

In practice, the meeting in Davos – as well as regional meetings – are used by both funding- and non-funding corporations and smaller firms to meet and at least talk about possible deals, if not closing them. At each meeting there is a 'networking area' where people mingle, date and talk, oftentimes about business. During the three days that we spent in relation to a regional WEF-meeting in Turkey in the networking area, where we were observing and chatting with participants (wearing white badges) and 'hangarounds' (such as ourselves without badges), we observed a flow of examples of markets in action. As Hans Klerk explained to us – working for a networking company that had applied, but was refused attendance at the meeting, but was welcomed to approach people in the networking area – he would do business from there. His interest was to deliver as many leads as possible back to his company, that is, names of people they could contact as possible business partners. A young fashion designer from Turkey took the opportunity to show her collection to Annisa Darmadi, a 'young global leader' (one of the many Forum categories of people attending) from Indonesia who by Wikipedia is described as 'an influential media personality'. For the designer, the chat was a time for marketing; whilst for the Forum participant it was a time for coaching (and maybe getting some new inputs that she could use in her work). At an adjacent lunch table sat Jan de Vries, a participant/funder working for a socially oriented hedge fund, in the midst of a long row of scheduled meetings. Small-scale meetings were taking place all around us, in the interstices of formal, orchestrated meetings.

The Forum not only arranges the networking area, it also helps its funders out in many other ways. In Istanbul, Peter Andrade, a man from a global insurance company, sits down beside us on a sofa, declaring that he has accomplished what he had ultimately came for. So far, he had skipped the WEF-sessions, instead occupying himself with a number of prearranged business meetings. These took place not in the networking area but in a small room that the Forum had set up for him. He is happy with the arrangement, but says that the meeting in Jordan had been more efficient. Hakan Yilmaz, his colleague, still has some mingling to do. To him the most important thing is to meet people and to be seen. It is expensive, he says, but worth every penny. He will come home with new opportunities for business at the same time as he had learnt something of the political context.

The Forum is also willing to help out more directly in business deals. As one informant at the headquarters in Geneva explained to us, a government official from a country that is, for example, interested in rebuilding the telecom network, can contact them. The Forum can then arrange meetings in Davos or any other of their many meetings with the CEOs from relevant companies, to help them to start discussions.

A large share of the frenzy in Davos and other places where the Forum touches ground is thus about markets in action – selling and buying, but also embedding (trans)actions in social relations. In this sense, meetings such as the one in Turkey is staged by the Forum and deployed by both participants and others as a market fair. For the attendants, the market-related activities oftentimes legitimize their attendance at meetings that focus so much on political issues. Controlling the political environment is important for all companies, but if such an endeavor may be combined with concrete market actions, such as selling and marketing, it is a legitimizing bonus.

TESTIFYING AND INFORMING

The headquarters in Geneva and the people working there make up the organizational hub, framing the activities of the Forum. It is there that future funders are chosen, participants selected, publications written, indexes constructed and so forth. Usually, funding corporations do not have any of their staff placed in Geneva although they can come to visit for shorter or longer periods. This indicates that much of what is coming out of the WEF is shaped by the organization itself, not by corporations. In this sense, the WEF is mastering its own voice.

At the same time, the WEF offers many chances for the corporations to use their voices under the WEF-logo. In Davos, for example, an absolute majority of panellists, chairs, co-chairs and moderators come from corporations. In all the conferences and meetings held since 2011, business representatives accounted for just over 40 percent of the active participants. At the meetings, they inform and testify about their own experiences, frame panel debates in accordance with their world views and interests, take part in discussions on, for example, the Arctic, the need for education and global water supplies. Another example of how corporate leaders have an excellent opportunity to take active part is at the yearly event in Dubai (where we met with Mr Weiss), where WEF experts and its 'brain trust' – defined as the world's 1,500 smartest brains – gather in small groups for three days deliberating on given themes. The outcome of these deliberations may be booklets, indexes, suggestions for organizational changes or merely suggestions for the next Davos event. Since the groups are working under the Chatham House rule (always applied at WEF activities), governing confidentiality of the source, it is not possible to link perspectives to a particular sender. The product bears the WEF logo, and WEF has framed it by bringing in the people and asking the questions. What the group contributes is to provide the more specific content.

The WEF logo is also put on the many reports that emanate from the Forum. Often Forum staff in Geneva write these but in tandem with representatives of funding corporations. As the Forum raises new initiatives it will gather a group to work on the theme. The group will have a WEF coordinator (who in turn has been assigned by a group at the headquarters) and a number of people from the stakeholder groups that WEF wants to conjure. As Pablo Pimentel, WEF manager in Geneva, explained to us, the initiative is more or less dependent on somebody within the group stepping up and taking the lead. The project may then be run by, for example, a WEF funder, a global corporation, who assigns someone from the corporation to do the job. The report is negotiated, so to speak, for all group partakers and the Forum. In the end though, the Forum will have the final say of what is stated in the text.

INSOURCING/OUTSOURCING

The credibility and authority of the WEF relies to a large extent on the 'brain power' of the individuals it can attract and keep in its orbit. The WEF positions itself as a platform for dialogue and knowledge-seeking around complex and urgent global issues. Onto this platform, intelligent, trusted and experienced people from 'all walks of life' are drawn for the WEF to tap into their ideas and expertise. The sheer complexity of global issues creates a continuous need for translators and interpreters of analysis, and for 'knowledge management' systems. In the WEF, staff who edit and vouch for the credibility of information and analysis enjoy important roles and become 'gatekeepers' in determining who meets its standards and who is let in. These gatekeepers are arguably highly influential in defining problems, shaping the agenda and enrolling organizations and individuals. In so doing, however, the Forum also draws upon its corporate funders, outsourcing knowledge production to them, and in-sourcing corporate knowledge.

The foundation for how WEF organizes its knowledge-seeking, deliberations and events is based on so-called 'communities'. Communities are, in essence, loosely organized groups of people, rather like networks of individuals and organizations joined together around issues. The Foundation Members are one such community, comprised of the Forum's 1,000 funding companies. 'Together, they form one of the Forum's key pillars of global business, address urgent issues, explore emerging trends and help facilitate the Forum's mission of improving the state of the world' (http://www.weforum.org, accessed 26 April 2016). In this way, large-scale corporations are drawn into the activities of the WEF in a continuous manner. The global chairs and chief executives of Foundation Member Companies are invited to participate in the Forum's Annual Meetings: the Annual Meeting in Davos, and the Annual Meeting of the New Champions in China. They have privileged access to the Regional Meetings across the world.

The Network of Global Agenda Councils makes up another 'community'. Involved in these are over 1,500 'experts' contributing to 'a network of invitation-only groups that study the most pressing issues facing the world' (www.weforum.org, accessed 26 April 2016). There are at present over 80 Councils, to which the Global Agenda Council Members commit their knowledge, expertise and willingness to jointly shape the global, regional and industry agenda. As stated on the web: 'The Network convenes the most relevant and knowledgeable thought leaders from academia, government, business and civil society to challenge conventional thinking, develop new insights and create innovative solutions for key global challenges' (www.weforum.org, accessed 26 April 2016).

Other such 'communities' are, for example, the Global Leadership Fellows, the Young Global Leaders and the Global Shapers. The Global Leadership Fellows network aims to attract 'outstanding individuals' to take part the Global Leadership Fellows (GLF) Programme. The programme is run in collaboration with partner universities, and involves both work and learning experiences. Fellows may have the chance to hold a full-time position as a senior community manager at the Forum, and to receive an Executive Master in Global Leadership. The Forum of Young Global Leaders is composed of more than 700 'bold, brave, action-oriented and entrepreneurial' individuals that 'commit a portion of their time to jointly shape a better future and thereby improve the state of the world' (www.weforum.org, accessed 26 April 2016). Conceived as representing 'the future of leadership' they are drawn from business, government, civil society organizations, arts and culture, academia and social entrepreneurship. These young leaders are said to go through a rigorous nomination and selection procedure, involving rounds of discussion within the Forum and with trusted partners. Once selected, they are involved in virtually all WEF initiatives, meetings and events for a period of time. Another community is that of Global Shapers Community. This network consists of 'young people who are exceptional in their potential, their achievements and their drive to make a contribution to their communities' (www.weforum.org, accessed 26 April 2016). Shapers are also selected based on what is described as rigourous assessment of their achievements, leadership potential and commitment to make a difference. As Klaus Schwab explained to us, this particular community has a key position in keeping the Forum young and up to date. The particular interest for the community is its perceived desire to work towards a more peaceful and inclusive world.

In all of these examples of multi-stakeholder communities all corporations are part of constructing the worldwide network of the WEF. To some extent, and taken together, the communities of the WEF form part of what Stone (2008 p. 24) refers to as 'transnational policy professionals'. They make up a diverse community of foundation officers, business leaders, academics and NGO executives. Insofar as WEF staff, funders and other participants together constitute something like a transnational community of policy professionals, it is through the communities and the events organized around them. By way of its communities, the WEF taps into the expertise of others, thus outsourcing part of their knowledge-seeking to other individuals and organizations. The knowledge actors involved have 'intrinsic governance capacities' (cf. Stone 2012) to define problems and to shape the climate of the debate. By the same token, the Forum also insources potentially valuable ideas and knowledge into its organizational core, where these ideas and visions are further elaborated upon, translated into the WEF vocabulary or discarded. By these double transfers, the WEF is inviting a mix of private and public sector actors into its activities. By interlocking activities, through the testing of ideas and crafting of knowledge, the writing of reports and policy statements, the WEF is thus partly shaped by, but also shaping, its funders and participants.

DEEP LOBBYING

Our corporate informants have aired the significance of the WEF as an arena for 'value creation' in the broad sense of the term. By this, they refer to the fact that engaging in the activities of the WEF, meeting other corporate and political leaders of similar weight, may not be instantly rewarding from a market point of view, but may in the long run shape discussions in a way that could have an impact on regulations and the structure of markets. This is 'deep lobbying' (Clemons 2003), in the sense that what happens is that the intellectual climate around an issue may be changed by a continuous process of social interaction and networking. By involving oneself in the WEF, one may contribute to the creation of 'talking points' and eventually to the shaping of a meeting agenda, or even better, be asked to give a speech at the Annual Meeting in Davos.

At the WEF Summit on the Global Agenda Council meeting in Dubai in November 2012, we met with a high-level director at one of the Strategic Partners of the WEF, Mr Bond. He had been involved in working groups, or 'communities', at the WEF for a number of years, and had attended the Davos meeting several times. Over dinner, he told us that it was actually at the off-agenda meetings in the interstices of the outlined program that the more interesting discussions happened. Once, he told us, his working group had gone out for dinner, and this was when the important breakthrough came about. 'It is really the informal gatherings that are value-creating,' he put it. Mr Bond talked at length about value creation. The WEF can, in his view, be strategically used in several ways. It may be used to the advantage of the corporation by extensive networking. The corporation may actively and strategically organize business meetings with partners and clients around WEF events. But it may also be useful on a personal level. He recounts being invited to give a talk on an island in the Caribbean as part of the WEF-network. Participating in WEF activities can thus function as a lever for one's own career and for furthering the ideas and positions of the corporation in front of an influential audience.

Another of our informants, Mr Gunnlaugson, a director of an influential foundation, whom we met at the Annual Meeting in Davos, asserted that 'If you are not here, you do not exist. Everyone who counts in our business is here. We are here to meet and to discuss.' In the cozy warmth of a pizza restaurant just inside the secured gates of the meeting ground, Mr Gunnlaugson brushed the snow from his long grey winter coat and took a seat at the table. To him, and to many others, he explained, the chief reason for coming to Davos is the fact that everyone else of importance will be here. The event is a magnet for influential leaders from all over the world, and a convenient meeting spot. With everyone's agenda filled up, attending the Davos meeting is synergetic, in combining time, place and issue. Over lunch and a beer, he also explained that going to Davos is a long-term investment, since nurturing and maintaining network ties takes a while, and one might not see the results immediately.

The Davos meeting has in social media been termed 'a glorified dating agency', by a Swiss banker and former attendee (http://www.economist.

com/blogs/newsbook/2013/01/wold-economic-forum-davos, accessed 21 September 2013). Indeed, it works to attract leaders from all corners of the world to meet other leaders, who also qualified through the slim needle's eye. Being among the selected few – knowing that oneself and all the other participants have been carefully scrutinized and judged to pass – one can rest assured that the ties nurtured within the realm of the WEF may work to influence people's perception of an issue, to raise awareness and to place the issue on a future agenda. It is deep lobbying among 'the best of brains', as WEF staff have it.

In Davos we once attended a closed lunch discussion, not announced in the official program. The lunch was organized as a possibility for a number of actors to meet and discuss questions regarding the Arctic. Participating at the lunch were among others a prime minister, a few members from the Arctic Council, scientists and CEOs from a number of corporations interested in the area. A few of the participants were offered the possibility of introducing their views on the topic, while the others were eating. Discussions around the small round tables were then encouraged and fed back to the larger group. In this small setting, the attending prime minister told the corporations about possible alternative conventions. The participating CEOs on the other hand talked about the challenge and the importance of establishing guidelines for corporations, perhaps headed by the WEF. Somebody else claimed that in the long run it will cost more to not use the oil in the Arctic, than to use it. The scientist rose and tried to inspire the participants to think of the environmental consequences.

Access to meetings such as this lunch is part of the deal between corporate funders and the WEF. Here you can combine business with politics. As such they are exemplary cases of deep lobbying, where all participants sit down at the lunch table as equals. Some have paid to come there (the funders), some are invited (the politicians and the scientists), but they sit down to eat and talk to each other. As opposed to more obvious forms of lobbying this lunch is not an attempt by the corporation to influence a specific decision. Rather, it is about molding the environment in the direction of a context that is favorable to the participating actors.

CONCLUDING NOTES: AMPLIFICATION AND SPIN

In this chapter, we set out to explore an organizational actor that operates freely on the global scene, but without the political mandate accorded to established actors such as nation-states and multilateral organizations. The notion of the policy bricolage was introduced as a way to capture the ambiguous, creative and agile role of the organization. Like the bricoleur in the Lévi-Straussian sense, the WEF has a broad repertoire of material and immaterial resources from which it associates funders and practices. The WEF is, as a non-profit foundation and civil society organization funded by corporate capital, strategically positioned to act as a bridgehead between representatives of nation-states, business and civil society. It foregrounds its resources, as it were, flexibly, to pursue its ends. As we have shown in this chapter, the 1,000 corporate funders make up a key resource in that respect, Drawing on corporations for its construction of 'communities', 'working groups' and 'events' – the Annual Meeting in Davos being prime among them – are arenas for influencing the intellectual climate around particular issues by working the network and for stretching the potential impact of what Granovetter (1973) calls 'weak ties'.

At the same time, corporations may make good use of the Forum. The WEF has built its position and reputation on providing an arena for large-scale business corporations and top-level political elites. The influence of corporations on the structure and content of activities should not be underestimated. Our analysis indicates a number of conduits through which business may deploy the WEF and its platforms. First, by paying large sums of money in funding dues, corporations gain access to the many communities and activities of the WEF and provide the central basis for its existence. Second, business finds the WEF to be a strategic place from which to market and sell their products and services. The communities and activities of the WEF provide a node in the network of business – it works like a magnet for clients and partners alike. Third, corporate leaders inform and testify based on their own experiences, frame panel debates in accordance with their world views and interests and take part in discussions on particular topics. Fourth, through the involvement of business people in the testing of ideas and crafting of knowledge, the writing of reports and policy statements, the WEF is thus partly shaped by, but also shaping, its funders and participants. In this way, knowledge is both insourced and outsourced. Fifth, the WEF is an arena for 'value creation' in the broad sense of the term, in that meeting other corporate and political leaders of similar standing may in the long run frame discussions in a way that may impact on deals and regulations. 'Deep lobbying' may thus change the intellectual climate around an issue through a continuous process of networking.

Corporations thus find a strategically positioned amplifier for their non-market interests in the WEF. The WEF functions to enhance and gain leverage for funder's ideas and priorities in a highly selective and resourceful environment. As many informants underline, there is hardly any better place to be, and to be seen, as a business leader with global ambitions. In the long run, both the market priorities and the political interests of business may be served by engagement in the WEF. In this, the WEF as the bricoleur may amplify the voice of corporations in the broader political landscape.

However, the WEF cannot only be conceived as the extended voice of corporations. The WEF also makes use of the corporations to organize and expand its own agency, which doesn't necessarily coincide with the interests of multinational corporations. By way of corporate financial resources, the tapping of knowledge and expertise and access to vast networks of business relations, the WEF is also able to amplify its own voice. On top, it is through the support and engagement of business, as well as that of political leaders and non-governmental high profiles, that it gets its spin. The global policy bricolage of the WEF is thus not just a complex form of global governance, but an intricate system of interweaving market and political interests, and one that both amplifies and blurs the choir of voices.

NOTE

1. For reasons of anonymity all names of our interlocutors, apart from Klaus Schwab, are fictitious.

REFERENCES

Baker, T., A.S. Miner and D.T. Eesley (2003), 'Improvising firms: Bricolage, account giving, and improvisational competency in the founding process', *Research Policy*, **32**, 255–76.

Barley, S. (2010), 'Building an institutional field to corral a government: A case to set an agenda for organization studies', *Organization Studies*, **31**(6), 777–805.

Braithwaite, J. and P. Drahos (2000), *Global Business Regulation*, Cambridge: Cambridge University Press.

Campbell, J.K. and O.K. Pedersen (2014), *The National Origins of Policy Ideas: Knowledge Regimes in the United States, France, Germany, and Denmark*, Princeton: Princeton University Press.

Clemons, S.C. (2003), 'The corruption of think tanks', *JPRI Critique*, **X**(2).

Fischer, F. and J. Forester (eds) (1993), *The Argumentative Turn in Policy Analysis and Planning*, Durham: Duke University Press.

Fligstein, N. (1990), *The Transformation of Corporate Control*, Harvard: Harvard University Press.

Granovetter, M.S. (1973), 'The strength of weak ties', *American Journal of Sociology*, **78**(6), 1360–80.

Hillman, A.J., G.D. Keim and D. Schuler (2004), 'Corporate political activity: A review and research agenda', *Journal of Management*, **30**(6), 837–57.

Lakoff, G. (2008), *The Political Mind: Why You Can't Understand 21st Century Politics With an 18th-Century Brain*, New York: Penguin Books.

Lawton, T., S. McGuire and T. Rajwani (2012), 'Corporate political activity: A literature review and research agenda', *International Journal of Management Reviews*, **15**, 86–105.
Lévi-Strauss, C. (1966), *Savage Mind*, Chicago: Chicago University Press.
Medvetz, T. (2012a), 'Murky power: "Think tanks" as boundary organizations', in D. Courpasson, D. Golsorkhi, and J.J. Sallaz (eds), *Rethinking Forms of Power in Organizations, Institutions, and Markets*, Bradford, UK: Emerald Group Publishing, pp. 113–33.
Medvetz, T. (2012b), *Think Tanks in America: Merchants of Policy and Power*, Chicago: University of Chicago Press.
Mittelman, J.H. (2013), 'Global bricolage: emerging market powers and polycentric governance', *Third World Quarterly*, **34**(1), 23–37.
Nye, J.S. (2004), *Soft Power: The Means to Succeed in World Politics*, New York: Public Affairs.
Pigman, G.A. (2007), *The World Economic Forum: A Multi-Stakeholder Approach to Global Governance*, London: Routledge.
Rich, A. (2004), *Think Tanks, Public Policy, and the Politics of Expertise*, Cambridge: Cambridge University Press.
Ruggie, J.G. (2004), 'Reconstituting the global public domain: Issues, actors and practices', *European Journal of International Relations*, **10**(4), 499–531.
Scherer, A.G. and G. Palazzo (2011), 'The new political role of business in a globalised world: A review of a new perspective on CSR and its implications for the firm, governance and democracy', *Journal of Management Studies*, **48**, 899–931.
Scholte, J.A. (2005), *Globalization: A Critical Introduction*, Basingstoke: Palgrave Macmillan.
Smith, J. (1991), *The Idea Brokers: Think Tanks and the New Policy Elite*, New York: The Free Press.
Stone, D. (2013), *Knowledge Networks and Transnational Governance: The Public-Private Policy Nexus in the Global Agora*, Basingstoke: Palgrave Macmillan.
Stone, D. (2012), 'Governance via knowledge: Actors, institutions and networks', in D. Levi-Faur (ed.), *OUP Handbook of Governance*, Oxford: Oxford University Press.
Stone, D. (2008), 'Global public policy, transnational policy communities and their networks', *Policy Studies Journal*, **36**(1), 19–38.
Stone, D. (1996), *Capturing the Political Imagination: Think Tanks and the Policy Process*, London: Frank Cass.
Stone, D. and A. Denham (eds) (2004), *Think Tank Traditions: Policy Research and the Politics of Ideas*, Manchester: Manchester University Press.

3. Policymaking as collective bricolage: the role of the electricity sector in the making of the European carbon market

Mélodie Cartel, Eva Boxenbaum, Franck Aggeri and Jean-Yves Caneill

INTRODUCTION

How can public policies be designed and implemented when they face strong reluctance from both the politicians that make them and the private corporations that influence them? This question is particularly vivid in the case of the European carbon market (EU-ETS).[1] The EU-ETS was adopted in 2003 as the corner stone of the European climate policy. Its development countered both the European Commission's intellectual convictions and the interests of industrial stakeholders (Newel and Paterson 1996; Wettestad 2005). Despite abundant scholarly work in multiple disciplines (Braun 2009; Cass 2005; Christiansen and Wettestad 2003; Damro and Mendez 2003), the making of the EU-ETS still represents a conundrum yet to be explained.

The failure to fully explain the making of the EU-ETS is partly linked to the lack of detailed empirical accounts of the policymaking process. The case of the EU-ETS epitomizes a general situation in the analysis of policymaking (Tyllström this volume). The lack of empirical case studies has limited the understanding of how corporations and policymakers interact and collectively shape public policies. Indeed, the tactics that corporations use to exert influence on the political sphere have become an academic blind spot. On the one hand, the research stream on corporate political activities focuses on corporations' internal motivations for influencing policymaking (Baron 1995, 1999; Baron and Diermeier 2007; Bonardi et al. 2005; Holburn and Vanden Bergh 2008). On the other hand, political scientists are primarily interested in governmental activities and less in strategic corporate action. So far, the collective dynamics of policymaking and how corporations manage to provoke radical opinion shifts during policymaking have been overlooked.

In an effort to address this blind spot, we pose the following question: How do private corporations provoke radical opinion shifts during policymaking processes?

To examine this question, we reopen the case of the making of the European carbon market with unprecedented empirical elements. Drawing on a rich set of archival data and interviews, we reconstitute the original strategy deployed by the electricity sector to implement a carbon market in Europe.[2] During the Conference of Parties at Kyoto, the European Commission opposed emissions trading (Cass 2005; Convery 2009; Damro and Mendez 2003; Skjærseth and Wettestad 2008; Wettestad 2005). As for industrial companies, they pleaded against any measure involving a price on carbon (Newell and Paterson 1996, 1998). Nevertheless, a handful of actors in the electricity sector believed that a carbon market could be an effective solution to manage carbon emissions at the company level. From 1999 to 2001, these actors organized two successive experiments where they invited industrial companies to build and test various carbon market prototypes. Our interviews indicate that these experiments triggered an intellectual shift among participants and considerably fuelled the policymaking process that led to the EU-ETS.

In this chapter, we discuss two aspects characterizing policymaking in the case of the EU-ETS. First, building on the literature on bricolage (Duymedjian and Rüling 2010; Lévi-Strauss 1962, 1966), we describe the role of collective bricolage as a key process for reaching consensus. The Greenhouse Gas and Electricity Trading Simulation (GETS) participants felt involved in the design of the market instrument as they had a possibility to add new features to the market's design and reshuffle its existing architecture. Collective bricolage proved key to gain participants' confidence as well as to ensure that the participants' interests were represented in the market design. Secondly, we describe the role of staging experimentations of policy innovations. Staging an experimentation of carbon markets with a restricted community demonstrated both their economic and environmental value. Such experimentation might not have taken place in more formal political arenas. Yet, it imbued carbon markets with legitimacy at a large scale. We believe that the concepts of collective bricolage and staging carry the potential to open new academic avenues in the analysis of policymaking.

THE SETTING

The empirical setting of this study is the Greenhouse Gas and Electricity Trading Simulation (GETS), an experiment organized by the European electricity sector to generate and test alternative designs for carbon markets. Eurelectric, the Union of the European Electricity Industry, organized two GETS: GETS1 in 1999 involved only the electricity sector while GETS2 in 2000 involved all the main stakeholders of the forthcoming European climate policy. Both in GETS1 and 2, Eurelectric invited a closed number of companies to participate in a role play on prototype carbon markets.

The original idea for organizing an industry-wide role play on carbon markets stemmed from a small group of colleagues at Eurelectric in 1998. After a conference on emission trading, members of the small group challenged each other to imagine rules for a carbon market that could be implemented in Europe. That afternoon, they sat down with a whiteboard and wrote the rules of the first carbon market prototype. Before returning home the small group agreed that it would be an opportunity to conduct a sector-wide role play on carbon markets so that electric utilities could learn more about these policy instruments. Consequently, they hired economists and experts to help them refine the rules they had imagined and organized a role play with the European electricity utilities. The initially small-scale initiative ended up two years later mobilizing all the main stakeholders of European Climate policy: top ranked economists and climate policy experts, members of the European Commission in charge of elaborating European climate policy, more than 40 major private companies in Europe and financial institutions. How did this wide-scale mobilization occur, given the initial reluctance of key stakeholders?

GLOBAL POLITICAL CONTEXT

The 1997 Kyoto conference acted as a political shock that destabilized private actors' historical positions towards climate change management. The Kyoto targets on carbon emissions were legally binding which restrained their ability to promote voluntary agreements and may quickly lead the European Commission to craft a European policy instrument to reach this objective. Eurelectric, the professional association in charge of defending the interests of the electricity sector in Europe, held several workshops with electricity utilities to decide on their next move:

> We all came back from Kyoto and we looked at what we were going to do. At that time, the industry's basic view was that we didn't want a tax. What we

wanted were voluntary agreements. [. . .] It became clear to us that the market-based mechanisms within Kyoto were going to drive the Commission towards implementing some kind of constraint on emissions in the power industry. We recognised then that the voluntary agreements were a good idea but were not going to get much political traction. Therefore we had the choice between a tax and some market based mechanisms. (Eurelectric 1, 2015, 22 October)

Except for British companies, most of European electricity companies shared a somewhat reluctant position toward carbon markets, whether or not this position was officially enacted through active political strategizing. Eurelectric, eventually launched the GETS as a way to accelerate collective learning at the sectoral scale, unify the sector's position towards carbon markets and work on a common strategy.

As shown in Table 3.1, the design that Eurelectric co-developed with the rest of the industry and with inputs of the European Commission in GETS2 was very similar to the policy that the European Parliament finally adopted in 2003.

Table 3.1 EU-ETS/GETS comparison

Rules	GETS2.1	EU-ETS Pilot
Market Type	Cap and Trade	Cap and Trade
Commodity	1 quota = 1tCO2eq	1 quota = 1tCO2eq
Coverage	Energy activities, Production and processing of ferrous metals, Mineral industry, pulp & paper industry	Energy activities, Production and processing of ferrous metals, Mineral industry, pulp & paper industry
Scope	6 Kyoto gases	CO_2
PROCEDURES		
Allocation	Grandfathering	Grandfathering
Permit Restitution	End of each engagement period	End of each engagement period
FLEXIBILITY		
Pricing Mechanisms		
Celling Price	No	No
Threshold Price	No	No
Temporal Flexibility		
Banking	Yes	Yes
Borrowing	No	No
MONITORING		
Penalties	Non-discharging	Non-discharging

Source: comparative analysis of GETS and EU-ETS pilot archives. See also Cartel, Aggeri and Caneill 2017.

DATA COLLECTION

We studied the two successive GETS exercises in the period running from 1998 (the year the system was designed) until 2001 (the year the first EU-ETS directive was proposed). We had exclusive access to the archives of the GETS role plays, which remain unpublished: report documents, internal communications and emails, meeting reports, etc. In addition, over a three-year period, the first author collected both physical archives classified in the basement of the companies involved in the GETS, and electronic archives. We supplemented the historical archives with a series of 28 semi-directive interviews (Eisenhardt and Graebner 2007) with key GETS protagonists: the managers of GETS, the participants and the observers.

Some informants said that the GETS played an implicit cognitive role in the formulation of the EU-ETS Directive. Others perceived the GETS role plays as a deliberate lobbying effort rather than a collective learning experience. Yet others claimed to have been deliberate pioneers of the European carbon market. We framed our interviews so as to understand how the various members of GETS participated in the elaboration of the prototype carbon market. We asked our interviewees which design element they promoted as well as why they considered this element important. Reponses varied widely according to our interviewees. Certain members of GETS promoted design elements related to 'sensitive industrial strategies' while others tested features they considered to be for the 'common good'. Others even introduced design elements to fulfil their 'personal curiosity'. We related the design elements tested by each member with the change in their strategic positions over time. We focused on changes in their positions over time, including the development of interests and strategies throughout the GETS role plays.

THE CASE STUDY

GETS1 (1999) – The Electricity Sector Initiating An Experiment

In December 1998, Eurelectric hired the International Energy Agency to collaborate in the design of a prototype carbon market (see Figure 3.1). The global architecture of the prototype carbon market took inspiration from the SO_2 market that had been successfully operating in the United States since 1995. For instance, the attribution of emission allowances was based on the SO_2 market model: the regulator distributes emissions allowances to each affected utility on the basis of historical emissions. The possibility for utilities

RULES for GETS1	
Market type	Cap and trade
Good	1 quota = 1tCO_2eq
Constraint	Up-stream
Coverage	Electric utilities
Scope	6 Kyoto Gases
PROCEDURES	
Allocation	Historical (grandfathering)
Permit restitution	At the end of each engagement period
FLEXIBILITY	
Carbon price mechanisms	
Ceiling price	No
Threshold price	No
Temporal Flexibility	
Banking	Yes
Borrowing	No
Grace period	Yes
MONITORING	
Penalties	Non discharging

Equipment

Trading Platform

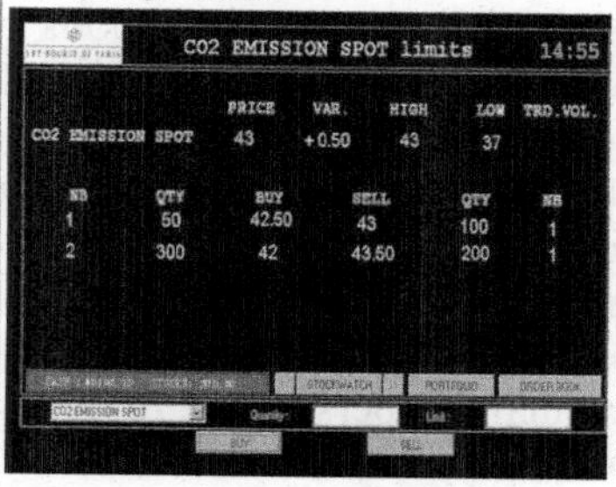

CO2 EMISSION SPOT limits 14:55

	PRICE	VAR.	HIGH	LOW	TRD.VOL.
CO2 EMISSION SPOT	43	+0.50	43	37	

NB	QTY	BUY	SELL	QTY	NB
1	50	42.50	43	100	1
2	300	42	43.50	200	1

Actors

Organizer: Eurelectric

Technical Support: ParisBourse

Game Master: IEA

Players: utilities

Source: adapted from GETS1 report 1999. See also Cartel, Aggeri and Caneill 2017.

Figure 3.1 The GETS1 carbon market prototype

to 'bank' unused allowances also took inspiration from the SO_2 market. Banking consists of setting aside allowances received in period A and using them in a further period B. Such an option had proven valuable to the political success of the SO_2 market (Burtraw and Szambelan 2009). Indeed, 'once firms have built up a bank of unused allowances, they have a vested interest in maintaining the value of those banked credits and thus in furthering the program itself' (ibid., p. 6). Aside from adapting these pre-existing principles to the European carbon emissions context, Eurelectric also introduced an original element in the prototype, namely the 'grace period'. The grace period authorizes utilities to comply with their carbon emission objective even after the deadline, in case they have not been able to comply before. The idea behind the grace period is to help companies that failed to reach their carbon emission target, by providing them with some extra time.

Eurelectric also hired Paris Bourse, the French stock exchange to help manage a role play on the prototype carbon market described above. Paris Bourse lent its experimental trading platform to carry out the role play. Indeed, Paris Bourse had designed an experimental trading platform to test financial products before launching real markets. The device operated as a simplified stock exchange: to buy carbon, company A would book an order, indicating both a quantity and a proposed price; to sell carbon company B would also book an order, indicating the available quantity of carbon and a selling price. If there was a match, the transaction took place. If not, both buyers and sellers would adjust price expectations by booking another order. Paris Bourse was particularly interested in carbon markets, which it perceived as novel and promising objects. Its main question toward GETS1 prototype was: 'does it allow for the fast emergence of a carbon price?' Celerity of price discovery is crucial from a financial perspective to demonstrate that markets are healthy. Fast price discovery enables economically efficient trading. As shown in Figure 3.1, GETS1 prototype consisted of a series of rules formulated by Eurelectric and the International Energy Agency as well as technical equipment to support carbon and electricity trading provided by Paris Bourse. The IEA was tasked to be the game master.

Staging an Experimentation of the First Prototype

The experience generated traction among 19 utilities. Every Wednesday for two months, the players connected to ParisBourse's experimental trading platform. Thirty minutes before the opening of the trading platform, participants received guidelines indicating their objectives as well as some key economic elements (for instance the price of raw material). Staging an experimentation of carbon markets through the role play had three types of impacts on the electricity sector's position in the carbon market. First of all, it raised awareness of carbon markets inside the participating companies. Second, it provoked a strategic shift in the industry by demonstrating empirically some desirable properties of carbon markets. Third, it created an atmosphere of camaraderie among the participants that pacified the debates at the sectoral level.

Participants would gather in teams to elaborate various compliance strategies. According to our informants, the need to gather multidisciplinary teams to perform the role play raised awareness on carbon-related issues inside the participating companies:

> The exercise also helped us make the issue known in the company because we formed a team from a different part of the company. For example we went to the trading people, when I talked to the head of trading at first he almost ruled me out of his office and said 'I have so much work to do here and you come with this stuff . . . !' but pretty quickly he realised that we had a point and he sent one of his people into our simulation group. In our team we had 4–5 people sitting in front of the computer during the trading sessions so that was important. (Electricity Company 2, 2015, 28 October)

Participants remember the 30 minutes preparation as intense because it was a very short time to design sophisticated strategies. For a period of two hours, participants could then trade both electricity and carbon via the trading platform supplied by Paris Bourse. Each session represented one or two years of activity. Over the eight weeks of the role play, the players simulated various time periods between 2000 and 2012. Participants generally found the role play engaging and fun. When meeting together in more formal occasions at Eurelectric, they would challenge each other on their performances in the role play, which favoured a friendly atmosphere among them.

This first experimentation triggered an intellectual shift from reluctance to endorsement within the electricity sector. The GETS had enabled electricity companies to learn in a practical way about carbon markets. Participants observed that carbon trading was cost-effective. Some of them even realized that they were making a profit by reaching their environmental targets. Electricity companies came to increasingly view carbon markets in an operational sense:

> The main learning from GETS1 was that a carbon market could help reduce compliance costs. (Eurelectric 1, 2010)

This experimentation convinced Eurelectric's members that they would benefit from carbon markets if such instruments were adopted at the level of the European Union.

Using GETS1 to Make Alliances with Key Stakeholders

After the experiment was over and the conclusions had shown to be positive, Eurelectric presented GETS1 in many political circles. The most decisive of them was the Conference of Parties on Climate Change when it met in Bonn in November 1999. Eurelectric publically and officially expressed their position in favour of carbon markets:

> In the room, Eurelectric explicitly took position as carbon market promoter. [. . .] And the electricity companies from other regions did not look very happy about it. (International Energy Agency, 2015, 23 September)

The Commission informed Eurelectric that it had been working on a Green Paper on carbon trading. Eurelectric immediately published a position paper in favour of the European Commission's Green Paper.

Since these developments and during the rest of the policymaking process, the European Commission considered the electricity sector as allies. Together with the European Commission, Eurelectric sought to organize a second GETS to convince the other industrial sectors of the usefulness of a carbon market. The relations between the electricity sector and energy intensive sectors were tense on the issue of carbon markets. First, energy intensive companies feared that electricity companies would pass through the cost of carbon and charge them more for electricity. Second, energy intensive companies thought of GETS as a threat – an instrument designed by the electricity industry to further its own interests. Eurelectric sensed that energy intensive sectors would gather and attempt to undermine the policymaking process. The European Commission encouraged Eurelectric to invite these reluctant actors to a second experiment:

> The electricity sector has always been very much on board with us, and allies with us, but we didn't want the electricity sector to be the only sector to participate in the ETS. We wanted it to include industry because industry produces a lot of emissions as well through other means than through power generation so we didn't want to stop with electricity and this is why we may have encouraged them to do a GETS2. (European Commission 1, 2015, 28 September)

GETS2 (2000): A Second Experiment with Key Stakeholders

Following the European Commission's Green Paper, Eurelectric invited companies from six energy-intensive sectors to redesign the carbon market prototype and test it altogether: metallurgy, oil and refining, chemicals, glass, construction materials and paper.

Collective Bricolage on the Prototype

Eurelectric decided to redesign the prototype through a process that we qualify as collective bricolage. Building on the first prototype, Eurelectric invited all the participants to make proposals and refine its architecture. The ambition was both to harmonize the relations amongst industrial actors that had diverging interests towards carbon markets. Associating key actors from these six industrial sectors would also ensure their understanding of the policymaking process. As a result, three carbon market prototypes were created with original features that integrated multiple strategic views.

As part of this collective bricolage, all the participants were invited to get involved in designing the rules of the new carbon market prototype. They could make any proposal to change the architecture of the original prototype. Eurelectric had hired a consulting company to coordinate the collective bricolage process. The objective was to accept as many proposals as possible, provided that it would be easy to implement. Only the experiment would reveal their robustness, not *ex ante* negotiations. This open-ended process was set up as a way to pacify relations amongst industrial participants and favour a bottom up appropriation process. A member of Eurelectric explains this design strategy as follows:

> There was no way that, as utilities, we would impose rules that would apply to other industrial actors. The process had to be much more creative. They [the energy intensive sectors] had to feel represented in the design. This is also why we chose a neutral agent to coordinate the operations. We did not want to give the impression that we were imposing our point of view. We wanted to produce collective knowledge on carbon markets so we could talk with the regulator. (Eurelectric 2, 2015, 23 September)

The collective design process was successful and yielded a wide variety of proposals. For instance, several companies suggested new allocation methods for carbon emissions allowances. Most industry players were in favour of prorating allowances according to previous emissions. The advantage of this system was that companies would receive their allowances free of charge according to their past emission profile, which enabled them to gradually reduce their emissions over time. A cement company advocated allocation according to a benchmarking system. This method consisted of calculating allocations according to a fictitious situation in which the production of the same quantity of cement would mobilize the most efficient technologies. This allocation method had the advantage of encouraging technology transfer. Such systems are most effective in sectors in which the carbon intensity of production technologies varies strongly from one company to another, which it does in the cement sector. Lastly, a member from a utility recommended testing auctions. The auction method was recognized by economists as the one that enhances the overall efficiency of market-based instruments.

The European Commission was also on board as an advisor in the design process. The role of the Commission in GETS was informal but did nevertheless provide considerable input. This cooperation helped Eurelectric to ensure consistency between the European Commission's view and the industrial view. Certain features of the prototype were also added to ensure consistency between GETS and other initiatives going on in Europe. Amongst others, a mechanism called 'gateway' was added to ensure consistency with the United Kingdom's initiative. This strategy proved crucial to enter into a dialogue with key institutional actors in Europe.

Staging an Experimentation of Three New Prototypes

The role play of GETS2 unfolded almost identically as in GETS1. To test the three prototypes, three separate role plays were organized. The complete exercise lasted 6 months, from January to July 2000. Each Wednesday, the participants would connect to an Internet platform designed by the organizers, and proceed to engage in carbon and electricity trading.

The Effects of GETS2: Alliance with Key Stakeholders

The participants understood that market-based instruments were not constraints per se but tools to help them reach compliance. The players had learned to use the carbon price as a signal to trigger investment choices and trading strategies. Compared to any other carbon regulation mechanism, emissions trading would make it possible to achieve carbon compliance at the lowest cost. Highlighting the role of a carbon price in economic optimization was a key achievement of GETS2:

> An electricity-carbon market made it possible to obtain a clear and objective price signal, allowing industrial companies to determine a cost of energy 'carbon included'. This cost, related to the various market prices played an important role and allowed economic optimisation strategies to be designed. (GETS2, p. 7)

The experiment also removed the negative view of carbon markets that had prevailed in some segments of the industry:

> The role play highlighted the key elements needed to convince the rest of industry. It disproved the negative connotations ascribed to this type of instrument, such as the concept of constraint and the right to pollute. (Electricity Company 1, 2012)

Most importantly, the previous process of collective bricolage had triggered appropriation. The participants had been involved in the detailed mechanics of each prototype. After testing each prototype, each participant had a personal understanding of the effects of each detail of architecture. For instance, they had experienced that auctions would be less advantageous than grandfathering in terms of allocation rule. They also relied on banking and had experienced the importance of this rule in order to devise long term strategies. After the experiment, having developed this pragmatic understanding through collective bricolage and testing, most of the participants expressed that their preferred option would be prototype 2.1. It is not surprising then that the EU-ETS pilot that was implemented after the stakeholder consultation was very similar to GETS2.1's prototype.

The Role of GETS in the Policymaking Process

In 2001, the European Commission launched a stakeholder consultation on emission trading. All key stakeholders, from both the private sector and the member states joined, exchanged points of view and learned about carbon markets:

> Many of us did not understand what carbon markets were and the Consultation process clarified many issues. (Cement Company 1, 2011)

Companies that had participated in GETS shared their experience with the ones that knew less about emissions trading. Eurelectric presented GETS on behalf of the European electricity sector. Government representatives from Denmark and the United Kingdom presented their national experiments. Finally, a number of companies among which BP and Shell had also run their own experimentations (Akhurst et al. 2003; Braun 2009; Christiansen and Wettestad 2003; Victor and House 2006; Wettestad 2005). Despite technical differences among them, all these experimentations played a considerable role in the collective sense-making that was necessary to push further the policymaking process:

> All these trading schemes, although very imperfect, were very important in building the consensus needed for this different policy instrument to be implemented . . . because there was a mistrust of it. But the models, the exercises we did, they helped familiarise, understand and even see the benefits and the advantages. (European Commission 1, 2015, 23 September)

According to our informants both at the European Commission and in the industry, GETS had more impact on the policymaking process than did the other prototypes. Among the factors that may explain this observation, we believe that the process of collective bricolage that was at play in designing the GETS prototype played an important role. Through this process, disagreements among key stakeholders had already been addressed and evacuated during prototyping. Moreover, key actors had a sense that they had participated in making the instrument which rendered the prototype more accepted. Finally, the appropriation of the prototype proved crucial in the negotiations since it provided a basis of shared knowledge. The most important stakeholders of the consultation understood the prototype, the way it worked as well as its practical implications because they had participated in its making. They had tested several prototypes generated from this process of collective bricolage and understood the impacts of each rule taken separately. Instead, the other prototypes that were presented during the consultation process, were not a product of collective bricolage. For instance, while the Climate Change Levy had been pushed forward by private companies too, the UK government officials then designed the scheme in isolation. They then tested with British private companies.

DISCUSSION: COLLECTIVE BRICOLAGE AND STAGING IN POLICYMAKING

The case described the efforts of a professional association to influence policymaking despite significant reluctance among both industrial players and policymakers. In many aspects, the case is a classical story of influence and power in political arenas where a skilled leading actor provokes a radical shift in the general opinion. The originality of the case is to reveal a rather unexpected influence strategy revolving around two elements: collective bricolage and staging. Here, collective bricolage served to dynamically recombine the interests of different stakeholders into a prototype for a carbon market. Eurelectric also staged an experimentation on carbon markets to diffuse the GETS results into key political spheres to convince wider circles of stakeholders to engage with, and support, the prototype.

Collective Bricolage

Collective bricolage played an important role in Eurelectric's initiative to co-construct a carbon market with other players in the industry. By collective bricolage, we mean the act of recombining heterogeneous propositions from multiple domains (for example from the cement industry, electricity sector, non-governmental agencies) into an original arrangement (Baker and Nelson 2005; Carstensen 2011; Højgaard Christiansen and Lounsbury 2013; Duymedjian and Rüling 2010). Eurelectric organized collective bricolage sessions with key stakeholders of the climate political arena as a way to engage them in the notion of carbon markets. All GETS participants were invited to make proposals to the carbon market's design and test these proposals through a role play. The design of the carbon market prototype used in GETS was thus the outcome of collective bricolage.

The composition of the prototype crystallized the political strategies of participants and their potentially conflicting interests and representations. For instance, some electricity utilities from the United Kingdom proposed to introduce a 'gateway system' that was being tested by their government. Their alternative proposal reveals their involvement in policymaking with their government. Indeed, since 1999, the electricity sector in the UK had been working with its national government on a semi-voluntary framework for carbon emissions management. Following the demand of the electricity sector in the UK, this system was introduced and tested in GETS2. Similarly, the request of Lafarge, a major European cement company, to implement technology standards reveals its political implication at the international level to promote sectoral agreements on carbon that are based on benchmarks. As it appears, the multiple orientations promoted by the participants for the carbon market design were not easily compatible with one another. To convince the cement sector, consultants were hired to design a sophisticated algorithm for benchmark allocations. To enrol the Italian industry, sophisticated carbon accounting methods had to be imagined to ensure environmental integrity. Testing the gateway proposed by the UK's electricity utilities also raised some arduous technical challenges for the organizers. The GETS role plays allowed heterogeneous actors to try out different proposals in practice and collectively construct a model that appealed to all, or most, participants.

We propose that collective bricolage – instead of a multi-stakeholder negotiation – helped alleviate the challenge of initial conflicting viewpoints and preferences. Instead of being negotiated, various propositions were tested in the role plays and their effects were discussed collectively afterwards. Every implementable proposition was tested, and promising features from different models were combined and tested as well. Collective bricolage worked as an instrument of dialogue that harmonized the interests of participants. Collective bricolage should not, however, be understood as a simple matter of integrating whatever proposition actors submit to a policymaking process. It requires considerable engineering effort to design tools and algorithms that enable selected features from multiple proposals to work well together.

To sum up, collective bricolage appears as a promising approach to analyse policymaking in as much as it allows stakeholders that do not initially share the same interests and understandings to work together towards the crafting of a collective model. In collective bricolage, stakeholders are encouraged to project and hybridize their respective representations and interests onto 'a boundary object' that operates as a negotiation device.

Staging

In the GETS case study, staging an experimentation of carbon markets was central to building influence, strategies and policymaking. It played two central roles: learning and demonstration. Eurelectric first used GETS as a learning device to provoke the intellectual shift that they needed in the private sector to promote carbon markets. All the participants in GETS shifted their point of view on carbon markets once they experienced it in practice. Before GETS, the participants would mostly be opposed to these market instruments that they perceived to be a constraint. After GETS, participants saw carbon markets as efficient tools for compliance instead. The two German companies that left the experiment after the first round were convinced too. They decided to promote voluntary agreements at the national level but they could understand the interest of carbon markets at the European level if such a regulation was to come.

The European Commission that closely followed the experiment was pleased that the results demonstrated that carbon markets worked the way they were supposed to work. Such demonstration was key to influence other key stakeholders that did not participate in the experiment. Along with the policymaking process, Eurelectric organized a large diffusion operation based on the GETS results. Eurelectric's representatives presented the GETS results in strategic political arenas such as the United Nation's climate summits and the stakeholder consultations organized by the European Commission. The European Commission officially invited Eurelectric during the United Nation's climate summit of Marrakesh to present the GETS results. Eurelectric's representatives also presented the GETS results to the European Parliament as well as to foreign governments and companies. The fact that GETS had actually demonstrated that carbon markets worked in practice proved crucial to convince key stakeholders in these instances.

If the experiment had depicted an unrealistic prototype, its results would not be relevant to 'real world' debates. For staging operations to be successful, considerable attention must be directed to technical details. In GETS, intense engineering helped the results spread outside the experiment. Apparently insignificant details had been reproduced with a high degree of precision. This mimicking of real conditions is very important, we contend, for the success of a staging operation.

CONCLUSIONS

This chapter describes two activities that companies strategically display to influence policymaking processes: collective bricolage and staging. These activities are by no means an exhaustive list of lobbying strategies that can be deployed at the organization level. Neither do they ensure success in influencing key stakeholders in political arenas. Nevertheless, we believe these components of effective policymaking to merit further investigation. They should be looked at in more detail if we want to better understand how the private sector influences policymaking (Bonardi et al. 2005).

We believe that collective bricolage is becoming an increasingly relevant concept for shedding light on the collective nature of policymaking, which is particularly visible in the field of environmental/climate regulations (Braun 2009; Callon 2009; Wettestad 2005). Indeed, emerging issues such as the climate change initiative that we describe in this chapter, and environmental issues more generally, are characterized by both unstable and lacunar scientific knowledge (Godard 2004). Under such conditions, policymakers rarely have the means to design regulations in isolation. These complex issues call for the participation of actors that are not traditionally involved in policymaking processes such as private associations and scientific NGOs. We propose that the concept of collective bricolage is particularly well suited to reveal the mechanisms at play when heterogeneous actors seek to find a consensus on policy alternatives. We thus call for further scholarly analysis of the processes of collective bricolage in policy studies.

Staging is the second analytical concept that emerged from our study for describing strategies of influence in the context of policymaking. Compared to collective bricolage, staging is more aligned with what is usually described as being classical lobbying strategies. Our case indicates that staging an experimentation of policy innovations that targets key audiences can be a highly influential activity. Studies of the role of 'demonstration' in the making of economic policies are gaining momentum in the social studies of market literature (MacKenzie et al. 2007). In particular, the very places where staging takes place, such as platforms (Muniesa and Callon 2007), hybrid forums (Callon et al. 2001) and political arenas in general merit attention in future studies of contemporary policymaking.

NOTE

1. EU-ETS stands for the European Emissions Trading System. It was launched in 2005 as a pilot carbon market.
2. For a detailed analysis on the role of the electricity sector in the institutionalization of the EU-ETS, see also Cartel, Boxenbaum and Aggeri (forthcoming).

REFERENCES

Akhurst, M., J. Morgheim and R. Lewis (2003), 'Greenhouse gas emissions trading in BP', *Energy Policy*, **31** (7), 657–63.

Baker, T. and R.E. Nelson (2005), 'Creating something from nothing: Resource construction through entrepreneurial bricolage', *Administrative Science Quarterly*, **50**, 329–66.

Baron, D. (1995), 'Integrated strategy: Market and nonmarket components', *California Management Review*, **37** (2), 47–65.
Baron, D. (1999), 'Integrated market and nonmarket strategies in client and interest group politics', *Business and Politics*, **1** (1), 7–34.
Baron, D. and D. Diermeier (2007), 'Strategic activism and nonmarket strategy', *Journal of Economics and Management Strategy*, **16** (3), 599–634.
Bonardi, J.P., A. Hillman and G. Keim (2005), 'The attractiveness of political markets: Implications for firm strategy', *Academy of Management Review*, **30** (2), 1209–28.
Braun, M. (2009), 'The evolution of emissions trading in the European Union – The role of policy networks, knowledge and policy entrepreneurs', *Accounting, Organizations and Society*, **34** (3–4), 469–87.
Burtraw, D. and S.J. Szambelan (2009), 'U.S. emissions trading markets for SO_2 and NO_x', *Resources for the Future*, Discussion Paper, DP 09–40.
Callon, M. (2009), 'Civilizing markets: Carbon trading between in vitro and in vivo experiments', *Accounting, Organizations and Society*, **34** (3–4), 535–48.
Callon, M., P. Lascoumes and Y. Barthe (2001), *Agir dans un monde incertain. Essai sur la démocratie technique*, Paris: Le Seuil.
Carstensen, M. (2011), 'Paradigm man vs. the bricoleur: An alternative vision of agency in ideational change', *European Political Science Review*, 3, 147–67.
Cartel, M., F. Aggeri and J-Y. Caneill (2017), 'L'histoire méconnue du marché européen du carbone: archéologie du secteur électrique. *Entreprises et histoire*, **86**, 54–70.
Cartel, M., E. Boxenbaum and F. Aggeri (forthcoming), 'Just for fun! How experimental spaces stimulate institutional innovation in mature fields', *Organization Studies*.
Cass, L.R. (2005), 'Norm entrapment and preference change: The evolution of the European Union position on international emissions trading', *Global Environmental Politics*, **5** (2), 38–60. The MIT Press.
Christiansen, A.C. and J. Wettestad (2003), 'The EU as a frontrunner on greenhouse gas emissions trading: How did it happen and will the EU succeed?', *Climate Policy*, **3** (1), 3–18.
Convery, F. (2009), 'Origins and Development of the EU ETS', *Environmental and Resource Economics*, **43** (3), 391–412.
Damro, C. and P. Mendez (2003), 'Emissions trading at Kyoto: From EU resistance to Union innovation', *Environmental Politics*, **12** (7), 71–94.
Duymedjian, R. and C.C. Rüling (2010), 'Towards a foundation of bricolage in organization and management theory', *Organization Studies*, **31**, 133–51.
Eisenhardt, K.M. and M.E. Graebner (2007), 'Theory building from cases: Opportunities and challenges', *Academy of Management Journal*, **50** (1), 25–32.
Godard, O. (2004), 'Le casse-tête de l'effet de serre au crible du développement durable', *Risques et management international*, **3**, 13–35.
Højgaard Christiansen, L. and M. Lounsbury (2013), 'Strange brew: Bridging logics via institutional bricolage and the reconstitution of organizational identity', in M. Lounsbury and E. Boxenbaum (eds), *Institutional Logics in Action, Part B*, Bingley: Emerald Group Publishing Limited, pp. 199–232 (Research in the Sociology of Organizations, Vol. 39 Part B).
Holburn, G. and R. Vanden Bergh (2008), 'Making friends in hostile environments: Political strategy in hostile environments', *Academy of Management Review*, **33** (2), 521–40.

Lévi-Strauss, C. (1962), *La pensée sauvage*, Paris: Plon.
Lévi-Strauss, C. (1966), *The Savage Mind*, Chicago: University of Chicago Press.
MacKenzie, D.A., F. Muniesa and L. Siu (2007), *Do Economists Make Markets? On the Performativity of Economics*, Princeton: Princeton University Press.
Montgomery, W. (1972), 'Markets in licenses and efficient pollution control program', *Journal of Economic Theory*, **5**, 395–418.
Muniesa, F. and M. Callon (2007), 'Economic experiments and the construction of markets', in D. MacKenzie, F. Muniesa and L. Siu (eds), *Do Economists Make markets? On the Performativity of Economics*, Princeton: Princeton University Press, pp. 161–89.
Newell, P. and M. Paterson (1996), 'From Geneva to Kyoto: The second conference of the Parties to the UN Framework Convention on Climate Change', *Environmental Politics*, **5**, 729–35.
Newell, P. and M. Paterson (1998), 'A climate for business: Global warming, the state and capital', *Review of International Political Economy*, **5** (4), 679–703.
Skjærseth, J.B. and J. Wettestad (2008), 'Implementing EU emissions trading: Success or failure?', *International Environmental Agreements: Politics, Law and Economics*, **8** (3), 275–90.
Victor, D.G. and J.C. House (2006), 'BP's emissions trading system', *Energy Policy*, **34** (15), 2100–12.
Wettestad, J. (2005), 'The making of the 2003 EU Emissions Trading Directive: An ultra-quick process due to entrepreneurial proficiency?', *Global Environmental Politics*, **5** (1), 1–23.

4. Lobbying in practice: an ethnographic field study of public affairs consultancy

Anna Tyllström

INTRODUCTION

Since the 1970s, a plethora of organizations devoted to political influence has emerged. Industry organizations, lobbying firms, think tanks and PR consultancies all assist corporations in public opinion building and getting in touch with policymakers, functioning as 'second hand dealers of ideas' (see Salles-Djelic in this volume). However, although called for more than three decades ago (Spradley 1980), ethnographic descriptions of lobbying have been conspicuous by their absence (Barley 2010). As a result, the actors surrounding political affairs, as well as policy outputs, have been readily studied, whilst the methods of 'second hand dealing' have not.

This chapter aims to shed light on this blind spot of corporate–political action studies. By drawing on ethnographic fieldwork from the realm of public affairs consultancy, my purpose is to provide insights into the practical nature of corporate lobbying, to discuss important aspects of lobbying practice and its role in society. In other words, I aspire to answer a quite straightforward question: How do public affairs consultants practice lobbying?

The text is structured as follows. In the next section, I detail my research context, the Politicians' Week in Almedalen, Sweden: I describe the setting, how I got there and the conditions for my study. Against this backdrop, I then flesh out my observations from one main lobbying case, in which I followed a senior consultant at a small consultancy, Strat PR, in his work with mapping the lobbying landscape around the issue of ethanol as a biofuel – a subject dividing political parties, advocacy organizations and industry into two camps.[1] As will become clear, this lobbying case unfolds as an intricate process where sophisticated arguments are formulated, gathered and linked, and holy and unholy alliances are formed. Finally, I reflect on the five main practices characterizing the lobbying work observed, and also on how those lobbying practices might be understood in a wider societal context.

CONTEXT: PUBLIC AFFAIRS CONSULTING AND POLITICIANS' WEEK

The empirical setting of my fieldwork is the Politicians' Week in Almedalen, a week-long annual political fair taking place in Visby, on the island of Gotland in the Baltic Sea, off the east coast of Sweden. Originally instigated in 1968 by former Prime Minister Olof Palme, who wished to hold summer speeches close to his summer house, the event has gradually expanded over the decades to comprise a whole week and all political parties. In recent years, its popularity has also grown exponentially. In 2001, 52 pre-arranged events were attended by fewer than 5000 visitors, whilst in 2016, 3800 events attracted 40 000 visitors, making the Week the largest single political event in Sweden. Virtually all Swedish politicians, business organizations, religious organizations, mass media outlets and to an increasing extent also industry leaders, academia and the general public, attend to engage in discussion in all fields of policy.

For professional lobbyists of all sorts, the Politicians' Week of course constitutes important business. One type of actor thriving during the Week is the young industry of public relations consultancy (Tyllström 2013; c.f. Walker 2014); a fairly new collective of strategic advisors, specializing in a broad array of services like media relations, product placements and investor relations, but also public affairs services.[2] Over the years, the visibility of PR agencies in Almedalen has increased in steady correlation with the event's popularity. Agencies help their clients to organize seminars, debates and parties during the Week. Some firms also have their own events and parties in Visby; to them, the Week is a marketing event. But far from all consultancy activity is formalized, with much of the work going on in between, under and after the formally listed events, such as networking and the booking of meetings with policymakers on behalf of corporate clients.

To me, a researcher interested in the practices of corporate–political action, the Almedalen Week constitutes a unique opportunity. Firstly, access is relatively informal. While access among PR consultancies in the normal Stockholm business setting is generally difficult to gain, Almedalen proved easier; the control over schedule and location is not as rigid as usual. But most importantly, the Politicians' Week is unique in terms of political intensity. In organizational terms, the Week could be termed a field-configuring event, in other words a periodical setting that bears considerable importance for how a field's identity and activities are constructed, defined and delineated (compare Lampel and Meyer 2008). Subsequently, the week constitutes a 'hyper-version' of Swedish political life, altering the basic course of events, but also speeding it up; the presence of a totality of actors causes great political momentum during a few days only. Studying lobbying in Almedalen transcends the border between organizational and industry-level ethnography (see Zilber 2007) and holds the promise of potentially unique insights into complex political processes.

MY ENTRY POINT TO ALMEDALEN: STRAT PR

Between 2009 and 2011, I conducted field studies in Almedalen during the Politicians' Week. I attended seminars, participated in various events and observed consultancy work. The last two years, I observed consultants at Strat PR, a small Stockholm-based PR agency with 12 employees working predominantly with media relations and public affairs for clients in the private, non-profit and public sectors. Originally planned as shadowing (Czarniawska 2007), these observations quickly became quite participatory, as I was given the role of a non-remunerated assistant. During fieldwork, I had a general yes-policy, accepting most tasks assigned to me in order to see as much of consultancy practice as possible. In a few cases, I declined participation referring to my researcher status, for instance when I was asked to perform tasks directly for the agencies' clients or the tasks were not evidently relevant to my research question. Throughout, I took double-layered notes, separating descriptive accounts of factual events from my own interpretations (Saldana 2013).[3] Strat PR, its clients and consultants are anonymized to guarantee confidentiality, but all other actors are called by their real names.

The case below unfolds during my last year with Strat PR in Almedalen, 2011. Head of the project is the agency's owner Magnus, whom I had got to know the year before. A trained chemical engineer in his mid-50s, Magnus had a long career as a trade journalist within high-tech behind him before he left for the PR industry, and eventually founded Strat PR together with a younger colleague in 2006. Magnus works predominantly with public affairs, and this particular case is about regulation of biofuel in Sweden. This is an issue of great importance to many actors, including political parties, companies in energy and transportation sectors, environmental NGOs, as well as millions of Swedish car owners and buyers. But of the specific details, I still know little as I meet up with Magnus on the first day of Politicians' Week 2011.

Seminar 1, Swedish Farmers' Confederation: Searching for 'Good Persons'

It is raining and quite windy, as Magnus and I meet outside a white plastic tent in the harbour. Even though the week has just started, the transformation of the normally quaint, seaside medieval town of Visby has already taken place: each corner of the town is occupied by organizations trying to get their message across, to someone. Every hotel, bar, office, school building or public facility is occupied – there is a plastic tent on nearly every lawn. The inhabitants of Visby sublet their gardens and homes to an invading opinion elite clad in blue shirts, sunshades and khaki shorts.

We say our hellos, and Magnus briefly summarizes the situation. One of his clients, a Nordic petroleum company, has bought a nationwide network of gas stations, previously owned by Shell. Now the company has plans for rebuilding all these stations to provide only biofuels, reinventing itself as 'the environmentally conscious gas station' on the Swedish market. The most advanced plans are for E85, a fuel consisting of 85 per cent ethanol, an alcohol produced from grains. But the client's plan also includes Mk1 or biodiesel, a local Swedish quality of diesel distilled from various types of organic fats (in contrast to normal diesel, Mk3, which is a by-product of petroleum processing). In the beginning of the 2000s, Sweden had had various tax waivers to drivers of biofuel-driven cars. But this system of fiscal advantages had recently started to be dismantled; tax discounts per litre had disappeared for ethanol, and been heavily reduced for biodiesel. The aim for Magnus this week, he explains, is to map the regulatory landscape around biofuel, and to identify opportunities to influence policy in the client's favour, before the company enters the Swedish market. To pave the way, so to speak. I will assist him in this.

The Federation of Swedish Farmers (LRF), a well-established lobbying organization in agriculture and forestry, is hosting this first seminar of the Week. About 80 people have come to listen. In the panel discussion there are representatives of LRF, two industry organizations for energy and forestry sectors respectively, and two corporations; truck manufacturer Scania, and Volvo. Several panellists mention a new pine oil refinery producing Mk1 in western Sweden. The plant is co-owned by forestry companies and Preem, a petroleum company competing with Magnus's client. Magnus listens attentively to the panellists, while taking sparse notes. About the LRF representative, I can see that he writes 'good person'.

The following Q&A session is busy. When the discussion touches on ethanol, a woman in her 50s stands up. In a frank, down-to-earth manner she starts off: 'Why is ethanol so degraded in public discourse?' She is referring to recent claims that ethanol, which is predominantly extracted from various crops, is occupying land resources that could be used for food production. 'Why is only ethanol said to compete with food? What about T-shirts, or golf courses . . .?' This woman is clearly used to speaking in public, backing up her rhetorical question with commensurable facts; 'Reports say that we can increase ethanol production yet another 15 per cent before the land use starts intruding on food!'

While the woman is still talking, Magnus takes up his mobile phone and starts writing a text message. Over his shoulder I can see the two words: 'Well spoken!'. He scrolls in his contact list until he finds the right number, and sends it off. The woman finishes her inflammatory speech, and sits down.

Once the seminar is over, Magnus moves fast towards the exit. The rain has stopped. We wait in silence while the audience drops off. When the woman with the ethanol question comes out of the tent, Magnus approaches her and gives me a wink to come along. He approaches her:

> M: Hi! Did you get my text?

The woman looks startled, as if she recognizes him but can't place him.

> W: Yes, I just replied, but I didn't know whom it was from. Thank you!
> M: No, but I mean it. You spoke extremely well. I was just lucky to still have your number.
> W: Thank you. I just get so angry when I hear ethanol being discredited like this!

Magnus explains his mission for the petroleum company and introduces me, without affiliation:

> M: This is Anna, working with me this week.

The woman presents herself as Annika, and suddenly I understand who she is; she is Annika Åhnberg, the former Social Democratic Minister of Agriculture. She explains how she has abandoned politics completely and also her top management position in a large Swedish MNC in the energy technology field. She now sits on the board of the Royal Academy of Agriculture and Forestry, and runs her own consulting company. Magnus listens attentively, then softly asks, with an air of it being the most natural question in the world:

> M: Maybe we could work together somehow?

Annika nods.

> A: Yeah sure, just call me. I am very eager to do something about this. I support all initiatives for this cause.

A while later, as we're walking towards the inner bay of the harbour, Magnus comments:

M: It's funny, that woman talking . . .
A: Annika Åhnberg?
M: Yes, you know her?
A: Well, she used to be in the government . . .
M: Well at first I didn't recognize her, but then she presented herself, and it just rang a bell. We used to work together, ten years ago or so. After leaving politics, she had an office in our PR agency. She is so sharp! She has such a good way of expressing herself, factual and clear. You get the feeling that her mind works faster than everybody else's in the room. A very good person. I hope she'll join us in this.

Just one hour into the week I am already startled; Magnus's play-it-by-ear strategy appears striking to me. There is no possibility Magnus could have known that Annika would attend the seminar, and he hardly recognized her at first. But from hearing her speak just a few sentences, he rapidly singled her out from all the other people in the audience, identified his old connection with her, found her number is his old phone book – where he must have thousands of old phone numbers saved, sent her a text, waited for her outside, re-established the personal connection, briefly presented his case and tied a potential ally to his cause. The whole series of events took a maximum of 20 minutes, but he drew on his whole professional arsenal to perform it: network contacts, political know-how, years of experience and last but certainly not least, his amiable personality. A beautiful display of lobbying in action?

We decide to sit down at a nearby restaurant on the Harbour Square. As we wait for our food, Magnus starts elaborating the mission to me in closer detail:

M: We need to do two things; to create a clear argumentation strategy and to identify which persons are good to have on your team.
A: So Annika could help you shape the arguments?
M: Exactly. As you heard this morning, all actors say the same thing: Policy in this area is too unstable, and developments are going in the wrong direction. And I have still not been able to figure out why ethanol is being dragged through the mud, where all the bad talk comes from. And we need to find allies, and find out which politicians have a say.
A: But on a concrete level, what does your client wish to accomplish? Policy decisions?
M: Partly that, like tax reliefs at the gas station. Then second, to crush this myth about the substitutability of ethanol for other grains. It is simply not true that ethanol is competing with food.

Magnus sounds like an echo of Annika's recent speech. I cannot judge whether this is his own view or a quick adoption of hers to make his argumentation look more orderly. He mentions that there are other 'auxiliary' taxes too that could be lobbied for, like tax reliefs for producing, buying and renting out 'green' vehicles, and exemption from car tolls and parking in major cities. In other words: measures indicating that using biofuels should be encouraged.

The project had started the previous spring, with the client approaching Strat PR for an overview of policy, regulation and actors in the biofuel field. A report was drafted, but Magnus felt that more could be done.

> We said to the client, 'You need to go to Almedalen.' And they replied, 'No, we don't have time.' So we figured that we'd go instead. So we're doing this mapping now, attending seminars and trying to identify people and angles.

Magnus points at his laptop screen, showing me his personalized schedule in the online platform of the Politicians' Week.

> See, I have listed the 7 most relevant events here. Already this afternoon there is one, at the same time that I need to attend to a telephone conference. Could you could go in my place?

I recognize the familiar sensation from earlier fieldwork, of simultaneously being trusted and feeling completely lost. After all, I am a researcher, not a policy expert. But I tell myself that Magnus must know what he's doing, and decide to say yes.

> A: Ok. But what should I look for?
> M: Good politicians, whether he or she might be interested in this. It is really about identifying good persons. Then there are two more seminars this afternoon. Tomorrow afternoon there is also something on ethanol. But I am double-booked then, actually triple-booked. Maybe you could attend one of these seminars too?
> A: Sure.

Magnus gives me his login so that I can see the details on the seminars. He continues to list some other projects he'll be working with during the Week: a cable TV provider, media training for a public authority and Strat PR's yearly party in a medieval church ruin for a few hundred guests. He also describes some projects that still lack a client. Such proactivity seems counter-intuitive to me. Being somehow instilled with the belief that lobbying consultancy work was based on clients' political needs, I ask him whether this is common practice, to come up with ideas for political campaigns *before* he has a client. Magnus looks up, honestly surprised: 'But why, yes. ALL the time.'

He explains how he often keeps track of regulatory changes in various policy areas that he is personally interested in, like youth science education, or digitalization of state television broadcasting. Sometimes he waits for political decisions, and then immediately contacts the affected organizations, who will need help in adjusting to the new policy. Other times, he is even more proactive. Right now, Magnus and his co-founder at Strat PR nurture a plan on how to reform the Swedish general pension fund system, providing a technical solution where less money could be lost in brokerage fees, and more money would go to the funds.

> M: It's awful right now! I mean, this is our money they're taking! Horrendous! It is a bit of a secret I guess, but we're sketching out a system where you'd have maybe three fund options – one a little more risky, and one that follows index etcetera. Actually, that would be a bit of a return to the old system, which was much better.
> A: But this sounds like a big project?
> M: Yes, it's huge! The ideal would be if we could find a consortium. We have some contacts with one of the large mutual funds, they might be interested.

Magnus and I work for a while side by side before I collect myself: I need to go off to the second seminar of the day. On my way out of the restaurant, I almost bump into the bodyguards of Prime Minister Fredrik Reinfeldt, escorting him down the boardwalk. I see him pass, a few metres away. Welcome to Almedalen, I think to myself.

Seminar 2, Green Car Owners: Identifying Alliances

I spend my afternoon in various seminars. The last one features the Minister of Trade from the Conservative Party. After the seminar, I meet Magnus for a debrief. He asks me specifically about the Minister of Trade, if I think she is 'a good person', in other words, if she has any reason to listen to ethanol producers. I answer truthfully that I do not have the slightest idea. Magnus laughs, and continues:

> I mean, we could take a Nordic angle on this. After all, this is a Nordic-owned corporation starting up in Sweden, of course they should talk with the Minister of Trade who also happens to be the Minister of Nordic Cooperation . . .

Magnus adds that he often does this; brainstorms with somebody junior – 'to get ideas' – and then he and his senior colleagues finalize the structure. He stresses that the profession is a craft, best learned by doing:

> They don't teach you this in Political Science 101. My colleagues are political scientists and they read. But I make calls. I don't stop calling until 5pm. I use

> my journalist background a lot. I could call 20 people, and they all describe the same thing but differently. Because that's reality, a bit different to everyone.

We discuss a bit further as we walk together towards the harbour and our next seminar venue, which is a boat. *Tre Kronor* is a 45-metre-long exact replica of a nineteenth-century navy cargo ship. She sails down from Stockholm every summer to serve as a seminar hall during the Week. Below deck, there is a small conference room for 50 people and the ship's handcrafted feel and natural use of wind power has made her an especially popular rental among environmentalist organizations. This afternoon's host is Green Car Owners, a lobbying organization for 'environmentally friendly driving'.

This seminar is spot-on; issues and representatives are highly relevant to Magnus's cause. It starts with a presentation by two lobbyists from Green Car Owners (GCO). I recognize one of them; he is a former Green Party politician and a former PR consultant, and I have previously interviewed him for research purposes. His and his colleague's style is quite demagogical – not unlike car salesmen, actually. Still, they provide many useful facts; statistics on car sales over time, distributed over different 'green car' classes and types of biofuels and an overview of recent policy changes. When they are through, two representatives from car producers Volvo and Nissan share their views. They are despairing, claiming to have spent big money on developing new, more efficient ethanol engines. But now, in time for the launch of these engines, tax benefits for ethanol are suddenly gone, and sales have plummeted; the share of ethanol-driven vehicles among new cars has decreased dramatically, from 50 per cent to below 5 per cent, in just three years. Also, the requirements for a car to be classified as a 'green vehicle', and hence qualify for purchasing discounts, have become considerably stricter. 'This is the engine everybody asked for three years ago, and now nobody wants it!' the Volvo representative laments.

Two local politicians, one from Gothenburg and one from northern Sweden, present themselves. They are both Social Democrats, and winners of the 'Best Green Car Municipality of the Year' contest, arranged by Green Car Owners. The Gothenburg politician agrees with the car industry representatives that the difficulty of predicting policy constitutes a major obstacle to efficient public traffic planning. The major bottleneck is the Ministry of Finance, she says; 'they simply don't want subsidies'.

The lobbyists from Green Car Owners end the session with an appeal to all actors in the room to unite in drafting a letter to the government. The letter would demand concrete policy changes and GCO have already prepared detailed bullet points: subsidies, tax rewards, classification limits in detail and so on. Magnus has somewhat of a poker face, so I cannot tell his reaction. But I reckon this must be a jackpot for him – an extant network of powerful organizations working towards the same goal as his client?

Afterwards, sparkling wine and crackers are served up on the deck, which is rather crowded. The rain has stopped. Annika Åhnberg is there, with her dog. For entertainment, Green Car Owners have hired an impersonator, who makes embarrassingly bad impressions of Swedish politicians. Magnus and I sit down a bit farther away by the railing. Magnus is contemplative, reflecting in a sort of think-aloud protocol:

> Maybe the smartest thing for my client would be to join these people. Maybe that would be the most honest thing. For me to say: 'You have to find allies, you can never do anything on your own. You need help in this.' That would be an advanced way of us saying 'Sorry, we cannot help you.' But that would be bad – for us of course, since there would be no work. But it would also be, like, as if we left them with nothing. Which is not fair. I mean, they come here, expect to get help and then we say that there's nothing to be done!

Magnus says that it might look like there is an established network around Green Car Owners, but he isn't so sure; it might look more fixed than it is. Perhaps his client could place itself in the outskirts of that nebulous group of actors? Joining GCO and the car producers around certain questions, while running its own lobbying race concerning others. 'That would be on a small scale, but a good scale,' he concludes.

From where he is sitting at the railing, Magnus has an overview of the deck. His gaze scans the crowd watching the impersonator, whose act seems to be coming along better now. The time is almost 7pm. We talk a bit more, and make some preliminary plans for the coming day. After agreeing to call each other the following morning, we part, and I go home.

Seminar 3, Car Sweden: Identifying Resistance

The next day is hot, over 30 degrees in the shade. I am attending a panel debate in Magnus's place, organized by one of Sweden's most dominant industry organizations, Car Sweden, on alternatives to fossil fuels for heavy transports. The relative importance of the hosting organization, built up over decades by Saab, Scania and Volvo and their subcontractors, is reflected in the setting; the rented main hall of University College of Gotland is huge, food is free and the air con is efficient. Also, participants are more distinguished; several members of parliament are present, head experts from the transportation and energy authorities, CEOs and vice CEOs of several energy companies, and Volvo. This time it's the big guys talking.

The outcome of the discussion is illuminating. The Volvo guy repeats his lament from yesterday, but meets resistance from two experts from the Swedish Transport Administration. They are very critical of ethanol, calling it a fad that politicians had been too eager to join too soon. Instead, they agree that the future lies in biogas and electric cars. This should be valuable information for Magnus; yesterday, the Ministry of Finance was identified as an enemy of ethanol, but obviously there are public experts also working against it. Resistance to ethanol is obviously occurring in multiple places in government administration, simultaneously.

Seminar 4, Environmental News: The Diesel War on Display

The morning of the last day Magnus and I work together, I open the country's largest newspaper to read the front page of its economic supplement: 'THE DIESEL WAR'. The phrase is directly stolen from media industry magazine *Resumé*, whose original headline the previous day had read 'Full Throttle in the Diesel War'. The rather lengthy original text had described the conflict in detail, focusing on the tax difference between biodiesel (called Mk1) and normal diesel (Mk3). Whereas ethanol has already lost its tax benefits, tax cuts on biodiesel had remained, although lowered. Two camps, represented by the two competing petroleum companies Preem and Statoil, now continue to fight over the remaining tax. Those who cherish tax benefits for Mk1-diesel and ethanol are headed by Preem, having made substantial investments in Mk1-diesel in its pine oil refinery on the west coast. The Social Democrats and the Green Party support Preem, as does the reputable NGO Swedish Society for Nature Conservation (SSNC). In the other camp, against subsidies, is Statoil, other producers of Mk3-diesel, the right-wing government, as well as the transport sector (*Resumé*, 6 July 2011). Complicating the conflict is the fact that Mk1 is a local Swedish fuel quality, and Statoil, owned by the Norwegian state, deems it protectionist by the Swedish state to subsidize it. The Statoil camp had also been behind the recent campaign resulting in abolished tax waivers on ethanol.

The article lists the PR consultancies working for respective camp, and ends by mentioning an Almedalen seminar where the two sides will meet in a panel discussion, organized by the magazine *Environmental News*, and finishes with a wordplay: 'When the diesel war comes to Almedalen, an already combustible area risks being considerably heated up.'

Just a few hours later, I aim for the very same seminar. When I arrive, I can't find Magnus, so I text him, and he replies: 'I'm in the back!.' I look around; he waves from where he's sitting. The panel is divided into exactly the two sides described in the article; Statoil and a conservative MP arguing against tax benefits, whilst Preem and a Green party MP are for them. Preem and Statoil immediately engage in polemics, and the whole seminar turns into an inflamed technical debate of how to measure CO2 emissions from the two types of diesel. According to Preem's way of calculating, the difference in emissions between Mk1 and Mk3 is considerable; according to Statoil's calculations, it is negligible.

Afterwards, Magnus and I sit down on a bench outside the venue. Suddenly, the image that had been so diffuse the first day is very clear to Magnus. I can't tell whether the article has informed him, or if he has been getting alternative information elsewhere. As we are talking, the Preem communication manager from the panel debate approaches us, together with her assistant. Why is she coming up to us? Had Magnus told her assistant that he wished to speak with her? He mentions the name of his client, that they're entering the Swedish market, and that they share the same political goal as Preem; tax subsidies for both ethanol and Mk1. He compliments her on her contributions during the panel. They continue talking about the conflict between Preem and Statoil, and then they proceed to educational background, stating that they are both trained chemical engineers but never worked as such. A common point of reference is established. Before the Preem woman turns to leave, she says: 'I am really happy to hear your client employed someone for lobbying! It was about time.'

Immediately after she's gone Magnus says: 'She is so sweet that girl! You know, when you meet ambitious women in technical companies, it's not uncommon that they are chemical engineers.'

We decide to go for a free coffee, offered by the client's nemesis, Statoil. Statoil's main argument against tax subsidies for the local Mk1 is that it is unfair, as it thwarts international competition and hence trade. To drive home the point, Statoil has rebuilt an electrical truck into a coffee wagon, serving free Fairtrade-labelled coffee outside the seminar venue. On the side of the truck, we can read the motivation behind the campaign in large letters: 'Because it gives you energy to modernize the diesel tax', with the subtitle 'Did you know that the diesel tax is being revised? Make sure your party votes for a competition-neutral and fair tax.' We have a latte each in takeaway mugs. It tastes quite horrendous, but Magnus is impressed by the wagon. He even takes a picture, to show his clients at the petroleum company an example of how the enemy works. I understand his fascination. The coffee truck mediates many things simultaneously; it promotes electric motoring, appeals to several senses and portrays Statoil as generous (offering free coffee) and globally aware (fairtrade label). Moreover, the wordplay with 'fair' in 'fair tax' and 'fairtrade' is pithy, all the while transmitting a corporate message to the targeted audience of politicians; to abolish tax waivers on Mk1. A textbook example of efficient PR, where both content and form communicate.

We return to the bench under the shade of the tree with the mugs in our hands. As we are about to conclude the week's collaboration, I decide to ask a question I had been wondering about:

> How common is it that you use personal contacts? You hardly seem to use personal contacts within government for example. Is this a conscious strategy, or you simply don't have them?

Magnus does not look offended as he replies:

> I mean, in general, all people are Greek,[4] thinking: 'I know somebody who . . .'. There's no doubt about that. We DO have these contacts. But we rarely use them. Our CEO knows a government member extremely well, they go on vacation together. I mean, could you possibly have a closer bond than boozing together for five weeks in Spain? But if our CEO then were to ask this guy, 'Look, could you push for . . .?' No! I think it works exactly in reverse. I mean they have a private, personal relationship. Imagine then if we would do that all the time! No, no.

He stops mid-sentence, pauses, then resumes to explain that such contacts are mostly good for marketing purposes.

> I mean the clients who come to a PR agency, knowing that we have the phone number of, say, 'Lars,' they go wild. 'Wow, these people know Lars!' they think. So it's like that with everything else, it works only because people believe in it. We allow ourselves to be Greek. See?

Magnus is clearly done talking about this, and moves on to hypothesize about the case at hand.

> Now with this assignment, I wonder . . . Should we take the Nordic angle? Or the political angle? Or go to the media? Should we go in and take the lead in environmental issues? But then we risk becoming a peeve of the right wing parties, and being perceived in the wrong way . . .

We don't reach any conclusion. I agree to email him notes from a seminar he'd missed, and then we are through for this year. We thank each other. The atmosphere is cordial now after working together in Almedalen for two consecutive years. Then I go off, quite exhausted after the past few days of lobbying.

THE PRACTICES OF LOBBYING

In many aspects, the case described above is a classical one: a powerful industry player wishes to influence policy, hires a consultant who uses classical tools to gain political influence such as identifying key players and enemies, good arguments and counter-arguments (Hillman et al. 2004; Kingdon and Thurber 2003). But the case also gives a rare account of how these tools are used by public affairs consultants. In generalized terms, I found the lobbying of public affairs consultants to revolve around five practices; information gathering, contact management, visibility management, role switching and ideological proactivity.

First, I found information gathering to be a central practice of lobbying work; corporate clients pay consultants to keep them informed of the latest developments in regulation, media and advocacy. The meticulous selection of seminars, reading of articles and taking notes were expressions of this. Perhaps to no great surprise, the management of contacts (second) is also essential. Magnus is in constant search for 'good people' who could help his client, probing existing networks for possible entries, to see whether his client could bring something that other actors want or need. But he also continuously establishes contacts outside the assignment; reconnecting with old contacts, forming new ties, entertaining relationships that might yield something in the future. Although not claiming to use his government contacts, he proves very aware of them and claims to use them for marketing purposes.

A third, practical feature of the work I observed was visibility management. A classic critique against lobbyists is that they act in secret; that their invisible work processes produce hidden influence (compare Dinan and Miller 2007). My material supports this point to some degree, as nothing is readily visible about Strat PR's missions. But on the other hand, it is difficult to know what is actually invisible. Goffman's metaphor of front stage and backstage, in which actors perform social life as a formal dramaturgy for an audience on stage, while refining their performance backstage without being seen, might be useful here (Goffman 1959; Kvarnström 2010). The Politicians' Week constitutes the front stage of thousands of political performances, with probably just as many backstage plays. In this spectacular setting, the intermediary nature of PR consultancy becomes clear. Magnus is not a formal actor in his own right. In most cases, he retains the low profile of an observer; he never asks questions during Q&A sessions and seldom talks to others in seminars. But neither is he a regular audience member for on chosen occasions, he approaches front stage actors, as in the case with the former Minister of Agriculture, or Preem's communications manager. In such instances, he reveals his identity and mission in backstage interaction. Likewise, despite being cordially open to me, sharing passwords and plans, Magnus keeps other things to himself and temporarily extends his confidence when he sees fit. Analytically, I argue that this passageway between front stage and backstage, between formal and informal, is a fuzzy yet institutionalized space where Strat PR and other lobbyists are operating; a grey zone where boundaries between visibility and invisibility are conscientiously managed.

A fourth, seemingly important, characteristic is role switching. Consultancy work in general is characterized by improvisation; consultants commonly alter the combination of techniques or appearances according to the situation (compare Furusten 2009). Public affairs consultancy is no exception. Throughout the Week, Magnus constantly switched roles between generalist and lobbyist, between observing journalist, chemical engineer and business-driven consultant, between working with others and working alone. By drawing on this whole repertoire of roles, Magnus could span more boundaries, and interact with more people on their own turf, make them open up and contribute with information, contacts or other resources promoting his clients' cause. He could do things that his clients simply couldn't, as these are bound up by their formal position in corporate structures.

Finally, the lobbying practice observed was to a surprising degree characterized by ideological proactivity. According to international ethical guidelines for PR consultancies, firms ought to 'help clients influence opinions, attitudes and behavior' and they are obliged to 'approach their clients with objectivity' (ICCO 2003). As I first entered the field, I held similar preconceived notions that consultancy was demand-driven, originating from clients' own problems. In my case, the observed consultant had clear personal political opinions of his own, around which he created projects, which he only later found clients for. My earlier interviews, outside the case described here, point to similar findings, suggesting that many PR agencies serve as originators of, and as arenas for, extra-parliamentarian political activity. According to my observations, public affairs consultants are hence not only to be understood as 'second-hand dealers' of ideas, but also first-hand initiators of policy.

These five types of practice are distinctly observable aspects of lobbying work, but they also feed into and amplify each other. Switching roles facilitates the establishment of contacts, which in turn enables the gathering of better, more valuable information. Moreover, the constant management of boundaries between invisibility and visibility, the rich contact networks and the constant adjustment of identities together makes it possible for consultants to launch their own political ideas into the opinion landscape. Understanding these qualities of practice and how they interact is crucial to understanding the resurgent critique against lobbyism concerning its hidden nature and role confusion. For fuzziness is not external to lobbying practices – it is at the heart of it. Lobbying is a process where roles, boundaries and mission continually blur and mesh, where allies team up for a while, and then no longer, unite in one issue but not another, and where actors use the identity most suitable to the specific context.

LOBBYING IN A LARGER PERSPECTIVE – A MARKETPLACE OF IDEAS

At this point, a caveat is necessary. Descriptions of lobbying should not be mistaken for illustrating the success of lobbying; opinions of the general public and political decision makers are not always easy to influence (Scott 2008). In the case of biofuel, various actors' efforts have not brought about radical change. As this is written, several years after the fieldwork ended, tax levels on ethanol and biodiesel are still intact. And even if they were altered, it would be hard to single out the role of Strat PR's, or other actors', endeavours. But the occurrence of lobbying is important in its own right, and after unveiling the main characteristics of lobbying practice, a second, equally straightforward question arises, namely: Of what is this a case?

The setting described, the Politicians' Week in Almedalen is a special context, but not unique. The template has increased exponentially in popularity the last 15 years, and has inspired several international followers; Denmark and Norway have recently started up their own Politicians' Weeks, and Finland and the Baltic countries have shown interest in doing the same. This recent dispersion of the format could be seen as a transformation of the old 'Scandinavian model' (Abrahamson 1999), a welfare regime where corporate–political interaction was centrally coordinated.[5] But since the 1980s, this controlled system has been gradually dismantled, in favour of a US-inspired pluralism (Lewin 2006; Naurin 2007). In pluralist societies, the political sphere is seen more as an open market-like arena where ideas and opinions compete with each other, and the best ideas 'win' the attention of the policymakers. The Politicians' Week in Almedalen is indeed close to a perfect analogy of an ideological marketplace of ideas – opinion actors professing their views, in competition with a multitude of others. From such a perspective, both the Politicians' Week and the emergent market for public affairs consultancy are signs of a transforming model of corporate–political interaction, and an intensifying field of organizations devoted to such activities. Moreover, Almedalen bears much resemblance to other non-parliamentarian meeting places for business and politics emerging on a global level, like the World Economic Forum (see Garsten and Sörbom, Chapter 2 in this volume). Such phenomena, and the practices analysed in this chapter, constitute in many ways a new situation for democracy, and new loci of political influence.

NOTES

1. For reasons of anonymity all names of the interlocutors are fictitious.
2. Unlike the US, there are no distinct lobbying firms in the Swedish context. Instead, the concept 'PR consultancy' encompasses lobbying and advocacy services. The term 'PR consultant' is used synonymously with 'public affairs consultant' and 'lobbyist'. Moreover, many PR agencies are founded by former politicians, and in the public affairs departments a political background is more common than not (Tyllström 2009).
3. In cases where I shared notes with the consultancy, it is the former type that is referred to.
4. Referring to ongoing political-economical crisis in Greece summer 2011, in the media often explained by intricate systems of nepotism and corruption instead of meritocracy.
5. Typical arrangements where business and politics met were labour negotiations between trade unions and business associations, corporate representation on government boards, government hearings with civil society organizations and so on.

REFERENCES

Abrahamson, P. (1999), 'The Scandinavian model of welfare: Comparing social systems in Nordic Europe and France', MIRE, Paris, pp. 31–60.

Barley, S.R. (2010), 'Building an institutional field to corral a government: A case to set an agenda for organization studies', *Organization Studies*, **31** (6), 777–805.

Czarniawska, B. (2007), *Shadowing: And other Techniques for Doing Fieldwork in Modern Societies*, Copenhagen: Copenhagen Business School Pr.

Dinan, W. and D. Miller (2007), *Thinker, Faker, Spinner, Spy: Corporate PR and the Assault on Democracy*, London: Pluto Press.

Furusten, S. (2009), 'Management consultants as improvising agents of stability', *Scandinavian Journal of Management*, **25** (3), 264–74.

Goffman, E. (1959), *The Presentation of Self in Everyday Life*, New York: Anchor Books.

Hillman, A.J., G.D. Keim and D. Schuler (2004), 'Corporate political activity: A review and research agenda', *Journal of Management*, **30** (6), 837–57.

ICCO (2003), The ICCO Stockholm Charter.

Kingdon, J.W. and J.A. Thurber (2003), *Agendas, Alternatives, and Public Policies*, New York: Longman.

Kvarnström, E. (2010), 'Medieträning: skönhets-operationen för att styra intrycket', in J. Pallas and L. Strannegård (eds), *Företag och Medier*, Stockholm: Liber Förlag, pp. 150–68.

Lampel, J. and A.D. Meyer (2008), 'Guest editors' introduction', *Journal of Management Studies*, **45** (6), 1025–35.

Lewin, L. (2006), 'The rise and decline of corporatism: The case of Sweden', *European Journal of Political Research*, **26** (1), 59–79.

Naurin, D. (2007), *Deliberation Behind Closed Doors: Transparency and Lobbying in the European Union*, Colchester: ECPR Press.
Saldana, J. (2013), 'An introduction to codes and coding', in J. Saldana, *The Coding Manual for Qualitative Researchers*, London: SAGE, 1–31.
Scott, W. (2008), 'Approaching adulthood: The maturing of institutional theory', *Theory and Society*, **37** (5), 427–42.
Spradley, J.P. (1980), *Participant Observation*, New York: Holt, Rinehart and Winston.
Tyllström, A. (2013), *Legitimacy for sale: constructing a market for PR consultancy*, Department of Business Studies. Uppsala, Uppsala University. Doctoral Thesis No. 162: 235 pp.
Walker, E.T. (2014), *Grassroots for Hire: Public Affairs Consultants in American Democracy*, Cambridge: Cambridge University Press.
Zilber, T.B. (2007), 'Stories and the discursive dynamics of institutional entrepreneurship: The case of Israeli high-tech after the bubble', *Organization Studies*, **28** (7), 1035–54.

5. Firms' political strategies in a new public/private environment: the Boeing case

Hervé Dumez and Alain Jeunemaître

INTRODUCTION

Relationships between firms and states are old and probably date back to the very origins of firms. Researchers have studied them since at least Epstein's book (1969). In recent years, however, firms have undergone major changes due to the widespread introduction of the private sector in areas previously reserved to the state (Mahoney et al. 2009). In such a context, firms have adapted their strategies. In addition to efficiency, they have learned to seek innovation, as well as, possibly, monopoly and influence rents (Ahuja and Yayavaram 2011), so as to organize to their advantage the new relations between the public and the private domains. Such a development is not without difficulties. The outcome of political strategies has turned out to be much more unpredictable than previously thought. The traditional view of firms' political strategies is that, by acting on the state, they will protect and expand firms' interests. But whereas in the classic game (to prevent the vote of an adverse law for example) corporate interest is from the outset clearly defined, in the new game companies frequently identify their interest only in the course of actions and interactions with politicians (Woll 2008). The context of political action is often deeply uncertain. Moreover, political action ends up being much more expensive than had been thought. Indeed, it consists not merely of lobbying or financing political life, but requires heavy investments and economic commitments (Bonardi 2008). Therefore, the traditional opposition between market and non-market strategies (Baron 2000), and between relational and transactional political activities (Hillmann and Hitt 1999) should be questioned. It is necessary to rethink the relationships between firms and the state, especially at a time of globalization. The transgression of the public-private divide must be approached as a global phenomenon.

This is what we propose to do in this chapter by examining Boeing's strategy in the late 1990s and early 2000s. Boeing is accustomed to the traditional strategies of lobbying (for example in the context of its rivalry with Airbus) and financing political life. But in the late 1990s, it developed very ambitious strategies aimed at building up influence rents. These strategies failed, but they help identify new types of relationships between firms and the state. We will first examine the methodological difficulties of researching firms' political strategies. Then, we will present recent theoretical contributions on the theme of firms' strategies and on the general framework for studying them. In the third part, we explain the methodology we followed in our case study of Boeing, which is presented in the fourth part. We then discuss the results of the case study in the fifth section.

METHODOLOGICAL DIFFICULTIES IN ANALYZING POLITICAL STRATEGIES OF THE FIRM

Since Epstein's pioneering work (1969), we know that a series of problems, later highlighted by Schuler (2002), makes the analysis of the relationship between firms and the state difficult. First, many things remain unobservable to researchers. This is particularly the case of contacts between business leaders and government officials and politicians. 'As a result, it is possible that researchers relying upon secondary source data are "missing the boat" as to the really important activities of political action' (Schuler 2002, p. 341). An indirect access to such contacts by means of interviews often proves disappointing: lobbyists exaggerate their influence to promote their role and function, while officials and politicians present themselves as guardians of the public interest who do not allow private interests to influence them. Defining an appropriate framework is also a challenge: should it be the firm, or the industry, a field including also interest groups, bureaucrats, politicians? (Oberman 2008, p. 251). We can then try to frame analysis around the mode of interaction between private and public officials. This is what Hillmann and Hitt (1999) proposed with their distinction between 'relational political activities' and 'transactional political activities' (which may take place only once and in connection with a specific issue). Their framework however raises two issues. The first, already mentioned, is that transactional political activities are easier to observe than relational ones. The second, more difficult, is that merely distinguishing between two types of activities is unlikely to account for firms' political strategies, which are complex, multidimensional and integrated.

Overall, research on firms' political strategies have focused on what is most easily observable — activities, such as lobbying or party and politician funding through political actions committees (PAC), which are governed by statutory provisions. Studies have tried for example to examine the link between tax provisions and firms' financing of members of Congress. But taxes are only one aspect of interactions between policy decisions and business strategies. What is being studied, namely the impact of lobbying and political funding in the well-defined framework of voting laws or taxes, is very limited and does not reflect all the issues involved in firms' political strategies. There is thus a field that remains to be explored, and the initial challenge is to figure out how to do that. One answer is to broaden the scope of the observation field. We will study a strategy developed by a big multinational firm, Boeing, to displace the public-private divide for its benefit. This strategy was not at all hidden, but observable, and the lobbying activity was not at the heart of it. It was a political strategy in that sense: a commercial strategy with the state as a client, based on technology, which moved the public-private boundary.

THEORETICAL FRAMEWORK

The field of research dedicated to political strategies by firms can be synthetized in two points, the framing of interactions and the strategies themselves.

Regarding the framing of interactions three elements are of main importance: the analysis of relations between the state and firms, the distinction between transactional and relational interactions and the frame of political subsystems, in which these interactions take place. The prior concerns the development of relations between firms and the state, which, as we mentioned, are hardly new. In the United States, they were part of the initial discussions between the founding fathers, especially Jefferson and Hamilton, then resumed steadily in the late nineteenth century with the vote of the Sherman Antitrust Act (1890). In recent years, however, the boundary between public and private has changed profoundly, as private players entered areas traditionally managed by the State (Mahoney et al. 2009). This is particularly the case for defense, previously considered as the heart of the state's domain. A major consequence of the increasing overlap between the private and the public domains is that the opposition between market strategies and non-market strategies (Baron 2000) in practice is difficult to maintain. Market and non-market factors are increasingly integrated, and this 'forces researchers to have a greater grasp of the overall strategy of the firm, as well as some of the behavioural and organisational elements that drive strategic behaviour' (Schuler 2002, p. 348).

The second element, as mentioned, concerns the distinction between relational and transactional political activities. Hillman and Hitt who formulated the distinction consider it solidly established and explain that the two forms of action 'differ in terms of the length and scope of continued activity and exchange' (Hillman and Hitt 1999, p. 828). In practice, the opposition is however not that clear cut. Rather, the two forms of activities are integrated. The transactional ones are based on relationships formed upstream of the transaction between the firm and the state, and the relationship thrives on successive transactions. This feature is particularly important in the context of a policy subsystem, which takes us to the third element of the theoretical framework.

The actions that concern us here take place in the framework of subsystems. Borrowed from political science, the notion of political subsystem can be used to analyze periods of stability – as when a branch of the state works with the same companies over long periods (for example the Department of Defense with firms specialized in an industry in which there are few new entries) – but also periods of abrupt change (as when a crisis enables a new entrant to disrupt the traditional operation of the subsystem). In this framework (Baumgartner and Jones 1991) stability and change are analyzed along two dimensions: images and venues. Images are beliefs and values associated with a policy. Venue refers to the existing set of institutions that conduct the policy. Within a subsystem, images and venue can be stable for a long time, when the public institutions in charge of policy and the associated private actors are both considered legitimate, and when the image of the policy is positive. Things change when images become negative and when institutions (the venue) appear less legitimate.

Regarding strategies undertaken by firms at the political level, three theoretical elements appear important to analyze. The first is the identification of a possible new form of rent linked to changes in the policy framework mentioned earlier. A rent is a source of supernormal profits. The literature identifies four types of rent: the monopolistic, related to the structure of the industry (natural monopoly, for example); the efficiency rent, rooted in a specific firm's own resources which competitors cannot imitate; the quasi-rent, due to transaction costs; and the Schumpeterian rent, due to innovation. Ahuja and Yayavaram identified a fifth type, the influence rent, defined as 'the extra profits earned by an economic actor because the rules of the game of business are designed or changed to suit an economic actor or a group of economic actors' (2011, p. 1631). Under the new relationships between firms and the state, firms are primarily looking for influence rents. These are linked to the proverb that 'In Washington, DC, if you are not at the table, you are on the menu!' (Ahuja and Yayavaram 2011, p. 1640).

The second theoretical element regarding the strategic analysis of firms' political action relates to the notion of interest. The traditional analysis of the topic is based on the idea that when a firm develops political strategies, it defends its interests; it would therefore seem that the firm has clearly identified its interests, and that these will not be mutually contradictory. However, if we take into account the fact that large firms are diversified, and that policy is fundamentally pluralistic and develops through subsystems, which are relatively independent from each other (see earlier), then it is conceivable that a firm can hold conflicting interests. Already Epstein (1969) suggested that internal conflicts could prevent a firm from developing a coherent, and therefore effective, political action. More recent case studies confirm that diversified firms can have incompatible political interests, and indeed experience great difficulties when trying to develop a political activity (Shaffer and Hillman 2000). Some researchers have gone further and shown that firms often do not know what their real interests are before entering in relation to politicians and regulators, they discover it while interacting with the world of politics and the state. In other words, firms engaged in political action are not defending a clearly identified interest, but developing this interest in the very course of action (Woll 2008).

The third theoretical element concerns the opposition between market and non-market strategies. It is generally assumed that these are separate, yet combined at the same time. This is indeed the case when non-market strategies consist essentially of lobbying and political funding. It is also assumed that investment in these areas is relatively small compared to the investment market strategies require. In fact, non-market strategies involve investments that are higher than usually believed: 'Because successful non-market activities require commitments of certain market inputs, these non-market activities often end up becoming substitutes to market activities. In that case, firms' managers face trade-offs and are likely to favor market strategies over nonmarket ones' (Bonardi 2008, p. 166). For example, politicians want to be re-elected. To support a re-election, a firm may be tempted not to close a plant in the candidate's constituency. But such a decision represents a very expensive market policy: 'The larger the overlap (dependence) between the two types of activities [market and nonmarket activities], the more likely managers will have to face difficulty in integrating the two types of activities' (Bonardi 2008, p. 168).

In sum, the last three decades were characterized by the introduction of private interests in areas such as defense, hitherto reserved for the state. Analysis should then look at how these areas have evolved as a result of firms' seeking influence rent. Such a strategy probably develops in a context of uncertainty. Firms may not be well aware of what their interest is; they therefore try to identify it in the course of trying to articulate market and non-market strategies, with likely trade-offs in terms of commitment.

METHODOLOGY

The analysis of firms' political action has generally focused on lobbying and political funding, which are the most visible parts of the field and allow quantitative analysis. Our question is whether and how we can explore the other, less visible part of firms' political strategies. The methodology adopted is that of the case study. We reconstruct a firm's strategy during the recent period of redefinition of areas between the public and the private domains; we see the firm trying to obtain influence rent in an uncertain framework that is neither limited to an industry or a policy, nor clearly transactional or relational.

The selected case is that of Boeing in the late 1990s and early 2000s. It offers several advantages regarding the issue as it has been defined. Boeing is a new entrant in a new political game. Of course, the firm has always had relationships with politicians, at the federal level (lobbying against Airbus, for instance) and at the local level (Seattle). However, in the early 1990s, Boeing is still a commercial company that does 80 percent of its business with private customers (the airlines), and only 20 percent in connection with defense. In the late 1990s, however, Boeing actively starts looking for political influence rent.

In terms of methodology, we will analyze a multidimensional strategic sequence and articulate market and non-market strategies (Dumez and Jeunemaître 2006; Dumez 2016). The collected material is mostly secondary. It is based on investigations about the restructuring of air traffic control (Depeyre et al. 2009) and about the strategies of defense firms (Depeyre 2009), and consists of annual reports, press releases and articles in the press. In the early 2000s, 20 interviews we also conducted with Boeing and FAA (Federal Aviation Administration) officials, managers of competing firms and financial analysts (these interviews were conducted by Colette Depeyre, Hervé Dumez and Alain Jeunemaître, mostly in the US). There was no direct or indirect access to relations between Boeing and US politicians. The analysis is based on the strategic observable facts, especially in the area of 'asset orchestration' (Helfat et al. 2007) in its two dimensions: internal (the reorganization of the company) and external (purchases or sales of assets). We assume that, contrary to what Schuler (2002) claims, an analysis of a firm's strategies based on secondary, public and observable data does not miss any essential relevant facts in a case when a commercial strategy by the firm aims at displacing the public-private boundary. In a sense, the adopted methodology is Dupin's one in Poe's *The Purloined Letter*: what seems hidden is before our eyes, as expressed in Seneca's epigraph – *nil sapientiae odiosius acumine nimio* (too much cleverness doesn't make good sense). The framing of Boeing's action was the US political system. But the strategy was global: Boeing had also contacts in Europe and in Asia. The US constituted the first, most important, step for a global strategy.

THE BOEING CASE

In the early 1990s, up to 80 percent of Boeing's turnover came from business with its main customers, airlines, and the remaining 20 percent through contracts in the military and spatial industries. The situation resulted from a deliberate strategy. During and immediately after World War II, Boeing focused on military contracts. Civilian customers, however, feared that the firm would favor military activities in the case of tensions between the two. To reassure them and grow in the field of civil aviation, Boeing decided to focus on this sector and invest in a complete range of civilian aircraft. It was the only manufacturer of civilian aircraft to have done so, and the strategy was successful. Its competitors, such as McDonnell Douglas, lost market shares. In the mid 1990s, the Boeing 777 is the biggest commercial success in the history of aviation. Yet the firm's strategy would again switch.

Crystallization

Two independent phenomena met and brought a dramatic change in the firm's strategy. The first was Boeing's interpretation of the success of its 777. This airplane was built under special conditions. On the one hand, it was the first commercial aircraft without prototype, designed exclusively by computer. On the other hand, it was built for and with customers (airlines, especially United Airlines), which designed with Boeing the aircraft they wanted. Finally, subcontractors were given the task of developing the different parts of the aircraft, its subsystems, while Boeing only defined the requirements, and tested and assembled them. The methodology was named the Working Together Team (WTT). Boeing interpreted its success in terms of an almost unique ability that differentiated it from its competitors: the ability to design for its customers large technical systems, and organize their development by coordinating subcontractors through a computerized platform.

The second element that rendered a new strategy possible was the rise of corporate acquisitions in the field of space and defense. The first one, in 1996, was the acquisition of the defense and space business of Rockwell International. The firm won the contract for the B-1 bomber in the 1980s and then grew in the spatial industry (manufacturing for example the space shuttle boosters). Discussions were held between Rockwell and McDonnell Douglas regarding a merger, Boeing's main competitor in the field of civil aviation. But Boeing ended up acquiring it in 1996, and thereby became capable of competing with Airbus. On 1 August 1997, McDonnell Douglas itself was definitely absorbed by Boeing, and that transformed the configuration of the firm. Indeed, McDonnell Douglas was primarily a manufacturer of military aircraft. With these two acquisitions, completed in 2000 through the purchase of the space and communication activities of Hughes Electronics Corporation, Boeing became a balanced company, with its activities evenly divided between the commercial and the military.

Officially, Boeing's aim was to offset cycles in commercial aircraft sales by independent cycles of military activities. A priori, Boeing can be analyzed as a diversified firm. Though specialized in the aerospace industry, half of its activities involved multiple political subsystems (for instance the US Air Force for military aircraft, the NASA for rockets and shuttles, the US Army for UAVs). Yet, this was not how the firm defined itself. Rather, in the late 1990s, the company believed it had a unique capability, embodied in the resounding success of the 777. Such a capability supposedly consisted in the company's capacity to identify the customer's need, design large technical systems to meet it, specify the requirements of the adequate subsystems, entrust the task of developing them to subcontractors, and finally test, integrate and assemble them. Boeing thinks this capability is generic and can therefore be applied by shaking up the traditional game of public subsystems. In 1994, Boeing's new military/civilian profile led the company to establish its defense and space business headquarters in Washington, DC and later, in 2000, to relocate its headquarters to Chicago, a city equidistant from the seat of political power and the historic seat of the company, Seattle.

The Construction of a Strategic Rhetoric

Boeing identified a domain to which its capability could apply. In the 1990s a new phenomenon emerged in the structuring of states' civil and military activities, known as Systems of Systems (SoS). The aim was no longer to develop a very sophisticated and complicated technological system, such as a nuclear submarine or a fighter, but to design systems capable of communicating and operating together at a more complex scale than that of its components. It therefore became necessary to develop monitoring, control and communication systems for allowing other systems, which were in themselves sophisticated, to operate together in configurations that could not be foreseen from the beginning and were expected to evolve. It was crucial to analyze the customer's needs and simulate them, to be able to design architecture for monitoring, communication and computation, and to organize the outsourcing and integration of the various subsystems. Boeing saw itself as the only company with the capacity to do so.

Boeing highlighted its position and tried to convince its customers, especially military ones, to institutionalize it. This took the form of the Lead Systems Integrator (LSI). Until then, the acquisition services of the Department of Defense (DoD) defined the requirements of the systems to be acquired, organized a competition among firms, selected the best offer, followed the development of materials and tested them. Now, in the SoS logic, a private firm would carry out most of the work. The first contract of LSI was awarded for the 1998 anti-ballistic missile program, the National Missile Defense (NMD), and it went to Boeing, which won against the United Missile Defense Company, an alliance formed by Lockheed Martin, Raytheon, Hughes and TRW. At the time, Boeing commented on its success saying:

> We have an unmatched history of first-time successes integrating large, complex military, commercial and space systems. For example, we are responsible for some of the largest systems integration programs in the world, including the Space Shuttle, AWACS (Airborne Warning and Control System) and the Boeing 777 commercial aircraft system. Our innovative design, rapid prototyping, end-to-end simulations and commercial processes developed for those programs will be applied to NMD. (Press Release 30 April 1998)

At first, Boeing promoted the WTT concept (Working Together Team), which had allowed the development of the 777, and tried to translate it in different areas. In every domain, Boeing spoke of 'systems' to try to convince the customer to trust its capability. This was for example the case in the field of Unmanned Aerial Vehicles (UAVs), a term used by everyone except Boeing:

> Boeing representatives (. . .) have a conscious political strategy, using the term 'system' rather than 'vehicle' when discussing UAVs; the company plans to leverage its expertise in systems integration as a selling point. And perhaps that strategy has already enjoyed at least a superficial success: the Department of Defense announced in July 2005 that it prefers the name 'UAS' for Unmanned Aerial System in place of the established term, UAV. Beyond the name change, though, Boeing hopes to build a coalition of supporters by promoting unmanned vehicles as part of the network, interoperable with other battlefield

> systems produced by Boeing and other defense companies. (Dombrowski and Gholz 2006, p. 83)

Boeing associated its approach to the idea of 'solutions' developed by other companies, that is to say, the idea that what the firm sells is not a product or a system, but a solution that mixes products and services to meet the customer's need. As is explained:

> Like IBM in computers, AT&T in telephony, Ford in automobiles, and GE across a mix of businesses, we are moving to a new business model. It is predicated on our ability to offer full-service solutions to an expanding array of customer needs. The opportunities that are opening before us play to two of our core competencies: detailed customer knowledge and large-scale systems integration [. . .] One thing is certain. The push into full-service solutions will put an even higher premium on our ability to think and act as one company. (Annual Report 1999)

Imitating GE Capital, the financial arm of General Electric, Boeing created Boeing Capital in 1997, taking over the assets of McDonnell Finance, founded in 1968. The strategic rhetoric was completed in 2002 with the emergence of the concept of 'government systems', as the company won the LSI contract for Future Combat Systems of the US Army, and announced an internal reorganization that 'assembled the necessary communications, intelligence, surveillance and reconnaissance capabilities as well as platform knowledge to be the preeminent government systems company in the world' (Press Release, 10 July 2002). Thus, Boeing presented itself as designing government systems and as the world leader in that domain, firstly in the US but also worldly.

Shaking the Political Subsystems

Traditionally, as an aerospace firm, Boeing counted the US Air Force and the US Navy (for its onboard aircraft) among its customers. It was not very present with the US Army, except for Unmanned Aerial Vehicles. Yet in 2002, Boeing, together with SAIC, was awarded the LSI contract for the giant program of modernization of the US Army, the Future Combat Systems (FCS). Traditional subcontractors of the US Army, such as General Dynamics, would henceforth be managed by Boeing rather than directly by the military customer. For the US Army, using a LSI had several advantages. First, DoD lacked the skills to design and monitor a program of such complexity. Second, it saved costs. Third, the US Army knew that, due to its internal contradictions (helicopter pilots wanted more helicopters, artillery wanted more cannons, drivers of

UAVs wanted more UAVs and so on), it could not design a real SoS, and that only an outsider could overcome those internal rivalries and think in terms of SoS. Boeing and SAIC, although not having experience with land war materials, emerged as the most legitimate companies to assume such a role.

During the same period, Boeing shook up another political subsystem, air traffic control. Traditionally, this subsystem operated autonomously. The Federal Aviation Authority (FAA) identified a need to improve air traffic management and made firms compete (mainly Lockheed Martin and Raytheon) to provide the necessary materials (radars, control centers, computer systems). In November 2000, Boeing created a subsidiary in the field of air traffic control. Its official position was that ATC was a bottleneck for air transport and that if such a situation continued, aircraft sales would suffer. The traditional political subsystem was unable to find a solution. On 6 June 2001, the FAA announced its Operational Evolution Plan. A few hours later, Boeing presented to the press a revolutionary plan to transform air traffic control. A month later, in July, a Working Together Team was created and began to operate by gathering Air Traffic Services providers, airlines, military, general aviation and equipment suppliers. Boeing wanted to occupy informally the position of Lead Systems Integrator that did not officially exist in the air traffic subsystem, thus marginalizing the FAA, which it considered incapable of modernizing the area. Since the political subsystem appeared unable to move, the firm decided to shake it up and to take leadership.

The Failure

All these strategic initiatives were unsuccessful. In 2004, Boeing ATM was dissolved and research concerning air traffic control and air traffic management was repatriated to Boeing's common R & D unit, Phantom Works. The FCS program experienced considerable cost drifts and insurmountable technical problems, and on 23 June 2009, the DoD announced that it was abandoned. Even worse, the Boeing 787, designed and presented as an SoS (Wilber 2009) and not only as a commercial aircraft, experienced technical problems and delays in its development. It was as if Boeing had erred in depth on its ability to integrate large systems for its customers, whether public or private.

DISCUSSION

In the late 1990s and early 2000s, Boeing believed it was capable of shaking up a number of civilian and military policy subsystems, and tried to occupy a special place vis-à-vis the public client, dominating it with its financial and technological means, as well as vis-à-vis its competitors (we should rather say other firms: if Boeing had succeeded, there would no longer have been any competitors). This strategy consisted in seeking an influence rent (Ahuja and Yayavaram 2011), which implied developing the capacity to organize the interplay between the public and the private domains.

As highlighted by interviews conducted in the field of air traffic control, Boeing's strategy was never entirely clear. People in the various companies of the industry, such as Lockheed Martin, Raytheon and Thales, did not understand how Boeing would make money and how its ideas would be implemented. The business model of reference was indeed that of General Electric, that is to say, that of selling solutions to customers and making profits mainly on services, including financial ones. But no activity undertaken for the public customer actually implemented a 'solution' approach. Boeing Capital was finally used only for the sale of Boeing aircraft, while the remaining activities were, somewhat ironically, sold to GE Commercial Finance in 2004. In other words, Boeing seems not to have had a clear view of where its real interest was. However, the commitment to its chosen strategies (Bonardi 2008) had been high.

Such a commitment can first be measured by direct costs. In the field of air traffic control, for example, Boeing created from scratch a subsidiary of 250 engineers, without having a clear perspective of return on investment, apart from a few contracts with the FAA. Even if the investment was modest compared with the financial strength of the firm, the sunk costs were not negligible. The company's commitment can also be measured indirectly. Boeing banned itself from certain activities. To appear as an independent systems integrator, compared to other companies that sold the systems they themselves designed and produced, Boeing abstained from designing and producing systems and subsystems. It consistently refrained from vertical integration and from activities that could contradict such an image. Perhaps benefits would have remained at the level of design and production of (sub)systems, rather than at the level of integration into an SoS.

Another point must be emphasized. The quest of an influence rent by an actor is perceived as a threat by both political authorities and other firms. The company that wants to pursue such a strategy must therefore provide some reassurances. Boeing was aware that it could not monopolize the special position of lead systems integrator for the public client in different policy subsystems. If it won the FCS contract for the US Army, it would have to leave to others the contract of the Coast Guard and the US Navy. Also, Boeing knew that if it improved the functioning of the US air traffic control, it would work for both itself and its rival Airbus. Boeing also carried out not-for-profit actions. For example, to develop the SoS, it initiated the Network-Centric Operations Industry Consortium (NCOIC), which brought together actors from industry, government and academia.

In short, the strategies of influence rent seeking involved self-restriction and abandoning certain potentially profitable activities. Overall, Boeing's strategy aimed at selling to public customers a generic capacity that would drastically reorganize the traditional game of political subsystems proved costly and not very remunerative. Especially on a large scale, it is not clear whether such a strategy can ever be profitable. In Boeing's case, the merger of market and non-market, relational and transactional strategies, certainly did not work well.

Moreover, Boeing was shaken by several major scandals. The first one illustrates the commitment required by the pursuit of influence rent. It happened during the firm's first contract as LSI, the National Missile Defense. As LSI, Boeing organized a competition for a subsystem between Raytheon and one of its own subsidiaries. Firewalls should have been operating, but documents related to Raytheon's offer were found in Boeing offices. The outsourcing contract was finally awarded to Raytheon, and the overall contract became a National Industry Initiative in which Boeing lost its role as LSI. The second scandal involved Darleen Druyun, former Air Force's deputy assistant secretary for acquisition, who had awarded major contracts to Boeing. In October 2004, she was sentenced to nine months in prison for having favored Boeing and then having been hired by the firm. The settlement with the US Department of Justice cost Boeing $615 million.

These scandals raise issues for the researcher. Two interpretations are possible. The first one says that they were isolated situations, in different political subsystems, implying a limited number of people within the firm. A second, very different interpretation, states that the scandals were a symptom of Boeing managerial conduct during these years. From a methodological point of view, it is difficult to decide which interpretation is more credible. However, during one interview an informant from Boeing gave two insights. One is that at that time, there was a culture pushing people within the firm to gain procurements against competitors. This culture distinguished between 'big deals' (prohibited) and 'small deals' (tolerated). Actually, Boeing did not succeed to manage the boundary between both.

Our last point relates to the current situation. Boeing failed on all the strategies it developed with regard to the public domain in the early 2000s. However, the imbalance between public authorities and firms remains.

Boeing thought it mastered a capability it did not really have, but at the same time, public authorities indeed did not have the means of developing very large systems. The persistent imbalance must be resolved one way or another, and the possibility of an influence rent persists.

CONCLUSION

The new deal that developed between the public and private sectors, with the introduction of the private sector in many areas hitherto reserved for the public, left traditional activities relatively unchanged, such as lobbying and political financing. However, it opened the possibility of influence rents for firms, that is to say, positions in which they can set the rules for their own benefit. Strategies to conquer this type of rent challenge the opposition between relational and transactional political activities, as well as the opposition between market and non-market strategies. However, the Boeing case demonstrates the difficulty of pursuing influence rent. While direct costs are high, costs of commitment in the sense of Bonardi (2008) are probably even higher. These include self-restriction strategies necessary to make the influence rent work. The firm's interest, in terms of possible gains, is highly uncertain, and only discovered when implementing the strategy itself. We are then in the situation described by Bonardi, in which non-market strategies becoming risky substitutes for market strategies.

It is not unreasonable to suggest that Boeing could have developed less risky and more profitable market strategies. In the end, the case shows that the new conditions have not changed fundamentally in the past decades, a point already highlighted by Epstein (1969) and confirmed by more recent research (Bonardi 2008; Shaffer and Hillman 2000). It also indicates that influence rent strategies are more difficult to develop than generally thought, and that firms do not necessarily have a clear vision of the interest they actually pursue through such strategies (Woll 2008).

At the same time, it is not possible to generalize from the case study. Some methodological limitations identified by Schuler (2002) apply to it: we tried to follow Boeing's strategy in its many dimensions, but the case is probably too extreme to be generalizable. Nevertheless, it highlights a serious imbalance between the capabilities of public and private actors in the development of very large systems. Boeing's failure, followed by that of other LSI contracts awarded to its competitors, demonstrates that private actors can be wrong about their capabilities. But the situation remains unstable and by the same token opens the possibility of new strategies for seeking influence rents.

REFERENCES

Ahuja, G. and S. Yayavaram (2011), 'Explaining influence rents: The case for an institutions-based view of strategy', *Organization Science*, **22** (6), 1631–52.

Baron, D.P. (2000), *Business and Its Environment (3rd Ed)*, Upper Saddle River (NJ): Prentice Hall.

Baumgartner, F.R. and B.D. Jones (1991), 'Agenda dynamics and policy subsystems', *The Journal of Politics*, **53** (4), 1044–74.

Boeing (2001), *Air Traffic Management. Revolutionary Concepts that Enable Air Traffic Growth While Cutting Delays*. McLean VA: Boeing ATM, 6 June.

Bonardi, J.P. (2008), 'The internal limits to firms' nonmarket strategies', *The European Management Review*, **5** (3), 165–74.

Depeyre, C. (2009), *De l'observable au non observable: les stratégies d'identification, d'adaptation, de création d'une capacité de la firme. Dynamiques de l'industrie américaine de défense (1990–2007)*, Nanterre, Université Paris Ouest (Thèse de doctorat).

Depeyre, C., H. Dumez and A. Jeunemaître (2009), 'Entrepreneurial strategy and coopetition. Boeing's strategy in the air traffic management', Montpellier, International Workshop on Co-opetition and Entrepreneurship, 25 and 26 June 2009.

Dombrowski, P. and E. Gholz (2006), *Buying Military Transformation: Technological Innovation and the Defense Industry*, New York: Columbia University Press.

Dumez, H. (2016), *Comprehensive Research. A Methodological and Epistemological Introduction to Qualitative Research*, Copenhagen: Copenhagen Business School Press.

Dumez, H. and A. Jeunemaître (2006), 'Multidimensional strategic sequences: A research programme proposal on coopetition', Milan, 2nd Workshop on Coopetition Strategy, EURAM, 14–15 September 2006.

Epstein, E. (1969), *The Corporation in American Politics*, Englewood Cliffs (NJ): Prentice Hall.

Helfat, C.E., S. Finkelstein, W. Mitchell, M. Peteraf, H. Singh, D. Teece and S.G. Winter (2007), *Dynamic Capabilities. Understanding Strategic Change in Organizations*, Oxford: Basil Blackwell.

Hillman, A.J. and M.A. Hitt (1999), 'Corporate political strategy formulation: A model of approach, participation and strategy decisions', *Academy of Management Review*, **24** (4), 825–42.

Mahoney, J.T., A.M. McGahan and C.N. Pitelis (2009), 'The interdependence of private and public interests', *Organization Science*, **20** (6), 1034–52.

Oberman, W.D. (2008), 'A conceptual look at the strategic resource dynamics of public affairs', *Journal of Public Affairs*, **8** (4), 249–60.

Schuler, D.A. (2002), 'Public affairs, issues management and political strategy: Methodological approaches that count', *Journal of Political Affairs*, **1** (4), 336–55.

Shaffer, B.A. and A.J. Hillman (2000), 'The development of business-government strategies by diversified firms', *Strategic Management Journal*, **21** (2), 175–90.

Wilber, G.R. (2009), 'Boeing's SoSE approach to e-enabling commercial airlines', in M. Jamshidi (ed.), *System of System Engineering: Innovations for the 21st Century*, Chichester: John Wiley & Sons.

Woll, C. (2008), *Firm Interests: How Governments Shape Business Lobbying on Global Trade*, Ithaca (NY): Cornell University Press.

6. Corporate advocacy in the Internet domain: shaping policy through data visualizations

Mikkel Flyverbom

INTRODUCTION

Despite a growing interest in how corporations engage in political affairs – such as lobbyism, multi-stakeholder dialogues, standards development and corporate social responsibility initiatives – we still have limited knowledge of the varied, often subtle ways in which corporate actors seek to shape policies, regulation and their environments more broadly. In particular, the disparate forms of knowledge that corporate actors produce, circulate and rely on in advocacy efforts deserve more scrutiny. Partly, this gap results from an overly narrow focus on the most obvious and direct forms of lobbying, such as financial contributions and political action committees (Brasher and Lowery 2006). Although it is important to show how well-established Fortune 500 companies use money, strategic alliances and lobbyists to influence politics and policies, corporate advocacy takes multiple forms and explores new approaches that deserve attention if we want to enrich our understanding of the relationship between the corporate world and politics. This chapter contributes to existing research on the role of corporate actors in political affairs by investigating how companies at the forefront of the Internet industry engage in advocacy efforts and policy processes. Such companies introduce new data-based and visual approaches to advocacy that may reconfigure corporate attempts to shape political affairs.

Based on a broad understanding of advocacy, the chapter emphasizes the need for explorations of the variety and diversity of activities involved when corporations seek to shape their environment. These activities may range from very direct interventions and targeted statements to more elusive forms of advocacy, such as what has been termed the production of 'anticipatory knowledge' (Gusterson 2008). The chapter sets out to expand our conception of corporate advocacy by pointing to the growing importance of knowledge, data and visualizations. To appreciate and conceptualize this variety, insights from the literature on the politics of knowledge (Rubio and Baert 2012) and the importance of knowledge in governance (Foucault 1980; Stone 2002) are useful as they remind us of the intimate connections between knowledge, politics and attempts at control. Also, these insights pave the way for the more narrow focus on particular forms of knowledge production – such as data provision and visualizations – that Internet companies rely on in attempts to shape public perceptions, politics and regulation.

The focus on knowledge highlights how activities such as launching campaigns, arranging events, funding research, publishing reports and visualizing patterns in data all play potentially important roles in corporate advocacy. These can all be understood as forms of advocacy, that is 'efforts to assemble and use information and resources to bring about improvements in people's lives' (Given 2008 p. 9). Also, the focus on different forms of advocacy gives attention to the multiple and varied dynamics involved in advocacy activities. For instance, corporate advocacy efforts may be proactive or reactive, relational or transactional, as well as collective or individual. Focusing on these dynamics is useful when characterizing and contrasting different types and registers of advocacy, an issue that remains under-theorized in the existing literature on corporate political activities (Hillman et al. 2004).

The chapter does not provide an industry-level study or a very situated, empirical investigation of selected companies, but instead seeks to develop a conceptual entry point that may enhance our understanding of how Internet companies engage multiple forms of knowledge and visualizations as resources in their advocacy efforts. To this end, the chapter uses illustrations from a study of Google and Facebook.[1] In particular, the ambition is to discuss the intersection of multiple kinds of advocacy efforts in this area and to foreground the importance of data visualizations. Based on interviews with policy directors, participant observations in multi-stakeholder dialogues initiated by the UN, as well as documentary research, the chapter discusses the various forms of corporate advocacy that play out in this field. These are: 1) *relationship building*, often in the shape of organizational arrangements and other forms of presence and interactions in salient forums and networks; 2) *message crafting*, such as attempts to influence formal policy processes and negotiations through statements and targeted campaigns that frame issues sharply and seek to mobilize support or resistance and 3) *data provision*, such as the circulation of various forms of data visualizations that make issues, future developments and potentials visible and actionable.

The first contribution of the chapter is a conceptual elaboration of the resources and forms of knowledge at work in corporate advocacy. This conceptualization engages insights from the somewhat scattered literature on corporate advocacy. While the chapter uses this conceptualization to illustrate how Internet companies engage in corporate advocacy, it may be useful for studies of other types of organizations, different industries and alternative forms of advocacy. The second contribution is to show that Internet companies rely not only on more well-known resources usually associated with advocacy, but also on the provision of data, visualizations and technological platforms, often with possibilities for repurposing and new types of engagement by other organizations and individuals. This also implies a discussion of how the growing reliance on data-based, visual forms of knowledge may condition particular types of advocacy, policy processes and politics more broadly. Although the goal is not to discuss how effective or important visualizations are in advocacy, the chapter does offer some reflections about the possible ramifications of a growing reliance on visualizations in corporate advocacy efforts, such as what we may think of as post-political formations (Garsten and Jacobsson 2013) and troublesome forms of political and societal rationalization (Kallinikos 2013).

CONCEPTUALIZING CORPORATE ADVOCACY – VARIETIES AND RESOURCES

The conceptualization and analytical approach developed here integrates discussions of corporate advocacy and the politics of knowledge, data and visualizations. This involves both a clarification of the concept of corporate advocacy, an anchoring in current discussions of corporate political activities and a discussion of the value of focusing on knowledge and other resources. Taken together, these insights underpin the focus on varieties of corporate advocacy that this chapter revolves around.

Forms and Resources of Corporate Advocacy

We normally associate advocacy with quite direct attempts to shape policies, priorities and practices, such as when corporations engage in 'lobbying, making political action campaign contributions, offering testimony to Congress, and hosting political fundraisers' with the explicit goal to 'influence government official to take actions that influence business performance' (Lux et al. 2012 p. 307). For the purposes of this chapter, however, a more encompassing understanding of advocacy is a valuable starting point. Advocacy can be conceived broadly as different 'tactics that seek to make a difference' (Berg 2009; see also Ezell 2001), such as promoting particular causes, ideas and norms (Keck and Sikkink 1998) or attempting to change existing or planned policies, priorities or practices (Ezell 2001). This conception allows for relatively open-ended investigations of the intersection of multiple types of activities and resources involved when corporate actors seek to shape their surroundings. This investigation can also draw on insights from a variety of discussions of lobbyism, public affairs, issues management and advocacy playing out in a number of disciplines. Such research is somewhat scattered and embryonic compared to more established areas and topics. In part, this is due to disciplinary fragmentation, difficulties with empirical access and the historical dominance of more established research themes. Scholarly work on corporate advocacy is marked by disciplinary gaps between political science, communication theory and organization and management studies, and there is relatively little systematic integration of findings and theoretical developments across these bodies of literature. Furthermore, studies of corporate advocacy seem to lie at the margins of more established disciplines. For instance, organization and management studies have for a long time focused on how organizations are affected by their environments and neglected the question of how organizations shape the world around them (Barley 2010). The majority of research in political science, including public policy and international relations, has given primary attention to the state and thereby neglected the roles of non-state, private actors, such as corporations and civil society movements, in the shaping of legislation and politics (Cutler et al. 1999; Fuchs and Lederer 2007; Hansen and Salskov-Iversen 2008). Finally, while corporate communication research has a long tradition for the study of corporate advocacy, it has done so under a number of separate headings, such as public relations, public affairs and lobbyism, without exploring their intersections and shared characteristics.

If we examine these different discussions of corporate advocacy, some distinct themes can be identified. These include topics such as the foundations, antecedents and goals of advocacy, the various forms taken by advocacy, the processes and organizational routines involved and the outcomes of such activities. To develop the conceptualization of the various resources at work in corporate advocacy, many of these discussions could be useful starting points for a study of the emergent shape of corporate advocacy in the Internet domain. But the focus on *forms of advocacy* is particularly relevant for the attempt to conceptualize how corporate actors engage various forms of knowledge and communication in their attempts to shape politics and policies.

Discussions of the various forms and orientations of corporate advocacy distinguish between, on the one hand, funding and financial incentives and, on the other, the provision of knowledge and information (Drutman 2011; Hall and Deardorff 2006; Hillman et al. 2004). Another distinction concerns proactive versus reactive forms of advocacy. For instance, some authors use terms such as 'buffering' to describe corporations that engage in proactive attempts to shape policies and 'bridging' to refer to corporate political activities that can be considered reactions to changes in the environment, such as new policies or pressures (Hillman et al. 2004; Holyoke et al. 2007). Obviously, in practice, corporations rely on multiple forms of advocacy (Baumgartner et al. 2009), and to conceptualize the different resources at work in corporate advocacy in the Internet domain, we need to be aware not only of the intersection of money and ideas, but also the patterns of reactivity and proactivity shaping corporate political activities. Certainly, parts of the literature call for a broader scope than merely looking at 'political action committees' (Brasher and Lowery 2006). Still, studies that seek to push beyond the most visible and well-known forms of advocacy tend to keep focus on more tangible aspects of corporate advocacy, such as expenditures and participation in lobbying activities and forums. Often such research takes a quantitative route and seeks to account for the issues, money and forums involved in advocacy efforts and has very little to say about the intangible resources being used. To repair this myopia, some have argued for the need to connect understandings of the relations between lobbyism, advocacy and PR (Berg 2009), and to broaden the scope of our research to include questions about various forms of advocacy, the anchoring in networks and the historical contexts that shape corporate advocacy (Wedel 2009).

Discussions of the forms taken by corporate advocacy invite us to explore the variety of resources and registers involved in attempts to promote causes and ideas or change policies and priorities. These may take the shape of funding, organizational arrangements, social relations or forms of knowledge. Also, this part of the literature is useful when considering the role of data-based visualizations and the type of knowledge and influence they constitute in advocacy processes. Finally, it invites us to consider how and when such resources are used, such as if they are used reactively or proactively. This focus is also present in discussions of step-by-step models of advocacy, which also invite us to consider where and when particular resources play a role. To sum up, these insights from the literature on lobbyism, advocacy and corporate political activities are a useful starting point if we want to conceptualize the intersection of different resources at work in the advocacy efforts of Internet companies. But for the purposes of this chapter, we also need to engage insights from a different strain of literature that gives more attention to the production, circulation and visualization of knowledge.

Corporate Advocacy and Knowledge Production

In order to conceptualize the role of disparate forms of knowledge in corporate advocacy, we need an analytical and theoretical understanding of *knowledge as political*. This argument starts from the basic tenet that knowledge is constitutive of – and inseparable from – the political. That is, we need to recognize that the nature of the knowledge we produce affects the nature of political activity we engage in. This position challenges what has been termed the 'liberal view', claiming that politics and knowledge can and should be separable entities (Rubio and Baert 2012). Such positions consider politics to belong to the sphere of values and knowledge to the sphere of facts. Along these lines, knowledge is considered to constitute more or less objective representations of a pre-existing reality. In contrast, the conception of politics and knowledge that is relied on in this chapter sees knowledge as performative and productive in relation to politics and seeks to unpack these 'generative capacities' of knowledge in politics and governance (Rubio and Baert 2012). Conceptions of the entanglement of knowledge, power and politics have multiple sources, including Foucault's and other sociologists' work on the role of knowledge in contemporary forms of discipline and 'governmentality' (Foucault 1980; Miller and Rose 1990; Strathern 2006), more recent work in 'critical accounting' on auditing technologies and governance (Power 1997; Roberts 2009), and studies of valuation and commensuration showing how simplified and densely packaged knowledge circulates and shapes objects and subjects (Beckert and Aspers 2012; Levin and Espeland 2002).

Such work also gives more attention to the production of knowledge and the possibilities for action that knowledge creates. This implies a fundamental distinction between data, information and knowledge (Leach 2012; Strathern 2006), and the suggestion that:

> Data is what comes into the senses, it is unprocessed stuff. Information is that data organised in some way. Data grouped according to some logic or other. But knowledge is more than information, it is data organised in a way that has an *effect*. To know something is to have to take it into account (Strathern 1992, 1999), often to have to act because of it, in the light of it, or around it (if only to consider it irrelevant). (Leach 2012 p. 84)

Data can be considered a type of resource (although not a 'raw' material since all data is always, already 'cooked' in various ways (Gitelman 2013)) that needs to be collected, refined and classified into information, which in turn needs to be made valuable and applicable to specific contexts and efforts, that is be transformed into knowledge that can be acted upon. This focus on the production of knowledge out of data and the understanding of knowledge as actionable is fundamental to the argument that the production of knowledge needs to be a key concern in studies of corporate advocacy. Finally, work in science and technology studies (Hackett et al. 2008; Latour 2005), and medium theory (Deibert 1997; Hutchby 2001) has captured how technologies of all sorts become entangled with social and political formations, effectively blurring or undermining the distinctions between the material and the social, and the technological and the political that we normally rely on. Particularly in the context of the Internet domain, algorithms play important roles in the production of knowledge and advocacy efforts. Increasingly, data is made valuable and actionable through algorithmic calculations, and these largely opaque operations deserve further scrutiny (Flyverbom and Madsen 2015). The capacities of algorithms to include and exclude, organize and evaluate the relevance of information (Gillespie 2014) is so central to the work of Internet companies that any investigation of this domain needs to consider how such operations have consequences for the practices and politics of advocacy.

While there are important differences between these strains of research, they share an interest in the 'generative capacities' (Rubio and Baert 2012) of knowledge in the shaping of conduct, governance and politics. In the context of this chapter, this understanding of the knowledge-politics nexus translates into the more specific argument that new techniques and forms of knowledge production 'afford' new forms of political action and orientation (Hutchby 2001; Hansen and Flyverbom 2015). This focus on the production of knowledge and its generative capacities in the context of corporate advocacy constitutes the foundation of the discussions to follow.

This first part of the chapter has argued for a broader conception of corporate advocacy than the predominant and narrow focus on lobbyism through 'political action committees', direct relations to policymakers and the view of companies as profit-maximizing entities engaging in advocacy for very instrumental reasons. In order to grasp the variation and subtlety with which corporate advocacy is carried out, we need to cast a much wider net when trying to understand the organizational arrangements, activities and rationales involved. In the context of the Internet domain, this orientation involves a focus on the strategies and avenues used for purposes of advocacy, including participation in policy dialogues, the funding of research centers and research projects, and the setting up of lobby organizations, as well as a focus on the reliance and provision of technological platforms, data, visualizations as well as product- and user controls.

The integration of these discussions paves the way for a problematization and extension of the established focus on the role of *relations*, such as the building of alliances, networks and prolonged interactions with policymakers, and *messages*, such as campaigns, public statements and interviews. While both forms of corporate advocacy are important and widespread, what we see in the Internet domain is also the emergence of more subtle forms of advocacy that do not involve organized relations or carefully crafted messages. In the Internet domain, corporate advocacy also involves *the provision of data, technological platforms and visualizations*, and these constitute resources that need to be taken into account. Exploring advocacy along the lines of the typology developed further on highlights how companies such as Google and Facebook seek to contribute to policy shaping and policymaking, produce 'anticipatory knowledge' (Gusterson 2008), and explore other ways to shape the world around them. More generally, these discussions point to new developments when it comes to the shape of corporate engagements in politics.

VARIETIES OF CORPORATE ADVOCACY IN THE INTERNET DOMAIN

Although Internet companies such as Google and Facebook figure prominently in public discussions of the social and economic importance of new information and communication technologies, we know less about their engagement in advocacy efforts and policy processes. Partly, this is because the advocacy efforts of these companies have been somewhat scattered, and more organized and targeted activities have only emerged as a priority quite recently. In fact, both Google and Facebook seem to have considered traditional advocacy and policy processes to be outside the primary scope of their operations, or something to be transformed in more fundamental ways than simply setting up lobby organizations. For instance, Google's entry into Washington, DC in 2008 was described not only as 'the swankiest "office" party Washington has seen in years' (Graff 2008), but also as part of a plan to change the rules of the lobbying game altogether (Levy 2011 p. 329). Both companies now engage in well-known forms of corporate advocacy, such as setting up policy offices in Washington, DC and Brussels, and hiring policy managers and creating the trade association the Internet Association to advance their interests in US politics and public policies. Finally, it is indicative that in 2012, Facebook tripled its spending on lobbying efforts to approximately $4 million, while Google's lobbying budget amounted to $16–18 million in 2012, 2013 and 2014 (http://www.opensecrets.org/lobby/clientissues.php?id=d000022008&year=2013).

For a long time, technology companies have called for deregulation to encourage further growth in their areas of operation (Flyverbom 2011). Some of the more specific issues currently advanced by such companies include questions about 'net neutrality', 'user empowerment' and 'privacy', 'intellectual property rights', 'Internet freedom', 'multi-stakeholder participation' and 'industry self-regulation'. By exploring corporate advocacy in relation to these issues, the chapter highlights the growing importance of data, algorithms and visualizations in such efforts. Whereas more traditional forms of corporate advocacy revolve around exerting pressure through networks and lobbying regulatory bodies to ensure appropriations, policy maintenance, policy changes or new policies that benefit corporations (Lux et al. 2012), what we see in the Internet industry is an increasing reliance on data, technological applications and visualizations, in combination with design-based forms of advocacy such as user controls, engagement in multi-stakeholder dialogues, as well as other ways of shaping political affairs. The illustrations of the varieties of resources and forms of knowledge involved in corporate advocacy are organized around three themes, namely *relationship building*, *message crafting* and *data provision*.

Relationship Building

One shape corporate advocacy takes is the development, management and use of relations and organizational arrangements that provide access to valuable and significant spheres and domains. Corporate actors have always been present in the capitols, circles and corridors where important political decisions are made, and cities such as Washington, DC and Brussels contain a high concentration of lobby shops, policy offices and similar forms of organized presence. Internet companies such as Google and Facebook constitute no exception to this, and have set up offices and/or employed policy directors in these and other cities. In the case of Google, in 2005 the company set up what it refers to as a 'lobby shop-think tank hybrid' in Washington, DC that not only lobbies, but also arranges educational talks on technical and regulatory issues (with ties to its operations) and engages in other forms of policy shaping. Similarly, Facebook has hired a number of new policy directors operating out of regional offices, whose primary tasks are to engage with policymakers and to explain technical and regulatory aspects of Facebook services and applications (interview, Facebook policy director, 2012). Also, a group of Internet companies have set up the Internet Association, based in Washington, DC intended to act as 'an umbrella public policy organization dedicated to strengthening and protecting a free and innovative Internet and the unified voice of the Internet' (www.internetassociation.

org). The CEOs of both companies regularly go to DC to engage in direct conversations with members of Congress and policymakers, and to attend government hearings and meetings. Finally, in recent years Google has been present in UN-initiated efforts to address questions about global Internet governance in multi-stakeholder dialogues such as the Internet Governance Forum (Flyverbom 2011).

But relations are also built in less visible ways, such as through the hiring of former policymakers or the diffusion of former employees into government offices. Particularly Google developed close ties with the Obama administration. For instance, Google's former global policy director, Andrew McLaughlin, took up a position in the Obama administration as deputy chief technology officer of the United States and according to the Opensecrets.org website, 100 of Google's 124 lobbyists have previously held government jobs (http://www.opensecrets.org/orgs/summary.php?id=D000022008). These examples clearly contribute to the widespread concerns about 'revolving doors' between government and the private sector.

Another less visible way in which Internet companies do advocacy is by funding research centers and research projects. For instance, Google contributes to a range of different research initiatives, often with no strings attached, and supports researchers and others addressing questions related to Internet governance and policy issues in the realm of digital transformations. While such efforts primarily lead to events and publications, they also constitute valuable resources for the building of relationships between corporations, universities and other types of organizations involved in the shaping of the Internet domain. The types of knowledge produced as a result of such efforts are largely tied to particular organizational settings funded by corporate actors and often remain anchored in these settings. That is, reports, newsletters and visual material produced as a result of these arrangements will often remain tied to the organizations or be delivered directly to policymakers and others who the companies see as targets of their advocacy efforts. Policy directors will approach policymakers armed with particular arguments and messages or rely on research findings to frame a particular issue or problem. But the context-specific nature and targeted orientation of these resources means that the knowledge involved is relatively immobile, static and dissociated from the larger groups of stakeholders or communities involved in the domain. If found and taken up by someone actively searching for information, however, it can certainly circulate. Also, for instance the Internet Association is in the process of rebuilding its website with a number of more interactive features inviting people to 'take action' (http://internetassociation.org), such as providing links to bills that users can comment on, ways of locating and contacting members of Congress and so on. But they remain somewhat local and certainly US-centric, which is also in line with the statement of the Internet Association's president and CEO that the approach of the organization is 'hyperlocal' (Bachman 2012).

Relationship building and organizational arrangements constitute local and context-specific forms of corporate advocacy. They are driven by a wish to be present, vocal and connected in circles and domains that companies consider important. In this advocacy mode, resources are invested in social relations that may be used for attempts to exert pressure, qualify debates and engage directly in policy processes. Furthermore, this mode can both be reactive and proactive, but rarely provides new avenues for conceptualizing and developing governance arrangements and issues. Also, it primarily involves interactions between corporations and policymakers and rarely broader constituencies or users. With a long-term orientation, relationship building engages resources in the construction of organizational arrangements that make corporations part of the regulatory ecosystem, provide ways of having a unified voice on policy issues and position them as stakeholders in important policy dialogues.

Message Crafting

A second mode of advocacy revolves around more targeted, limited efforts to shape a particular policy or negotiation process through the production of messages and communication campaigns. By crafting and circulating messages through media and at events, corporations can communicate their positions on a given policy proposal or political development. In the case of Google and Facebook, such campaigning efforts have been visible in relation to recent discussions about trade negotiations with a focus on copyright issues, such as the US Stop Online Piracy Act (SOPA) and PROTECT IP Act (PIPA) and the European equivalent, the Anti-Counterfeiting Trade Agreement (ACTA). These proposals for new and more enforceable legislation in the area of intellectual property rights and copyrights were met with strong resistance from key Internet companies, including Google, Facebook, Wikipedia and others fearing that regulation with more teeth in this area would undermine their business models and halt innovation in the Internet industry, which feeds on the circulation, sharing and integration of digital material. As part of their campaigning to stop these acts and agreements, thousands of Internet companies arranged a coordinated blackout of their websites to raise awareness of the possible consequences of such new legislation.

Another illustration of this mode of advocacy is the resistance against the UN World Conference on International Telecommunications (WCIT) in Dubai in December 2012. Internet companies and other critics feared that the International Telecommunication Union (ITU) was using this negotiation over international telecommunications regulations (ITRs) as a way to position itself more centrally in Internet governance and regulation by defining the Internet as a form of telecommunication that would then fall under ITU mandate. In response to these concerns, Internet companies, including particularly Google, set up an elaborate set of campaign activities targeting this event. In online videos and at the dedicated website freeandopenweb.com (now defunct and subsumed under the Google site www.google.com/takeaction), the campaign described the meeting as an event seeking to increase censorship and regulate the Internet through old-fashioned governmental means that would halt innovation and put an end to Internet freedom and openness. The company also sent its 'chief Internet evangelist' Vint Cerf (whose fundamentally important work on the TCP/IP protocols positions him as one of the 'fathers' of the Internet) campaigning: in op-eds, interviews and at events related to the meeting in Dubai, Cerf called for multi-stakeholder participation, transparency and openness in Internet governance matters and argued that the ITU process was an attempt to undermine these principles (Cerf 2012). While these arguments and attempts were a collaborative effort involving a large number of Internet companies, it is important to keep in mind that these corporate actors entered the discussion rather late and when civil society actors and others had already created a lot of momentum for the resistance towards stronger ITU engagement in Internet governance issues.

In terms of the type of knowledge produced in this mode of corporate advocacy, it often takes the shape of carefully crafted messages or narratives engaging historical information (such as the origins and libertarian foundations of the Internet), contemporary political concerns (such as the need for economic growth and innovation) and highly simplified portrayals of foes and allies (such as describing a possible ITU engagement in Internet governance as a way for repressive governments to justify censorship or cut off parts of the Internet). Message production constitutes a very visible and direct form of corporate advocacy. Such efforts tend to target specific policy processes that do not affect only the individual company, but may also have consequences for the entire industry. Along the same lines, such messages and campaigns rely on industry or technology-based arguments, such as by pointing to the negative consequences for innovation and the Internet in its entirety. It is also a largely reactive form of advocacy taking issue with policy developments at the final stage where decisions are made and not when the issue is raised in the first place. While such forms of corporate advocacy certainly aim to engage and mobilize constituencies, they do so by very traditional means that we recognize from advertising and political campaigning. That is, they package very carefully selected data and information into simple narratives that are hard to unpack or engage with beyond agreeing or disagreeing.

Data Provision

A third mode of advocacy – data provision – operates in more subtle ways and introduces very different resources into attempts to shape policies and regulation. Rather than serving to build relations through organizational arrangements and presence or to shape issues via very direct messages and campaigns, this mode relies on data, applications and visualizations. Unlike more direct and overt forms of corporate advocacy, the provision of seemingly neutral, factual and undisputable data and visualizations allows companies to remain out of sight and establish themselves as sources of information rather than actors with vested interests. Invoking large amounts of real-time data and algorithms in the production of visualizations, this mode of advocacy not only seeks to shape policies and politics in subtle ways, but also applies the particular competencies and innovations characterizing Internet companies to the field of advocacy as such. Particularly Google seeks to shape its environment through the provision of data, technological platforms and the production of extensive data crunches that illustrate key concerns of the company. This development is very visible in the emergence of www.google.org as a 'philanthropic arm' of the company with a primary focus on 'data philanthropy'. The issues at stake include various threats to the continued existence of an open Internet and a broader vision about increased openness and transparency in societies and politics, for instance in the shape of free flows of and access to information and ambitions about advancing transparency, legibility and openness in corporate affairs and governments. Access to data and an open Internet infrastructure are central to the business operations of Google and as its policy director points out, increased transparency 'would be valuable for us, if more made information available and were transparent, it would be easier for us to realize our mission, and this goes for governments also' (interview, 2011). The close ties to the Obama administration around the idea of open government (Levy 2011) and Google's various activities to strengthen what they term 'open data' are also central aspects of the corporate political activities of the company. Such attempts to shape policies and advance transparency have taken the shape of rather elaborate initiatives, such as M-Lab, a project involving the New America Foundation, the PlanetLab Consortium and Google that 'provides the largest collection of open Internet performance data on the planet' (www.measurementlab.net). M-Lab offers multiple types of open data about the Internet and advanced network measurement tools for researchers and policymakers, but also more simple ones that allow users to test their Internet connection and gain other insights into the workings of the Internet.

Google has developed what they term Transparency Reports as a way to capture and disclose how and when governments around the world make requests for user data and other types of information. These reports disclose when and where the Internet has been blocked, where outages have happened or particular services have been made inaccessible by governments. The reports are consistently presented as a tool to promote the 'free flow of information' and the need to provide transparent and open decision making in government bodies around the world. Transparency Reports also feed into newspaper, television and online reports about government attempts to block Internet access, filter information and censor content, such as those seen most recently during the so-called Arab Spring. Along similar lines, Facebook stresses the role it has played as a platform for mobilization and advocacy in relation to the Arab Spring and puts some efforts into documenting activity on its pages in the area (Facebook interviews, 2012). Increasingly, and particularly in the wake of the Snowden revelations of the surveillance schemes of the NSA, other Internet companies have started to publish similar reports of government interventions and attempts at control.

Such advocacy efforts constitute attempts to shape policies and world-views in more fundamental ways. For instance, we can see this as one incarnation of what may be termed the 'transparency evangelism' that Google and Facebook engage in. Transparency Reports contribute to such efforts because they make information about government activities to limit the open flow of information available and legible. Transparency Reports also constitute one pillar in Google's ambition to shape policymaking through data provision. That is, Google advocates what they term 'policy by numbers' rather than 'policy by emotions' (interviews, Google, 2011) and seeks to influence policy developments through the use of calculations, measurements, indexes and other forms of data aggregation. For instance, Transparency Reports are intended to show policymakers the results of legal and regulatory initiatives and to help pave the way for 'policymaking through data, instead of policymaking on emotions and feelings', such as recent trade agreements like SOPA and PIPA (interview, Google, 2011). By providing data about the effects of particular regulatory initiatives, Google seeks to shape legislation and to 'illuminate possible futures' (ibid). At the same time, they tie in with other attempts at making data available, such as the M-Lab, Google's Data Liberation Front and efforts in the area of 'data philanthropy' that seek to shape politics more fundamentally by advocating data-driven policymaking or as one policy director puts it, to help policymakers 'start creating policy based on numbers, based on metrics'.

This mode of advocacy focuses on the production of what Gusterson (2008) refers to as 'anticipatory knowledge', that is attempts to visualize and make current and possible future scenarios legible and actionable. In contrast to the two modes of advocacy described earlier, visualizations are thus more proactive in orientation and can be considered deeper forms of lobbying. By engaging algorithms, big data and digital visualizations in corporate advocacy, Internet companies seek to shape not only policy positions, but also worldviews, cognitive patterns and representations of the world around us. Obviously, corporate advocacy in general involves the production of reports, compilations and presentations of data and a search for numbers that can serve as evidence for the issues or arguments at stake. But in contrast to more traditional forms of corporate advocacy relying on words and numbers, the types of knowledge involved in visualizations are largely repurposable, mobile and visual. They thereby allow for a high degree of participation by others who can tweak and combine data for their own purposes. The production and circulation of such visualizations is central if we want to understand the current and possible future shape of corporate advocacy. The emergence of big data forms of advocacy raises important questions about the relationship between knowledge and politics and more fundamental questions about knowledge production.

CONCLUDING REFLECTIONS

Based on insights from the literature on advocacy and knowledge production, this chapter has conceptualized how corporations seek to shape politics by outlining three modes of corporate advocacy, namely *relationship building*, *message production* and *data provision*. This typology does not exhaust the multiple ways in which companies engage in advocacy, but it offers an analytical vocabulary for the study of resources and knowledge – and their intersections – involved in corporate political activities. The distinction between three modes of advocacy invites us to consider how Internet (and other) companies pursue advocacy efforts by relying on a variety of means and modes. But the conceptualization also stresses the relationship between knowledge and policy orientations, that is, how particular forms of knowledge may be associated with particular understandings and visions of politics.

The first contribution of the paper is thus the suggestion that corporate political activities in the Internet domain relies on multiple and discernible forms of knowledge production and advocacy. While the first two – relationship building and message crafting – are well established, the focus on the provision of data, algorithms and technological platforms adds a new dimension to our understanding of corporate advocacy. This typology and the empirical illustrations serve as the basis for a conceptual and contextual embedding of visual numbers- and data-based forms of knowledge production and advocacy in relation to prevalent forms and understandings of corporate political activities.

The second contribution of the paper is thus to consider how the growing reliance on such visual, numbers- or data-based forms of knowledge has consequences not only for those producing and circulating them, but also for users, stakeholders and policymakers they seek to mobilize or engage with, as well as for policy processes and politics they afford and shape more broadly. The conceptualization and illustrations of these three modes of corporate political activity and the different forms of knowledge production and circulation involved paves the way for some preliminary reflections on the intersection of corporate advocacy resources, knowledge production and political *imaginaries.* While largely addressing the same issues, the three modes of advocacy take very different shapes and engage very different resources and forms of knowledge. In particular, the visualization mode invites us to consider the possible effects of data and crunching technologies for practices and outcomes of corporate advocacy. For instance, the particular features of data-based attempts at 'deep lobbying' include interactive data sets and applications that target not only issues and policymakers, but also engage wider constituencies in their circulation and potential workings as fuel for campaigns, stories and policy guidance. The growing understanding of data as a resource and value – such as the hype about data constituting the 'new oil' of our times and the emergence of 'data philanthropy'– requires us to probe deeper into the ways in which data works as a resource for corporate advocacy and mobilization.

Looking across these three modes of advocacy, they involve rather different ways of sourcing data, synthesizing information and circulating knowledge. They offer different opportunities for participation and reuse and thus allow for different degrees of mobilization and political reimaging. That is, they produce different forms of knowledge and – by extension – politics. Thus, we need to address questions about the political ramifications of what Porter (1995) has termed the widespread 'trust in numbers', and the problematic forms of governance and unintended consequences that such attempts at rationalizing politics and governance tend to produce (Scott 1998). Data visualizations, like numbers, appear to be 'superior in objective reality than "mere" words' or messages (Hansen and Mühlen-

Schulte 2012). This calls for discussions of the possible ramifications of relying on data visualizations in policymaking, including the distance to experience and other situated forms of insights and the simple fact that many parts of life and the world are not subject to 'datafication' (Mayer-Schönberger and Cukier 2013). Also, we need to explore such algorithmic forms of knowledge production in terms of the politics they afford. For example, data visualizations contribute to what Garsten and Jacobsson (2013) term 'post-political forms of governance' that re-articulate politics by using other registers (Flyverbom 2015). For instance, we can understand the call for 'policy by numbers' as an attempt to turn political conflicts into a matter of data supply. These and related beliefs in data as truths may lead to the emergence of troublesome forms of political and societal rationalization (Kallinikos 2013) that make it more difficult to understand and assess advocacy efforts and corporate influence in the political arena.

NOTE

1. The empirical material related to Google and Facebook consists of a multi-sited investigation of the two companies in the period 2011–2014. The material consists of interviews with policy directors, policy managers and higher-level staff, carried out at Google in Mountain View, CA and Reston, VA, as well as at Facebook in Palo Alto and its new headquarters in Menlo Park, CA, and with Facebook and Google employees located in Europe. Another important source is the official blogs of Google and Facebook, and various documents and publications by the two companies. Finally, various public meetings, hearings and events constitute a third source.

REFERENCES

Bachman, K. (2012), 'Fast chat: The internet association's Michael Beckerman head lobbyist for 14 web giants readies for new Congress', available at http://www.adweek.com/news/technology/fast-chat-Internet-associations-michael-beckerman-145137. Accessed 3 May 2017.

Barley, S.R. (2010), 'Building an institutional field to corral a government: A case to set an agenda for organization studies', *Organization Studies*, **31** (6), 777–805.

Baumgartner, F.R., J.M. Berry, M. Hojnacki, D.C. Kimball and B.L. Leech (eds) (2009), *Lobbying and Policy Change: Who Wins, Who Loses, and Why*, Chicago: The University of Chicago Press.

Beckert, J. and P. Aspers (eds) (2012), *The Worth of Goods: Valuation and Pricing in the Economy*, Oxford: Oxford University Press.

Berg, K.T. (2009), 'Finding connections between lobbying, public relations and advocacy', *Public Relations Journal*, **3** (3).

Brasher, H. and D. Lowery (2006), 'The corporate context of lobbying activity', *Business and Politics*, **8** (1).

Carusi, A. (2012), 'Making the visual visible in philosophy of science', *Spontaneous Generations: A Journal for the History and Philosophy of Science*, **6** (1), 106–14.
Cerf, V. (2012), '"Father of the internet": Why we must fight for its freedom', available at http://edition.cnn.com/2012/11/29/business/opinion-cerf-google-internet-freedom/index.html. Accessed 3 May 2017.
Cutler, A.C., V. Haufler and T. Porter (eds) (1999), *Private Authority and International Affairs*, Albany, NY: State University of New York Press.
Deibert, R.J. (1997), *Parchment, Printing and Hypermedia – Communication in World Order Transformation*, New York: Columbia University Press.
Drutman, L. (2011), 'A better way to fix lobbying', *Issues in Governance Studies*, Brookings Institution, Number 40.
Ezell, M. (2001), *Advocacy in the Human Services*, Independence: Cengage Learning.
Flyverbom, M. (2011), *The Power of Networks: Organizing the Global Politics of the Internet*, Cheltenham: Edward Elgar.
Flyverbom, M. (2015), 'Sunlight in cyberspace? On transparency as a form of ordering', *European Journal of Social Theory*, **18** (2).
Flyverbom, M. and A.K. Madsen (2015), 'Sorting data out – unpacking big data value chains and algorithmic knowledge production', in F. Süssenguth (ed.), *Die Gesellschaft der Daten. Über die digitale Transformation der sozialen Ordnung*, Verlag: Bielefeld.
Foucault, M. (1980), *Power/Knowledge: Selected Interviews and Writings 1972–1977*, New York: Pantheon Books.
Fuchs, D. and M. Lederer (2007), 'The power of business', *Business and Politics*, **9** (3).
Garsten, C. and K. Jacobsson (2013), 'Post-political regulation: Illusory consensus and hybrid forms of governance', *Critical Sociology*, **39** (3), 421–37.
Gillespie, T. (2014), 'The relevance of algorithms', in T. Gillespie, P.J. Boczkowski and K.A. Foot (eds), *Media Technologies: Essays on Communication, Materiality, and Society*, Cambridge, MA: MIT Press.
Gitelman, L. (2013), *'Raw data' is an oxymoron*, Cambridge, MA: MIT Press.
Given, L.M. (2008), 'Advocacy research', *The SAGE Encyclopedia of Qualitative Methods*, London, UK: Sage.
Graff, G. (2008), 'A night out: Google opens a DC office', available at http://www.washingtonian.com/blogs/capitalcomment/scene/a-night-out-google-opens-a-dc-office.php. Accessed 3 May 2017.
Gusterson, H. (2008), 'Nuclear futures: anticipatory knowledge, expert judgment, and the lack that cannot be filled', *Science and Public Policy*, **35** (8), 551–60.
Hackett, E.J., O. Amsterdamska, M. Lynch and J. Wajcman (eds) (2008), *The Handbook of Science and Technology Studies*, 3rd ed., Cambridge, MA: MIT Press.
Hall, R.L. and A.V. Deardorff (2006), 'Lobbying as legislative subsidy', *The American Political Science Review*, **100** (1), 69–84.
Hansen, H.K. and M. Flyverbom (2015), 'The politics of transparency and the calibration of knowledge in the digital age', *Organization*, **22** (6), 872–89.
Hansen, H.K. and A. Mühlen-Schulte (2012), 'The power of numbers in global governance', *Journal of International Relations and Development*, **15** (4), 455–65.
Hansen, H.K. and D. Salskov-Iversen (eds) (2008), *Critical Perspectives on Private Authority in Global Politics*, Basingstoke: Palgrave Macmillan.

Hillman, A.J., G.D. Keim and D. Schuler (2004), 'Corporate political activity: A review and research agenda', *Journal of Management*, **30** (6), 837–57.
Holyoke, T.T., J.R. Henig, H. Brown and N. Lacireno-Paquet (2007), 'Institution advocacy and the political behavior of charter schools', *Political Research Quarterly*, **60** (2), 202–14.
Hutchby, I. (2001), *Conversation and Technology: From the Telephone to the Internet*, Cambridge: Polity Press.
Kallinikos, J. (2013), 'The allure of big data', *Mercury Magazine*, **3**, 40–3.
Keck, M.E. and K. Sikkink (1998), *Activists beyond Borders: Advocacy Networks in International Politics*, Ithaca: Cornell University Press.
Latour, B. (2005), *Reassembling the Social: An Introduction to Actor-network Theory*, Oxford: Oxford University Press.
Leach, J. (2012), '"Step inside: knowledge freely available" – the politics of (making) knowledge objects', in F.D. Rubio and P. Baert (eds), *The Politics of Knowledge*, London: Routledge, pp. 79–96.
Levin, P. and W.N. Espeland (2002), 'Pollution futures: Commensuration commodification and the market for air', in A.J. Hoffman and M.J. Ventresca (eds), *Organizations, Policy, and the Natural Environment: Institutional and Strategic Perspectives*, Stanford, CA: Stanford University Press.
Levy, S. (2011), *In the Plex: How Google Thinks, Works and Shapes Our Lives*, New York: Simon & Schuster.
Lux, S., T.R. Crook and T. Leap (2012), 'Corporate political activity: The good, the bad, and the ugly', *Business Horizons*, **55** (3), 307–12.
Mayer-Schönberger, V. and K. Cukier (2013), *Big Data: A Revolution That Will Transform How We Live, Work, and Think*, Boston: Eamon Dolan/Houghton Mifflin Harcourt.
Miller, P. and N. Rose (1990), 'Governing economic life', *Economy and Society*, **19** (1), 1–31.
Porter, T.M. (1995), *Trust in Numbers. The Pursuit of Objectivity in Science and Public Life*, Princeton: Princeton University Press.
Power, M. (1997), *The Audit Society: Rituals of Verification*, Oxford: Oxford University Press.
Roberts, J. (2009), 'No one is perfect: The limits of transparency and an ethic for "intelligent" accountability', *Accounting, Organization and Society*, **34**, 957–70.
Rubio, F.D. and P. Baert (eds) (2012), *The Politics of Knowledge*, London: Routledge.
Scott, J.C. (1998), *Seeing Like a State. How Certain Schemes to Improve the Human Condition Have Failed*, New Haven, CT: Yale University Press.
Stone, D. (2002), 'Global knowledge and advocacy networks', *Global Networks*, **2** (1), 1–11.
Strathern, M. (2006), 'Useful knowledge', *Proceedings of the British Academy*, vol 139.
Wedel, J. (2009), *Shadow Elite: How the World's New Power Brokers Undermine Democracy, Government and the Free Market*, New York: Basic Books.

7. Talking like an institutional investor: on the gentle voices of financial giants[1]

Anette Nyqvist

INTRODUCTION: MONEY TALKS

At an Annual General Meeting in Sweden: One after another representatives of large institutional investors step up to the microphone to question, critique and sometimes praise the company in front of its CEO, Board of Directors and an auditorium full of other shareholders.

At the offices of a financial ethics consultant: Some of his clients are large institutional investors and he talks at length about how 'dialogue' is the most important and efficient tool in his line of work. He claims that dialogue is a powerful instrument and key to all change.

At an international conference on responsible investments: Hundreds of representatives of institutional investors from around the world work the room between sessions. They introduce themselves, exchange business cards and pleasantries. The networking is intense and the small talk polite but brief and really swift.

This chapter pays attention to the talk of a certain kind of financial market actor – the institutional investor. I listen to what institutional investors say, to whom and where they speak. And I will discuss why they say what they say and what tone of voice they use. The paramount objective of this chapter is to describe and discuss some of the ways in which organizations with the primary goal of 'making money' increasingly also embark on projects of 'doing good'.

Institutional investors, such as mutual funds, insurance companies and pension funds, are large shareholder organizations commissioned to manage other people's money. These have emerged as influential front figures of the responsible investment industry claiming to make money and make a difference and positioning themselves as the 'active' and 'responsible' do-gooders of finance. These are intermediary organizations that in a relatively short time have grown in size and scope and now dominate corporate ownership globally (Clark 2000; Drucker 1993; Gold 2010; Hawley and Williams 2000). Institutional investors have, at that, become leading figures of the responsible investing industry. They are normative and fostering financial actors that aim to, in their view, better the way companies conduct their businesses (Gold 2010; Welker 2014; Welker and Wood 2011). Institutional investors are actors on a global financial market that not only aim at making money but also make a difference and as such they set out to pressure corporations to change: They are financial actors with political aims.

I suggest that 'voice' rather than 'exit' must be seen as a defining feature of institutional investors. I show how institutional investors use 'voice', 'dialogue' and 'small talk' with the intent to: (1) define and position themselves as a particular type of financial market actor, (2) foster and try to change companies that they own shares in and (3) set new standards for the investment industry.

The diverse practice of talk is at the core of any organization and salient in the very construction of the organization. Erving Goffman (1980) paid specific attention to the critical role of verbal face-to-face exchange and an important point in Goffman's analysis of, as it were, 'utterances and hearings' is that talk bear the marks of the framework in which it occurs (1980, p. 4). Deirdre Boden too places emphasis on the structural character of talk as she argues that: 'talk [. . .] is the lifeblood of all organizations and, as such, it shapes and is shaped by the structure of the organization itself' (Boden 1994, p. 8). In other words, everyday interaction in general, and talk in particular are constituent features of organizations. This chapter is about the talk of institutional investors; how they, with voice and dialogue, attempt to reshape and foster the companies that they have invested in and how they, with small talk and networking (Garsten 2013; Moeran 2005, 2013), strive to amplify their voice and increase their vocal range.

The notion of 'voice' is here used both literally and analytically in the organizational theoretical sense where 'voice' as well as 'exit' are strategies for dissatisfied members of any organization. Albert O. Hirschman argues (1970) that members of any type of organization have two possible options if they are in some way dissatisfied with the organization: they can either withdraw as a member of the organization – exit. Or members can stay and attempt to restore or improve that which they are not satisfied with – voice. The twin concepts of 'exit' and 'voice' can be said to represent economical and political action respectively. 'Exit' is commonly associated with neoclassical economic theory in which buyers and sellers are market actors in perpetual relationship with each other and that they are constantly shaped, reshaped and destroyed by the market. 'Voice', on the other hand, is a more political option that does not involve the selling and buying practices of the market but instead aims at 'from within' pressuring the organization to change. The role of the third concept in Hirschman's writings, loyalty, is to be seen in relation to the two others, in that loyalty is a variable that influences the possibility of exit and voice. The essence of the three possibilities that Albert O. Hirschman proposed – 'exit, voice or loyalty' – has been effectively summarized to entail: 'leave, protest, or keep quiet' (Sunstein 2013).

This chapter focuses on the talk of contemporary capital. I am interested in the voice of a particular type of financial actor, and I here provide insights into how the discourse of an alternative, responsible and engaged investment logic is being promoted with metaphors and practices that have to do with speech, and that the speaker's corner is dominated by this new and powerful financial market actor – the institutional investor. Given the normative and fostering projects that institutional investors launch, aiming to better the way corporations conduct their business as well as alter the ways of financial market actors, I view them as organizations that are, with Saskia Sassen's terminology, 'sites of normativity' (Sassen 1998) that have emerged on a global scene. In this chapter I will listen to what these normative and fostering financial actors say, and how they say it.

LISTENING TO ORGANIZATIONS

Institutional investors are interesting, important and intriguing objects for ethnographic inquiry for at least three reasons. First, institutional investors manage other people's money, and that, in itself, sets them apart from traditional financial actors driven by self-interest and makes them interesting entities to investigate. Second, the fact that there has been a shift in ownership on the world's financial markets and institutions during the past three decades by which institutions have emerged as major financial actors that now dominate corporate ownership worldwide makes them not only interesting but also important to study and understand. Third, institutional investors, acting in the best interest of others, position themselves as financial actors with a somewhat different agenda than traditional financial actors. By forwarding notions of what it means to be a fiduciary, institutional investors worldwide have emerged as prominent figures of the responsible investment industry.

As part of my ethnographic fieldwork among major institutional investors, I have 'followed' (Marcus 1995) some of the larger organizations to the main types of sites where they present and position themselves as 'active', 'responsible' and 'engaged' financial actors. I here focus in particular on what representatives from the Swedish National Pension Funds and one of the larger insurance companies, Folksam, do and say. My focus has been set on how these institutional investors use voice to present and position themselves as 'active' and 'responsible' financial actors, and on how they join forces with others in order to 'spread the word'.

The 'voice' of institutional investors is 'heard', that is made observable, in mainly two arenas: the Annual General Meeting, AGM, and the responsible investment conference (Nyqvist 2015a, 2015b, 2017). The empirical examples in this chapter are drawn from observations of and interviews with key informants at the First National Pension Fund, The Ethical Council of the National Pension Funds and at the insurance company Folksam, all of whom I have heard, at AGMs and conferences, officially 'speak for' the institutional investor that they represent and/or work for. I have also interviewed key informants at the consultant firm that all of the institutional investors that I have focused on use as their expert of ethical and responsible investments. Before listening to how institutional investors use 'voice' and variations of speech to both influence the companies in which they own shares and to set new standards for the investment industry in general, it is necessary to know more about those who are talking.

POOLING MONEY IN BETWEEN

Institutional investors are organizations that pool large amounts of money from many minor, individual investors. The idea of pooling several minor assets into a larger entity and thereby enable collective investing has been traced back to 1774 and Dutch businessman Adriaan van Ketwich who created an 'investment trust' and named it 'Eendragt maakt magt', which roughly translates to 'unity makes power' (Rouwenhorst 2005), thus already at the onset implying the political aspects of collective capital allocation schemes. This form of collective investment initiative spread and gained popularity in other European nations during the latter part of the seventeenth century and reached the USA towards the end of that century, where the collective investment in mutual funds became increasingly popular during the 1920s. What soon came to be called 'the fund industry' has since then continued to grow impressively. The growth and spread of mutual fund investments is viewed as constitutive for the ongoing development and increased significance of financial markets since the 1970s and 1980s (Rouwenhorst 2005).

As investors that manage other people's money institutional investors are, as opposed to individual market actors, intermediaries between lenders and borrowers, between the many minor, individual, investors and the companies in which the institution invests the pooled capital. I have elsewhere described and discussed the intermediary position of institutional investors and dubbed them 'ombudsmen' of capitalism (Nyqvist 2015a), since they are commissioned to act as investors solely in the best interest of their beneficiaries. The position and role of the broker, intermediary or middleman is interesting in that it enables for shifts in responsibilities and affects the agency chain. The broker position and role has previously been described and analysed by anthropologists as one that, in various ways, serve as a connection that mediate and disseminate knowledge between the local and global (Bailey 1969; Callon 1994; Geertz 1960; James 2011; Randeraad 1998; Wolf 1956). Further, economists have written about intermediaries and middlemen in markets and show how intermediaries work as nodes between buyers and sellers (Popp 2000; Spulber 1999).

When institutional investors use 'voice' in order to influence companies and set new standards for the investment industry they as shareholders show what is known as 'stakeholder's concerns' (Clarkson 1999; Donaldson and Preston 1995; Hawley and Williams 1997, 2000). Institutional investors have the responsibility to manage the economic assets on behalf of others. In this role they seek change and improvement in the way business is conducted, and many actively engage in social and environmental issues. I argue that they, by so doing, constitute a new, hybrid, type of financial market actor – the shareowner/stakeholder. David Westbrook, professor of law, assets that legal frameworks construct various actors and analyse how these, then, play different roles on the 'corporate stage' (Westbrook 2007). Institutional investors play several roles; they are brokers, agents, shareholders and stakeholders in one. They are mediators of capital and have been described as 'pass-through financial intermediaries' (Gold 2010, pp. 8–9), and they are norm-setters and knowledge producers and agents of change that seek to influence, shape and change other market actors (Brunsson and Jacobsson 2000; Sassen 1998; Sjöström 2010).

'CRAP' IN THE PORTFOLIO

Institutions, such as mutual funds and pension funds, manage other people's money and are thus legally and/or ethically – as well as by tradition and 'practice' – bound to do so 'prudently', as it were, and in the interests of its many beneficiaries. The fiduciary duties of mutual and pension funds are explicitly written down and legally specified in both British and US common law, albeit not in Swedish where, as my informants have accounted for in interviews, the fiduciary duties of institutional owners are, instead, 'implicit', 'fundamental but taken for granted' and 'normal behaviour'. Implicit or explicit – the notions of what it takes to manage other people's money are the same, and expressed as virtues and values such as 'trust', 'prudence', 'loyalty' and 'care'.

The concepts of 'duty of loyalty' and 'duty of care' are central here. 'Duty of loyalty' places on the fiduciary the responsibility to act solely in the interests of the beneficiary, while 'duty of care' requires that the fiduciary discharge his or her duty in the manner of a 'prudent investor' (Hawley and Williams 2000, pp. 18–19). The 'caring' conducted by fiduciaries such as institutional investors is pragmatically rooted. Owing to their sheer size and the fact that the largest institutions have portfolios that usually mirror those of other large institutions, most major fiduciary capitalists cannot sell their holdings as easily as smaller and/or individual investors. Institutions are, in other words, locked into the market and into the shares they own, on behalf of others. As a consequence, they cannot easily use 'exit', so they aim for 'voice', or as Hawley and Williams puts it: 'if they cannot sell, then they must "care"' (2000, p. xiv).

In interviews my informants at large institutional owners talk about how they, as one of them put it, handle the fact that there is 'crap in the portfolio'. Says one key informant: 'If you buy according to a global index, you'll get 4000 holdings. Bang! And that's how we get all of these problem companies.' The informant continues to explain how the institutional investor he works for, a large national pension fund with explicitly ethical investment strategies, handles the situation of such unwanted holdings, without selling them:

> Our ethics consultants make sure we're not involved in anything really, really bad. If there is something that is bad we need to evaluate what we can do. The AP funds don't exclude at once. Instead we stay put and see what we can do. What is it that has happened? How can we get this company to handle this properly and take their responsibility? That, we hold, is true ownership responsibility. To just say: 'No, we don't like this. Bye, we're leaving.' That, we think, does not solve any problems.

Another informant also talks about 'ownership responsibility' and says: 'Those of us that work with responsibility and sustainability issues, corporate governance or shareholder activism do it from a responsibility perspective. We consider this to be part and parcel of being an investor on a global market. You take responsibility for the investments you make.' This informant then goes on to reason more generally about ownership and responsibilities and says:

> When you buy something you take care of it, don't you? If you buy a house you take good care of it. If you buy a car you take care of that. You take

> responsibility. You take care of what you own and make sure you get what it's worth.

Another informant explained:

> Sure, it would be much better not to have, as we do, up to 4000 companies in the portfolio, but just maybe 400. We would still have crap in the portfolio because there will always fall down stuff you don't want. But we'd have less of that. Now we have everything! As soon as something pops up, it's in the portfolio. All scandals out there are in the portfolio. We get the whole market in our portfolio.

The 'voice' of pooled capital is enacted due to the fact that their passive, index-based asset management leave them with less wanted holdings. In their investment portfolios institutional investors hold a broad cross section of the economy; they do so on a long-term basis and on the whole do not trade except to maintain its index. The long-term return of such a large institution, owning a cross selection of the entire economy, is determined not merely by the performance of each individual firm it owns, but by the performance of the economy as a whole. It has been argued that because the portfolio of a large institution mirrors the entire financial market they have the potential of 'moving markets'; through its market activities it may potentially change and shape the market it acts upon (Hawley and Williams 2000, p. 3; Monks and Minow 1995). Hawley and Williams point to the intertwined economic and political powers and intentions of institutional investors as they hold that: institutional investors 'have come to occupy a quasi-public policy position as having an economic interest in the long-term health and well-being of the whole society' (Hawley and Williams 2000, p. xv).

Shareholders owning stocks in companies that they, for various reasons, do not believe will meet their expectations have two main options: they either sell the shares, that is 'exit' with Hirschman's (1970) terminology, or they keep the shares and use 'voice', that is, attempt to influence and shape the company in a direction that the shareowners consider better. The large and broad holdings of institutional institutions are, for economic reasons, predominantly managed passively, meaning they are linked to indexes rather than hand-picked through active financial management. To compensate for this passiveness in management and in order to handle some of the less wanted shares in the broad portfolio large institutions have come to practise what is now known as 'active ownership'. Active ownership can take a variety of forms: from publishing 'black lists' and making use of the news media, what has been called 'corporate governance by public embarrassment', to attending and voting at Annual General Meetings, and engaging directly with the companies (Gold 2010, p. 143; Hawley and

Williams 2000, pp. 101–24; Koppes and Reilly 1995). In what follows I pay particular attention to the varying practices of 'voice' used by institutional investors to influence companies in which they own shares and at the same time position themselves as 'responsible' financial market actors.

GATHERINGS OF VOICES

Spring is meeting season in corporate Sweden. At the Annual General Meeting, AGM, company executives, Boards of Directors and shareholders gather to vote on important issues such as electing, or re-electing, the Board, assembling an election committee and choosing accountants. In Sweden all shareholders owning a minimum of one share are invited to the meeting and one share equals one vote. The AGM is also where company representatives inform shareholders of previous and ongoing activities of the company and where shareholders vote on any company issue requiring their approval. Here, an AGM is an opportunity for shareholders to pose questions, file complaints or make proposals regarding the company in which they own shares.

There are the small, measured in amount of shares, voices of individual shareholders. Some shareholders take the opportunity to speak their mind or open their heart; once a man stepped up to complain about the opening hours (at a Nordea meeting), at another meeting a man asked the CEO to explain his phone bill (at a TeliaSonera meeting), and at another a woman expressed her unhappiness about the quality of thread being used in bras (at an H&M meeting). Another type of voice is the equally small but forceful and demanding one of shareholder activists that with one share acquire access to the meetings and bring about large albeit usually specific issues. Commonly, it is representatives of environmental or human rights organizations that with one share at hand attend the meetings and when given the microphone point to specific activities that the company is involved in and/or responsible for. Here voices of particular protest may be about the environmental damage caused by a mining company in Southeast Asia (at a Nordea meeting), or about the concern that the company has closed deals with partners in nondemocratic nations (at a TeliaSonera meeting).

Minor and personal or major and global, the voices of small individual shareholders do not resonate or carry as far as the voices of institutional investors do. When a person representing an institution that own several millions of shares speaks that voice is heard – not least, of course, because each share represents a vote at the AGM.

In 2010 and 2011 (and 2009 according to minutes of that year's meetings) remuneration packages, or bonus systems, to corporative management was the main topic of discussion. As in many places, in the aftermath of the financial crisis of 2008, the soundness of financial markets in general and ethics of financial actors and corporate managements were widely questioned and critiqued, and up for debate – so too at AGMs in Sweden.

The Swedish government had, in 2009, called for a total ban on bonuses to top managements, and while many minor individual shareholders sided with this stand the institutional investors instead sided with companies' position that remunerations packages of various designs are necessary. At most of the AGMs the institutional investors gave a silent approval by voting for the company's remuneration policies, and thus against the proposed ban, agreeing with companies that bonus systems are needed as incentives to 'attract the best people out there' and to 'retain competence within the company'. But at the 2010 AGM of Lundin Petroleum, a Swedish oil and gas company, the issue of remuneration deals stirs a heated debate where many institutional owners raise their voices. It is not bonus systems per se that is up for debate but the particular design of the remuneration packages used at Lundin Petroleum. The institutional investors object that the company is 'not transparent enough' and 'not linked to performance'. One of my key informants, head of corporate governance at the First National Pension Fund, leaves his red velvet seat on the second row in the turn-of-the-century theatre where the AGM is held. He steps up to the podium on stage, turns to the CEO and chairman of Board behind the desk on centre stage and says:

> We see some problems with the remuneration system you use. We have had this discussion with you before, last year for example, and we still want you to specify how the bonus systems you use work. As you know, we do not find them to be transparent enough. What are, for example, 'exceptional accomplishments'?

As the representative of one of the largest institutional investors in Sweden returns to his seat the chairman of the Board of Directors replies: 'If you want good people in the company, you must pay them to stay! I know that you institutions want sticks to measure with but we make it simple and general. Our guys know that if the company does well, they'll get a bonus.' Now the man representing the Third National Pension Fund stands up in the isle and seconds the First National Pension Fund comments and critique by stating: 'We agree with the demands for clearer and more precise performance incentives in your remuneration packages. These are unclear as they are now formulated.' He sits down and the chairman of the Board rolls his eyes and says: 'This is a tiresome discussion. What is important is that we pay out enough so that we can employ and retain good people. I can understand that you as institutional shareholders want other yardsticks. But oh, we could talk about this for ever!' He turns to the CEO and says, almost reassuringly: 'You're worth the package that you get.' This is when the representative of the Fourth National Pension Funds stands up and states: 'We see no connections to measurable accomplishments. We object to your remuneration packages.' As he sits down the representative of the Second National Pension Funds stands up, and says simply: 'We see no specified performance linked incentives. We will vote against your remuneration packages,' and sits down again. The woman representing the insurance company Folksam stands up: 'We also object and will vote against this.' A man from Nordea Funds, a private fund company and institutional investor, is the last to stand up and voice his opinion before the voting procedure: 'We want a better account for how your bonus systems work. The performance incentives are too unclear as it is.' Since the Lundin family controls a majority of the shares everyone knows that the existing remuneration plans will be approved and the institutional voices, raised one after another before the actual and official shareholders' voting procedure are thus raised in protest, without hopes of actual change.

At AGMs institutional investors do not solely raise their voices to question and critique, but also to praise and compliment. The insurance company Folksam is one of the more vocal institutional investors in Sweden. A representative from their department for responsible ownership is present at all AGMs, often referring to Folksam's customers when talking to CEOs and Boards of Directors: 'Our customers want to know why . . .' or: 'This years' customer survey shows that they are concerned with . . .' But sometimes, as in this example from the AGM of H&M 2011, the representative from Folksam has nothing but praise to voice as she enters the stage. She compliments the company for their 'engaged work with sustainable issues' and reads from a list of the different projects that H&M are involved in. She turns to the CEO and says:

> You have contributed to the process of raising salaries for employees in Bangladesh, you are engaged in projects aimed at abolishing child labour in Uzbekistan, you have educated 300000 employees in labour rights, and you employ and educate women in Saudi Arabia – where women do not even have voting rights!

The CEO looks a bit embarrassed as the auditorium is filled with applause and the chairman of the AGM moves to the next speaker.

Another example of such an approving voice is the one delivered by the representative from the First National Pension Fund at the AGM of Ericsson 2011. At this meeting, where Folksam incidentally delivered harsh critique of the company's involvement in Belarus, the First National Pension Fund takes to the stage and says: 'We have discussed remuneration plans with Ericsson for years and now . . . If you look at page 129 in their Annual Report . . . Look at how exemplary they account for their systems and the purpose of them! This is exactly how things should be done. Thank you. Well done!'

In an interview conducted after the AGM the woman from Folksam says they decided to do so for two reasons – to show support for H&M: 'it is one of the good companies. They do a lot but are often critiqued by media', and to critique others: 'By showing how much H&M does we also critiqued others for not doing enough.' The man from the First National Pension Fund says in another interview:

> We wanted to compliment Ericsson on having done a really good job with their incentives scheme. But to be really honest I did, of course, have an ulterior motive with that speech. This type of transparency was our idea; we have demanded this from companies for a while. So by saying to Ericsson: 'You did well' we also say that: 'Oh, by the way, it was our suggestion they should do this'. That, in some sense, improves our reputation. I tried to brag in a nice way.

I suggest that voice here is used not as protest by a dissatisfied member of an organization, but as a fostering technique and as part of a positioning act. This use of voice makes public that the institutional investor has made previous demands on the company and that the company has listened, obeyed if you will. The public praise in the earlier examples is also used to position the institutional investor as an 'active' and 'responsible' investor, implying that they are different from traditional investors.

MULTIVOCAL DIALOGUES

'Dialogue' is commonly described as a 'tool' and 'instrument' in the 'active', 'engaged' and 'responsible' work of institutional investors, and the amount of ongoing dialogues is often invoked as a measurement of the degree of engagement and level of responsibility.

If dialogue is a tool it is a multifunctional one, more like a Swiss army knife than a hammer. Here is how the CEO of a major ethical consultant firm, contracted by most institutional investors in Sweden, explains what 'dialogue' is:

> 'We listen to them [the companies] and hopefully they listen to us.' When asked to elaborate he says: 'It is often about posing questions to the company. Sometimes we just send an email, other times we meet and discuss with company representatives. We usually want them to explain things and answer questions and we often have suggestions on what they should do.'

When I, in a later interview ask the chairman of the Ethical Council, to explain what 'dialogue' is his answer, too, sheds light on the multifunctionality of 'dialogue':

> You can send email. You can make a phone call. You can have phone conferences. You can have meetings. You can meet with investor relations people. You can meet with the CSR departments. You can meet with the Chairman of the Board or with the CEO. You can enter the company at a number of different levels. You use different ammunition depending on the situation. The important thing is that you have a dialogue.

Apart from letters, emails and different types of phone conversations 'dialogue' also entails, as it were, going to 'the field'. 'We go out and look at the actual situations. We'll go down into a mine, or whatever, to try to grasp what the difficulties are. There are things you can't understand until you've been there,' says another ethics consultant.

Ethics consultants claim that an important component of dialogue as a tool for change is to listen to companies. Here is how the CEO of the ethical consultant firm puts it:

> We all have incredibly large ears. I think what we are doing with companies is a bit like what diplomats do with nation states. It is a negotiation and we want to reach results. This means we have to be careful with what we say and how we behave. We cannot stand in a corner and yell at them. We have to be humble and in nice ways inspire them to change.

Dialogue is a multivocal concept and instrument used by 'active' and 'responsible' institutional investors. Engaging in dialogues, institutional investors seek to persuade and coerce companies to correct their behaviour and better themselves. I have here noted the manifold meanings of dialogue as an instrument for fostering and change. It is time to eavesdrop on the chit-chat and small talk that institutional investors engage in as they network at conferences.

THE RESONANCE OF SMALL TALK

Besides raising their voices at AGMs and attempting to have dialogues with the companies in which they own shares, institutional investors also actively look for other institutional investors to collaborate with. Responsible investment conferences are important meeting grounds for institutional investors (Nyqvist 2017). Here they not only seek new knowledge but also new partners. Institutional investors attend conferences in order to 'find friends' and 'join forces' to, as one informant put it 'have a bigger say' when they pressure companies to change. Collaboration is key and in interviews several of my informants, all working at or with the largest institutional investors in Sweden, stress the importance of joint efforts and striving to work together with other institutional investors to be able to, as it were, speak louder. 'We work hard to form alliances with other, bigger actors,' says one informant. 'It is easier to listen to a larger group of shareholders,' says another. 'If a few of us join forces, we can become maybe ten times bigger. Then I think companies will listen better,' says a third informant. When I ask how they know which other institutional investors might be good to collaborate with, I get answers such as: 'Well, you get to know the other institutions and how they think,' and: 'Somehow you find groups where you feel like "Hey, these might be my buddies".' When I ask where, more precisely, these large Swedish institutional investors find their potential collaboration partners they say that conferences are the best places to 'meet people'. 'There are plenty of conferences! I could go to conferences all year round,' exclaims one informant. Another says: 'There are conferences all the time. We meet there. All of us that are interested in this [responsible investment] meet and talk, share experiences and discuss pros and cons.'

I have also attended conferences. Upon my visit to the PRI in Person conference PRI had over 900 signatories, and in September 2011 many of them gathered for two days at a hotel in Paris. Here, according to official PRI information, 'all PRI signatories meet, collaborate and learn with peers'. It is where 'PRI signatories, industry experts and thought leaders' meet and engage in 'thought provoking sessions and peer-to-peer dialogues' and, says the conference catalogue, 'there is plenty of time to network'. Between each session, which lasts an hour, there is a scheduled 30 minutes coffee break in the vast area called 'Gran Foyer'. Here several hundreds of conference attendees crowd around the many Nespresso machines and tables with pastries scattered in the large and brightly lit reception hall. There are mostly men, and every single one is dressed in a suit in one of surprisingly many shades of grey. The few women in the room are also dressed formally in either a feminine version of the traditional suit or a dress or skirt and jacket in a grey suit material. It is the ties, the odd scarf (around women's necks or shoulders), and one turban that bring some colour to the room. The sound of large institutions engaged in small talk resonates in the Gran Foyer. A name tag is clipped on to the collar or breast pocket of every suit in the room displaying not only the first and last name of the bearer but also, more importantly, what institution or organization he or she represents. There are two UN-people talking to an IMF person, OECD and the World Bank are engaged in conversation, several European pension funds stand around the large US pension fund. Service providers look for asset owners and policymakers try to spot the decision makers. The smaller institutional investors look for larger, and large institutions pair up with each other. It seems everyone who is anyone in the responsible investment industry is here to 'find friends', 'join forces' and 'collaborate' while simultaneously trying to choose coffee flavour and eat croissants. In the collaborative work at conferences connectivity is central and it is as we have heard, and as Christina Garsten elsewhere has stated, 'all about ties' (Garsten 2013, p. 139). Brian Moeran has written specifically about the role of connections in the act of networking and points to the distinction of this concept used as a verb as opposed to a noun (Moeran 2005, 2013). It is in between conference sessions that the institutional investors work on making connections; it is here, with intense small talk and business card swaps, the networking is done.

The networking at PRI in Person is intense, almost aggressive. All eyes scan the room by quickly reading name tags. If there is something on the name tag that catches the attention and seem interesting in one way or another there is immediate eye contact, a broad smile, verbal contact and formal introduction. The 'Hello's and 'How are you?'s echo in the room. After such initial and affable contact one's affiliation and position, aims and missions are dealt with: 'I work with such and such at this and that and I'd really like to get more involved in something or rather. How about you?' The polite small talk and nice chit-chat that follow is focused entirely on business and the apparent objective is to find partners with whom one might initiate a business relationship. Then there is the mandatory and ritualistic exchange of business cards. Some have their card out already at 'Hello', others reach into their pocket during the small talk, and yet others hand over their card as a parting motion as they already scan the name tags around them. Although PRI in Person has lots of networking opportunities time is still limited and no one engages in lengthy conversations. This is organizational speed dating and if there is no immediate promise of a new affair or potential partnership you politely but quickly move on to the next person. I am out of business cards already by the first afternoon's coffee break. A man that I exchanged pleasantries and cards with in the morning passes by, we recognize each other and on the go he says: 'Isn't it fantastic?! This is such a great social networking opportunity.' As part of my swift small talk during networking breaks I ask what he or she think of the event as an opportunity for making new contacts. 'It is really good to meet people face to face like this,' says one man. 'I can find the information I need on the Internet but actually meeting people is invaluable,' says another. 'You make contacts. Everyone's here. Everyone!' says yet another. 'Collaboration is good!' exclaims one man before he dashes off to make contact with someone else.

For institutional investors collaboration is seen as an important activity for both learning the ropes of the responsible investment industry and searching for peers to team up with in order to become even larger actors on the financial market (Leivestad and Nyqvist 2017; Nyqvist 2017). It is at events like PRI in Person that institutional investors meet, get to know each other and form alliances in order to work collaboratively and get a bigger voice so that they can put more pressure on companies.

CONCLUDING NOTES: THE GENTLE VOICE OF GIANTS

Institutional investors such as pension funds, mutual funds and insurance companies, are financial actors commissioned to manage money on behalf of others. These intermediary organizations dominate corporate ownership on a global scale and have become leading figures of the responsible investing industry. They are normative and fostering financial actors that aim to 'actively' better the way companies conduct their businesses and set new, more 'responsible' standards for the investment industry as a whole.

At AGMs institutional investors, and other minor shareholders, not only vote on issues concerning the company's management and business strategies but also use 'voice'. Here institutional investors publicly announce their disapproval or, as we heard, approval. They pose questions and place critique when dissatisfied with something the company has done, or not done, but they can also applaud and praise if they are pleased. The voice that institutional investors use when speaking directly to companies' CEOs and Board members at AGMs is a fostering voice. It is a parental voice seeking to correct the behaviour of a minor. It is a caring voice that scolds for bad conduct and compliments for good behaviour.

'Dialogue' is the multifunctional tool of choice when institutional investors work as 'active' and 'responsible' financial actors. By engaging in dialogue institutional investors demonstrate that they are 'active' and 'responsible' investors and financial actors. But dialogue is first and foremost a way of using 'voice' and thus to show the companies in which they own shares that they are not pleased with the way business is conducted. To initiate 'dialogue' with a company means that the institutional investor seeks change. Dialogue is, however, a conversation and not a list of demands. Dialogue is conducted with an understanding and compromising gentle tone of voice; it is the negotiating voice of a pragmatic diplomat seeking to come to terms in agreement.

Another type of talk that 'active' and 'responsible' institutional investors employ is the small talk used to find friends. Collaboration is seen as a way to gain knowledge of how the responsible investment industry works and as a way to place even larger pressure on companies to change. By joining forces institutional investors amplify their voice and increase their vocal range. A group of institutional investors can send one single representative to an AGM somewhere in the world to voice their common concerns. They can also decide to, as a group, initiate a dialogue with a company that they all own shares in and are dissatisfied with. Collaboration, then, is an amplifier of the voice that institutional investors use to place demands on companies and to set new standards for the investment industry. The louder voice of collaborative efforts is also gentle and fostering and it resonates when institutional investors find partners through networking and small talk.

At the core of this discussion are the workings of contemporary capitalism and the emerging moral position of venture capitalists such as institutional investors. As institutional investors set out to shape corporations and whole industries they have become front figures of the responsible investment (RI) industry, where other, moral, values are taken into account, alongside the strictly economic ones. The contribution of this chapter is an attempt to begin scholarly investigation and analysis of how contemporary financial organizations increasingly engage in political endeavours aimed at influencing and reshaping policies and practices.

NOTE

1. This chapter draws on research conducted within projects funded by The Swedish Research Council and The Swedish Foundation for Humanities and Social Sciences.

REFERENCES

Bailey, F.G. (1969), *Stratagems and Spoils. A Social Anthropology of Politics*, Oxford: Basil Blackwell.

Boden, D. (1994), *The Business of Talk. Organizations in Action*, Cambridge, MA: Polity Press.

Brunsson, N. and B. Jacobsson (eds) (2000), *A World of Standards*, Oxford: Oxford University Press.

Callon, M. (1994), 'Is science a public good?', *Science, Technology and Human Values*, **19**, 395–424.

Clark, G. (2000), *Pension Fund Capitalism*, Oxford: Oxford University Press.

Clarkson, M. (1999), *The Corporation and Its Stakeholders*, Toronto: University of Toronto Press.

Donaldson, T. and L. Preston (1995), 'The stakeholder theory of the corporation: Concepts, evidence and implications', *Academy of Management Review*, **20** (1), 65–91.

Drucker, P.F. (1993), *Post-capitalist Society*, Oxford: Butterworth-Heinemann Ltd.
Garsten, C. (2013), 'All about ties: Think tanks and the economy of connections', in C. Garsten and A. Nyqvist (eds), *Organisational Anthropology: Doing Ethnography in and among Complex Organisations*, London: Pluto Press.
Geertz, C. (1960), 'The Javanese Kijaji: The changing role of a cultural broker', *Comparative Studies in Society and History*, **2** (2), 228–49.
Goffman, E. (1980), *Forms of Talk*, Philadelphia, PA: University of Philadelphia Press.
Gold, M. (2010), *Fiduciary Finance. Investment Funds and the Crisis in Financial Markets*, Cheltenham, UK: Edward Elgar Publishing.
Hawley, J.P. and A.T. Williams (1997), 'The emergence of fiduciary capitalism', *Corporate Governance: An International Review*, **5** (4), 206–13.
Hawley, J.P. and A.T. Williams (2000), *The Rise of Fiduciary Capitalism. How Institutional Investors Can Make Corporate America More Democratic*, Philadelphia: University of Pennsylvania Press.
Hirschman, A.O. (1970), *Exit, Voice, and Loyalty: Responses to Decline in Firms, Organizations, and States*, Cambridge, MA: Harvard University Press.
James, D. (2011), 'The return of the broker', *Journal of the Royal Anthropological Institute*, **17** (2), 318–38.
Koppes, R. and M. Reilly (1995), 'An ounce of prevention: Meeting the fiduciary duty to monitor an index fund through relationship investing', *The Journal of Corporation Law*, Spring, 1995.
Leivestad, Hege Høyer and Anette Nyqvist (eds) (2017), *Ethnographies of Conferences and Trade Fairs. Shaping Industries, Creating Professionals*, New York: Palgrave Macmillan.
Marcus, G. (1995), 'Ethnography in/of the world system: The emergence of multi-sited ethnography', *Annual Review of Anthropology*, **24**, 95–117.
Moeran, B. (2005), *The Business of Ethnography. Strategic Exchanges, People and Organizations*, Oxford: Berg.
Moeran, B. (2013), 'Working connections, helping friends. Fieldwork, organizations and cultural styles', in C. Garsten and A. Nyqvist (eds), *Organisational Anthropology: Doing Ethnography in and among Complex Organisations*, London: Pluto Press.
Monks, R. and N. Minow (1995), *Corporate Governance*, Cambridge, MA: Basil Blackwell.
Nyqvist, A. (2015a), *Ombudskapitalisterna. Institutionella ägares röst och roll*, Stockholm: Liber.
Nyqvist, A. (2015b), 'The corporation performed. Minutes from the rituals of annual general meetings', *Journal of Organizational Ethnography*, **4** (3), 341–55.
Nyqvist, A. (2017), 'Scheduled Schmoozing: Notes on Interludal Practices at Responsible Investors' Conferences', in H. Høyer Leivestad and A. Nyqvist (eds), *Ethnographies of Conferences and Trade Fairs. Shaping Industries, Creating Professionals*, New York: Palgrave Macmillan.
Popp, A. (2000), '"Swamped in information but starved of data": Information and intermediaries in clothing supply chains', *Supply Chain Management*, **5**, 151–61.
Randeraad, N. (ed.) (1998), *Mediators between State and Society*, Hilversum, Holland: Verloren Publishers.
Rouwenhorst, K.G. (2005), 'The origins of mutual funds', in W.N. Goetzmann and K.G. Rouwenhorst (eds) *The Origins of Values: The Financial Innovations that Created Modern Capital Markets*, New York, NY: Oxford University Press.

Sassen, S. (1998), *Globalization and Its Discontents: Essays on the New Mobility of People and Money*, New York: New Press.
Sjöström, E. (2010), *Ansiktslösa men ansvarsfulla? Institutionella ägare och en hållbar utveckling*, Forskning i fickformat, Stockholm: Stockholm School of Economics.
Spulber, D.F. (1999), *Market Microstructure: Intermediaries and the Theory of the Firm*, Cambridge: Cambridge University Press.
Sunstein, C. (2013), 'An original thinker of our time', *New York Review of Books*, 23 May 2013.
Welker, M. (2014), *Enacting the Corporation. An American Mining Firm in Post-Authoritarian Indonesia*, Oakland, CA: University of California Press.
Welker, M. and D. Wood (2011), 'Shareholder activism and alienation', *Current Anthropology*, **52** (3), 57–69.
Westbrook, D. (2007), *Between Citizen and State*, Boulder, CO: Paradigm Publishers.
Wolf, E. (1956), 'Aspects of group relations in a complex society', *American Anthropologist*, **88** (6), 1065–78.

8. Leading the war on epidemics: exploring corporations' predatory modus operandi and their effects on institutional field dynamics

Sébastien Picard, Véronique Steyer, Xavier Philippe and Mar Pérezts

INTRODUCTION

Research on corporate political activity (CPA) focuses on the political attempts by corporations to shape regulations according to their economical interests (Lawton et al. 2013). Recently, critics have underlined the limits of this functionalist approach, arguing that both corporations' global impact and (relatively weak) legitimacy on such issues question this reduced and exclusively calculating vision of corporations' political actions. For instance, Palazzo and Scherer (2008) consider corporations as full political actors involved in shaping global governance. This perspective calls thus for a better understanding of the key political mechanisms through which corporations act, their broader implications and consequently how they are articulated (Crouch 2011; Walker and Rea 2014). In this chapter, we propose considering corporate political behavior as being of an institutional nature. How and through which mechanisms does CPA contribute to maintain and modify institutional fields? How do these actions actually underpin institutionalization processes?

To tackle these issues, we first build on both CPA literature (Lawton et al. 2013) and an institutional perspective (Scott 2008) to highlight the institutional reach of corporate activities. We then introduce Lallement's (2008) theoretical framework that underlines the incompleteness of institutions. This allows opening the black box of the institutionalization processes at work and the institutional dynamics associated to CPA. Using data from an in-depth ethnography in VaxCorp, a leading corporation in the vaccine industry, we analyze how it shapes its institutional field by imposing the dominant 'vaccinology' imaginary, a modus operandi that goes beyond the mere maximization of VaxCorp's interests to organize actions and behaviors of other institutional actors (for example, State, WHO) when it comes to 'protecting people against epidemics and infectious diseases'.

This chapter offers an enlarged vision of CPA, highlighting its institutional reach, and describing its concrete institutionalizing effects. It also addresses Walker and Rea's (2014) call to further examine how the different modes of corporate engagement and activities are interrelated and mutually reinforce corporations' increasingly dominant role. Finally, this institutional perspective sheds light on corporations' legitimacy issues (Deephouse and Suchman 2008), as the incomplete reach of institutionalization processes explains the difficulty for the market imaginary to secure legitimacy over the long run.

CORPORATE POLITICAL ACTIVITY AS HAVING AN INSTITUTIONAL REACH

The idea that corporations seek to shape their environment is not new (for example, Hickson et al. 1980), but has recently attracted the interest of organizational scholars (Barley 2007, 2010; Walker and Rea 2014), seeking to understand the broader implications of such phenomena. Here, we argue that through their political activities, corporations are actually modeling their institutional environment beyond the market structures in which they operate. This thus implies considering the other mechanisms through which corporations manage to constitute themselves as significant political actors of our contemporary world.

Corporations – From 'Doing Some Politics' to Being Political Actors

The CPA literature has analyzed corporations as engaging in political activity in order to influence public actors – governments, international organizations – in the hope of shaping self-serving regulations or at least avoiding too adverse regulations (Lawton et al. 2013). Scholars have successfully shown how corporations have developed sophisticated political strategies and engaged in networks of corporate lobbyism (Barley 2010; Hillman et al. 2004) in order to improve their economic performance (Lawton et al. 2013). However, this would imply that CPA does not go beyond mere lobbyism in the broad sense of the word and that corporations 'are not political actors in a strict sense' (Palazzo and Scherer 2008 p. 580).

This functionalist perspective, focusing mostly on the outcomes for policy and performance with less attention on the mechanisms underlying

CPA, may thus appear as a reduced vision of the political role of firms (Palazzo and Scherer 2008). Palazzo and Scherer (2008) stress that the influence of corporations on regulation, for instance of patent protection or on political attempts to fight global warming, contributes to building those global issues that have collective consequences and bindings. Yet, simultaneously, these corporations may present themselves as part of the solution (Nyberg et al. 2013). Indeed, addressing these issues implies collective actions where corporations hold an increasingly important place. For instance, recent studies show how 'political CSR' plays an active role in shaping global governance (Palazzo and Scherer 2008), how companies are now viewed as indispensable partners in preparing for major collective risks such as the threat of an influenza pandemic (Steyer and Gilbert 2013) or how banks play an essential role in implementing anti-money laundering (Pérezts and Picard 2015).

Therefore, corporations should not be perceived 'as depoliticized private business actors' (Palazzo and Scherer 2008 p. 580) since, whether their CPA only intends to maximize their private goals or not, they have broader impacts on society. In fact, evidence keeps building up on how corporations assume direct political responsibilities (Crane et al. 2008), where governments are unable or unwilling to intervene, filling institutional voids pertaining to basic social services in emerging countries with weak, corrupt or disorganized states (Boddewyn and Doh 2011; Calderón et al. 2009; Khanna and Palepu 2005). In fact, as Barley's (2007) and Nyberg and colleagues' (2013) studies illustrate, CPA seems in the end to be part of a wider phenomenon. These authors show that corporations are engaged in a movement seeking to establish their hegemony (Levy 2008). They detail how some corporations capture regulative agencies and take over certain things pertaining to 'public good' that were previously under the aegis of the State (for instance, the outsourcing of certain state missions and critical services to private military firms). Nonetheless, this inevitably raises the question of the corporation's legitimacy in undertaking such social functions (Palazzo and Scherer 2008), as this could constitute a drift and a danger for modern democracies (Walker and Rea 2014). This points to the need of a 'more enlarged concept of politics', that could take into account such actions by private actors (Palazzo and Scherer 2008 p. 578; Young 2004).

Therefore, in this chapter, we conceptualize corporate political activity as a series of mechanisms of a political nature exceeding in its reach and significance the simple optimization of firms' performance or maximization of their own interests. CPA may for instance involve power games (Djelic et al. 2005) aiming at shaping global governance (Scherer and Palazzo 2011) but also at imposing neoliberalism as a dominant ideology through the spread of technical and practical apparatus in organizing significant economical, but also social issues (Crouch 2011; Salles-Djelic, this volume; Nyberg et al. 2013). We thus believe that more attention should be brought to the processes by which corporations 'organize collectively to regulate or transform some aspects of their shared social conditions, along with the communicative activities in which they try to persuade one another to join such collective actions or decide what direction they wish to take' (Young 2004 p. 377). It is in that sense that beyond 'doing some politics' through activities such as lobbying for self-serving regulation in order to enhance performance (Bonardi et al. 2006), we argue that corporations can be considered as political actors in themselves.

CPA as an Institutional Activity

The roles of firms and industries as political actors thus appear rooted in deeper social, organizational and cultural processes, beyond the mere consideration of their interests in the marketplace (Levenstein 2004). Through diverse means, they in fact achieve dominance over our 'way of thinking' and organizing our social life. This claim echoes French sociologists' and Hickson and colleagues' (1980) statement that organizations, and more specifically corporations, can be seen as political actors that may constrain the behaviors of other actors in their institutional environment (Castoriadis 1975; Lallement 2008). This institutional reading of CPA is consistent with the 'enlarged concept of politics' suggested by Young (2004). We shall therefore seek to further our understanding of how corporations act politically in this broader sense and what the broader institutional impacts of their political activities are.

In the extant CPA literature, studies have mostly focused on the relational influence between institutions and CPA (Lawton et al. 2013). Yet, in line with recent studies, we argue that the main CPA identified by the literature – among which engagement in electoral politics and campaign contributions, political action committees, direct corporate lobbying, collective action through associations and coalitions (Lawton et al. 2013; Walker and Rea 2014) – demonstrate that corporate actions have a broader reach, beyond the immediate influence on and/or reaction to policy. For instance, corporations attempt and sometimes succeed in shaping the regulative framework of the institutional field in which they operate. Further actions, such as voluntary agreements (Walker and Rea 2014) could also be read as actions reflecting, maintaining or changing norms in broader environments. Finally, we suggest that when firms manipulate ('incorporate' in Nyberg and colleagues' words) individuals' identities, interests, roles and activities, in order to channel them into forms that align with corporate desiderata on specific issues – for example climate change by 'channeling citizens as responsible consumers' (Nyberg et al. 2013 p. 445) – such actions can be considered as aiming at molding the cultural-cognitive structure of a given institutional field. These different CPAs, taken together, actually depict an attempt to secure the dominance of the market imaginary as the solution to such problems, and strengthen 'a capitalist imaginary of "rationality" and "efficiency"' (Wright and Nyberg 2014 p. 4).

In this chapter, we aim at highlighting the institutionalization processes backing the increasingly dominant role of corporations in our contemporary (and global) societies. More specifically, we want to explore how corporations' political activities are contributing to maintaining and modifying institutional fields' underpinnings and, as such, are contributing to institutionalization processes. Answering these questions would contribute to better understand Nyberg and colleagues' (2013 p. 449) insight of corporations as engaged in a move paralleling the capture by the State of the civil institutions since the nineteenth century (Gramsci 1971), and also address Walker and Rea's (2014) call of further examining how different modes of corporate engagement and activism are interrelated and mutually reinforce the hegemony of corporations.

Distinguishing the Institutionalization Processes Supported by Firms' Political Actions

Institutions 'both arise from and constrain social action' (Barley and Tolbert 1997 p. 95). They are constituted by an ongoing local production and reproduction of practical understandings (Lawrence and Suddaby 2006), providing stability and meaning to social life (Scott 2008). They appear to be the enduring backbone for organized social behaviors within organizational fields (Barley and Tolbert 1997).

Institutions are sustained by three 'pillars' – regulative, normative and cultural-cognitive – that ensure legitimacy by providing a legal frame, normative support and cultural alignment (Scott 2008). These pillars keep institutions in place through a constantly rearranged equilibrium among them, possibly varying over time and predominantly supported by one or another (Caronna 2004; Wicks 2001).

Recent developments have highlighted the need for a deeper exploration of these processes of institutionalization that create, maintain and disrupt institutions through small, ongoing events and daily actions at the individual level (Lawrence and Suddaby 2006) or at the societal level (Djelic and Quack 2010). These process-oriented views thus avoid falling into a rigid structuralism that reduces the institution to 'a socializing authority, capable of infusing a set of values and norms, in a top-down movement' (Lallement 2008 p. 69, our translation).

Table 8.1 The four subprocesses of institutionalization, adapted from Lallement (2008, our translation)

Division process	Individuation process
Refers to 'the way institutions inform our judgments on the world thanks to the categories they support' (2008 p. 70). These common representations act as 'major points of reference to classify practices and individuals', and in that they structure our way to see the world (2008 p. 45).	Comes with the 'production of typical identity forms' and consists in 'instilling capacity to acquire the clearest conscience of the foundations of their action in the individuals, in such a way as to bring them progressively to moral existence and endow them with an willingness autonomy' (2008 p. 70). This explains how institutions create subjects within a collective.
Integration process	**Regulation process**
Meant to 'adjust the articulation between the individual and the society' (2008 p. 45). Institutions offer individuals anchoring within sociability spaces, they include them into a collective, sharing common values.	Refers to a collective activity of rules setting and negotiation. This rules production activity ensures the discipline within the collective, produces legitimate social hierarchies and is thus accompanied by constraints. To be legitimate, these rules must 'rely on morals that justify their existence and their effectiveness' (2008 p. 71).

With an enlarged definition of politics (Young 2004), this perspective allows focusing on the impact of CPA on surrounding environments, thereby understanding the role of corporations in modifying or maintaining their institutional fields. In this regard, Lallement's recent approach (2008), based on Durkheim's works, offers a deeper understanding of how such processes may unfold. He suggests reading institutional phenomena as constituted by a set of four interrelated institutionalizing subprocesses (see Table 8.1).

Studying a nineteenth-century experimentation, Lallement (2008) shows how Godin, a French manufacturer, tried to transform a mere factory into a whole living place for its workers including accommodation, school, shops and associations. This place, 'the Familistère', was created in order to institutionalize all life activities around a common activity structuring identity: work. While this attempt was not a complete success, illustrating the fact that institutions are never total, Lallement (2008) examines how the four aforementioned subprocesses structured workers' lives. This highlights how the cognitive, normative and regulative 'pillars' were intertwined and reinforced each other. For instance, if we consider the individuation process, Lallement (2008) underlines that the prototypical identity of Familistère's workers emerges from a professional system in which autonomy takes precedence over serving market requirements (normative pillar) rather than from an opposition to the capital, nor as an enlightened partnership of the employer. Yet, Godin's figure and leadership remain dominant. Owing the symbolic attributes of a father, no one at the Familistère really contests Godin's legitimacy, and eventually only state disagreements by leaving the room when meeting the employer (cultural-cognitive and normative pillars). This presence is even a coercive dimension in defining workers' identities as the many registers of the Familistère's shops report domestic quality of female workers as daughter of X or wife of Y, X and Y being reported as good or bad father/husband, assessing their identities' 'performance' (regulative pillar).

In fact, the four subprocesses are not sequential, but operate simultaneously to determine the efficacy of the institutional influence on individuals and collectives, as well as tensions that can alter it, at least partially (Lallement 2008 p. 71). Their concrete operating modes allow opening the 'taken-for-granted' black box of institutions and are an opportunity for enriching our understanding of CPA's impacts.

With the four subprocesses framework in mind, we will now highlight the institutionalization processes at work in the vaccine industry, and show how vaccine corporations are able both to shape the institutional field in which people vaccination takes place and to take over significant state functions.

A CASE OF CORPORATE PREDATION

Despite growing interest, the way corporations actually perform political activities is still not well understood. We consequently designed an inductive, longitudinal, field-based case study (Yin 2003), which is suitable for developing grounded theory (Glaser and Strauss 1967), and for uncovering political mechanisms that quantitative methods are unable to capture (Dieleman and Boddewyn 2012).

The study was designed with an ethnographic approach that allowed for accessing larger social processes that personal interviews may not completely cover. The approach also allowed capturing the forces bridging CPA and the larger institutional process at work (Suddaby and Greenwood 2009). We chose the vaccine industry because it is a 'revelatory' case (Yin 2003) that opens opportunities to make phenomena more transparent and temporally comparative.

Research Setting

In order to delve into the process by which private organizations shape the dynamics of their institutional field, we studied a leading corporation, who played a significant role in shaping the institutional field dedicated to the protection of people against epidemics and infectious diseases. Looking at epidemics and infectious diseases is a way to investigate the (dys)functions of our world because virus and bacteria have always accompanied humanity, strongly hitting the demography, spawning fears, social hazards, and doubts of moral references, values and virtues (Moulin 1996). Inquiring into the historical evolution of the fight against epidemics thus reflects human development, in its biological, religious, political, cultural and economical dimensions. To fulfill the social need of 'protecting people against epidemics and infectious diseases', a complex institutional field has developed over time, with many stakeholders trying to achieve different objectives, sometimes coexisting but often conflicting (see ibid.). This field thus offers a privileged observation site to grasp the role of private organizations in shaping their environment. The first author shared the organizational life of a multi-professional team dedicated to developing strategic and political affairs of VaxCorp, one of the historical leaders in the vaccine industry.

Data Collection and Analysis

Over one year, the first author collected rich and multilevel data, earning a diversified insight into VaxCorp's political activities: internal archives such as presentations and meetings minutes, and reports from hired consultants, in combination with publicly available archival material such as press releases, policy releases or competitors' and analysts' notes. This qualitative dataset was complemented with regular and subsequent interviews (all recorded) to ensure internal reliability of collected data and of the analysis that followed. Altogether, these multiple sources made it possible to grasp the global pattern behind VaxCorp's CPA.

In order to trace institutionalization processes at work in VaxCorp's CPA, we first analyzed VaxCorp's archives and other historical documents to make sense of this complex institutional and economic field. The historical analysis allowed us to map the multiple actors active in the field, their roles, relationships and actions which, together, underlie the dynamic fulfillment of the social need of protecting people against infectious diseases. Yet, our analysis reveals the recent centrality of 'vaccinology', and the way it places industrials at the center of our modern protecting apparatus. We then use Lallement's (2008) work to sharpen our analysis of the VaxCorp's political actions, and to uncover the organizing mechanisms underlying the way the world is protecting people against epidemics and infectious diseases today.

VAXCORP'S ATTEMPTS AT IMPOSING A DOMINANT IMAGINARY

The way societies have responded to epidemics over time is intrinsically linked to our beliefs about what epidemics and diseases are. From an 'act of god' to 'the outcasts' fault' to 'germ theory', we can observe that the social imaginary about these scourges is greatly determined and reinforced by the actors we consider legitimate to embody the appropriate social actions that should be taken to ensure stability to social life nevertheless. Using words and sentences collected on the field as raw material, we wrote a narrative presenting the way vaccine corporations are progressively imposing the 'vaccinology' paradigm as the dominant imaginary.

Integration Process: Building on Human Fear and War Culture

In 1977, when Dr Salk introduced the term 'vaccinology' as a new paradigm to protect people against infectious diseases, the war against smallpox was about to be won. Its basic principle lies in the belief that epidemics and infectious diseases should be fought and eradicated with vaccination campaigns mixing medical, political, social and industrial means. The proponents of this new approach, such as Dr Mérieux, CEO of the leading vaccine firm at that time, portrayed it as a war against an invisible and blind enemy – also two characteristics of terrorism – requiring a global coordination of forces. In fact, the war terminology, highlighted here, was already common in the scientific community to conceptualize how virus and bacteria survive through fighting and plundering the immune defense system, but it was also apparent in the state apparatus that has always been inclined to quarantine measures and restricted areas such as bio-safety laboratories. Even now, this modern and global imaginary about virus and epidemics has a strong hold in Western collective beliefs as it emerges from and articulates the above noted previous imaginaries associated with epidemics.

The 'vaccinology' paradigm, using the shared 'war' representation, integrates the different actors, allowing them to articulate their role and actions (Lallement 2008), while giving a key role to industrial actors. Then, unsurprisingly, corporations, with VaxCorp leading the way, became ardent advocates of the 'vaccinology' paradigm, for instance by spreading it through their affiliated research institutes and training centers.[1]

Division Process: Setting the Stage for Responding to the Threat

Following smallpox eradication and VaxInstitute's (now VaxCorp) 1974 success in containing a meningitis outbreak striking 90 million Brazilians by coordinating its industrial power with the Brazilian military logistic and World Health Organization's (WHO) medical staff, Dr Salk realized that epidemics could not be fought without industrial means and, consequently, organizing efforts had to be rethought according to the basic principle of 'vaccinology'. This reinforced the division of the field into four main categories: medical, political, social and industrial. Yet, if, taken together, these categories form a legitimate global system; under each category lies a specific logic of action.

The medical sphere described by Salk represents the health scientific community, today best represented by the WHO as 'the directing and coordinating authority for health within the United Nations system [. . .] responsible for providing leadership on global health matters, shaping the health research agenda, setting norms and standards, articulating evidence-based policy options, providing technical support to countries and monitoring and assessing health trends'.[2]

The mission of the health scientific community is operated in the political sphere through close relationships with local regulative institutions and agencies, such as Food and Drug Administrations (FDAs getting WHO certification). In fact, FDAs that ensure 'the safety, efficacy and security of health goods and services'[3] establish the link with local governmental institutions such as Ministries of Health and Centers for Disease Control, principal agencies for following disease evolution and providing essential health services.[4] The basic tenet in the political sphere is to ensure countries' stability and security in ensuring public health for citizens.

The division operates at the level of the population. This is clearly visible when there is an outbreak, as with the 2014 Ebola epidemic. When states consider citizens and suspicious outcasts, 'vaccinology' segments the population into three categories: (1) healthy people, (2) confirmed or suspected cases (of illness) and (3) patient zero. The latter category, more a concept than a reality, is tracked and studied, as 'vaccinology' assumes that finding the initial point of contagion is critical for producing vaccines with high potency.

Finally, vaccines appear to be, since Louis Pasteur, the ultimate weapon to fight the horde of pathogenic microorganisms. Yet, a significant firepower is required. The belief that the industry is more efficient in providing the needed level of effectiveness found its roots in the above-cited historical successes against outbreaks. Since the mid-twentieth century, most states have relied on industrials to supply them with qualitative and numerous, but also affordable vaccines. For instance, the WHO and UNICEF could never have implemented their Expanded Programme on Immunization (EPI) if VaxCorp and its competitors were not able to keep prices low.

In this way, 'vaccinology' has imposed several common representations that have acted as 'major points of reference to classify practices and individuals' (Lallement 2008 p. 45) in this institutional field.

INDIVIDUATION PROCESS: THE CENTRAL ROLE OF CORPORATIONS IN THE 'VACCINOLOGY' APPROACH

As the industrial corporations took more and more autonomy and traction power in the field, vaccinology in fact laid ground for a new 'subject' in the collective. However, the 'vaccinology' success would not have been possible without a myth about vaccines – the idea that any disease is due to a single pathogenic agent that vaccines can kill or at least render inefficient. This myth builds partially on VaxInstitute's actions to contain disastrous epidemics of foot and mouth disease that devastated European livestock. A vaccine had been available since 1925 but it was impossible to economically scale up the production at the level farmers required. In 1947, VaxInstitute, improving Dr Fraenckel's new *in vitro* technique, succeeded in producing up to 300,000 doses of vaccines at viable economic costs, both for the company and the farmers. Following this success, Dr Koprowski and Dr Plotkin collaborated with VaxInstitute to develop new industrial vaccines against rabies and rubella to stem these endemic diseases. VaxInstitute then started to create subsidiaries around the world to increase population access to vaccines and to be closer when outbreaks started, achieving corporate legitimacy and introducing economics into public health care.

Individuation was reinforced by the fact that new vaccine development had been proved to be proportional to the investment intensity. As the above-cited virologists, many scientists joined private organizations to find the funding necessary to accumulate knowledge, develop new vaccines and make a difference for public health. In Europe, VaxInstitute was the first to create its own advanced research center, while in US Dr Hilleman created eight of the 14 most recommended vaccines in national immunization programs, saving certainly millions of lives, but also enriching Merck & Co. Inc. for which he eventually became the scientific director. Consequently, both in France and in the US, private interests, strictly enforcing intellectual property rights and industrial secrets, gradually took control of both knowledge and knowledge-creative networks. Step by step, national laboratories were pushed to bankruptcy or acquired by corporations who became the main engine for vaccine development and forced governments and the WHO to accept vaccine producers' conditions.

These corporations also came to play a significant role in ensuring the efficiency of vaccination programs. Indeed, in many countries, where epidemics and diseases have been well controlled or even eradicated, people, through traditional media and websites, today more easily learn about deaths due to vaccines' side effects than about deaths caused by the disease. As a result, governmental vaccine policies, mixing paternalist and liberal approaches, are increasingly facing individual resistance, while they have to maintain an 80 percent coverage rate to insure population protection. Some government officials then confess their helplessness against rumors spreading through social media. Officially, corporations cannot do much about that, as they are not allowed to communicate directly with the public. Yet, while governments have difficulties to see people beyond the notion of the citizen, corporations created marketing departments in the 2000s to segment the market into coherent world regions through the analysis of prescription systems and behaviors, practitioners' expectations and population behaviors toward vaccines. They also enhanced the identification of key opinion leaders, price negotiations with health insurance companies and finally started to propose vaccination plans to governmental agencies. As a result, corporate knowledge about the social dynamics behind epidemics and infectious diseases was increasingly leveraged to influence governments not only on which vaccines should be developed but also how the vaccination policies should be organized.

As industrialization and, subsequently, privatization of vaccines developed, commercial considerations have replaced public health considerations. Industry executives rather than public health officials seem now to make decisions, as VaxCorp did when meeting M. Chen Zhu in 2011, China's minister of health, and some officials in charge of the Global Polio Eradication Initiative (GPEI):

> Polio is a highly political topic for China (incl. for security reasons). As a result, building on this contact and previous work, we should pursue a political approach at governmental level. We could start discussing this topic [. . .] and try to put together an approach very similar to the one that was developed for the nuclear industry. (VaxCorp CEO, after his meeting with Minister Zhu)

This evolution clearly stages the development of the vaccine corporations as new autonomous subjects (Lallement 2008) with their own ethics of how to organize the field.

Regulation Process: The Market as a Way to Conduct Public Health

How come corporations found in 'vaccinology' an approach that fits their industrial and commercial logic? An explanation could be that 'vaccinology' is, in many regards, pushing for the market as the only viable allocation system for protecting people against epidemics. Besides national immunization programs that are organized as a complex economic system between vaccine producers, taxpayers, governmental agencies, medical practitioners and insurance firms, the Global Alliance for Vaccines and Immunization (GAVI) ecosystem is characteristic of the marketization of preventing infectious diseases.

In the 1990s, many vaccine producers started to disinvest as expectations on affordable prices, rising R&D costs and volatile demand were rendering this business economically too risky. They were also increasingly bearing social responsibilities, leading some to bankruptcy (for instance the US Thimerosal class action lawsuits). This situation resulted in some vaccine shortages and, consequently, in a drop in vaccination coverage for a number of childhood diseases. Beyond unethical behavior (which is not our concern here), the world of vaccines had thus to find a fairer mechanism for allocating resources and responsibilities in order to improve and accelerate vaccination progress.

The GAVI was created in 2000, bringing together WHO technical expertise, buying power for UNICEF vaccines, the financial expertise of the World Bank, private donors such as the Bill & Melinda Gates Foundation, knowledge of research and development laboratories, as well as the scale-up technology of vaccine corporations. This global health initiative was conceptualized as a global marketplace where information, technologies, money and products could circulate efficiently and render possible sustainable transactions. The voice of developing countries (that is nations and local vaccine producers) and the financial power of large States such as the USA, UK and France were also fully included in the GAVI governance. From 2000 to 2010, the GAVI has helped to immunize 288 million children against six life-threatening diseases, saving five million children from a premature death.[5]

The GAVI model is now replicated everywhere. For instance, in 2014, the US FDA awarded more than $19 million 'to boost the development of medical device, drug, and biological products for patients with rare diseases, with at least a quarter of the funding going to studies focused solely on pediatrics'.[6]

In fact, this specific apparatus emerged as a new basis to regulate the interactions between the actors and the functioning of the system because corporations succeed in strengthening the central place of the market imaginary in the 'vaccinology' paradigm. The normative way of protecting people against infectious disease, corresponding to Lallement's (2008) regulation process, is now applied to other global diseases and threats, such as poliomyelitis, pandemic influenza or bioterrorism attacks.

In the end, building on Lallement's (2008) four institutionalizing sub-processes, our case reveals that 'imposing a dominant imaginary' rests upon numerous political actions. Vaccine corporations, VaxCorp leading the way, succeeded to reassemble a collective around a shared representation of the issue at hand, to structure and divide this world into specific practices and expected behaviors, enabling actors to become autonomous subjects. The dominant role played by corporations sediments and reinforces their corporate vision of 'vaccinology', pushing market mechanisms (regulative process) to articulate individual behaviors within a coherent system. The case thus shows that 'imposing a dominant imaginary' is a modus operandi that not only aims at filling the gaps left by weak institutional actors, but also at infiltrating the incompleteness of rival institutions to spread and diffuse the corporate imaginary as the basis of social organizing.

DISCUSSION AND CONCLUSION

If corporations are to be acknowledged as political actors (Palazzo and Scherer 2008), it is crucial to further understand how they concretely shape our political systems (Garsten and Sörbom this volume) – through which activities and on what issues – as well as the implications of such mechanisms (Walker and Rea 2014).

We sought to contribute to this endeavor first by arguing that corporate impact is of an institutional nature. To this end, we used a theoretical framework based on Lallement's work (2008) to open the black box of institutionalization processes pertaining to CPA. Second, we delved into a specific mechanism of what we identify as corporate predation over the imaginary to show how these political actors secure both the broader scope of their CPA and their own legitimacy in their institutional field. To do so, we built on a rich empirical illustration of how the corporate imaginary underlines what corporations do when they engage in political action and how this imaginary has shaped their institutional field over time. More specifically, by explicitly adopting our institutional perspective, we identified a corporate modus operandi that attempts to secure the dominance of corporations over other institutional actors.

Indeed, what is of particular interest in our case is the absence of weakness from the state. It is not because there is a missing institutional regulator that the corporation intervenes. CPA is instead developed in a subtler manner to exploit the weaknesses of other institutions. More than filling institutional voids (Calderón et al. 2009), our study shows that CPA may also aim at organizing the way other institutional actors implement their actions.

This institutional perspective renews the approach to explore CPA and identify other aspects of political activities until now neglected in the literature, besides 'classic' political actions already identified such as lobbying (Hillman et al. 2004). Imposing a dominant self-serving imaginary goes beyond shaping local regulations (Lawton et al. 2013) in view of enhancing performance: it aims essentially at infiltrating the incompleteness of rival institutions (Lallement 2008). More broadly speaking, in our case study, it is about diffusing the corporate imaginary as the basis of social organizing, as a mechanism towards which other actors will converge. This echoes Wright and Nyberg's (2014) work that shows how corporations attempt to secure the market imaginary as the solution for climate change. Yet, our study highlights that 'vaccinology' step by step had influenced other institutional actor's views towards the adoption of market mechanisms, illustrating the institutional predatory nature of the market and how corporations have secured the dominance over this institutional field.

In Scott's (2008) terms, we show that CPA supports the market imaginary not only through shaping the regulative pillars of an institutional field, but also by articulating them with the cultural-cognitive and the normative pillars. Our analysis points to the fact that a dominant imaginary through CPA emerges from but also intertwines institutionalizing processes into a larger and coherent pattern, which eventually legitimizes corporations' dominance in an institutional field. To the extent that this addresses Walker and Rea's (2014) call, we wonder about the intention behind the political actions of corporations. Our case shows that corporations' members, beyond the organization, acknowledge having a political role, more than implementing simple political activity toward the mere quest of financial performance. What we describe here may appear to be *political activism*, which can be defined as a purposive action by an organization to influence and to transform its institutional field durably. In this sense, organizations are not only interpretative mechanisms but also 'institutional architects' (Hay and Wincott 1998 p. 955).

In the end, this case allows an even deeper theoretical reflection on corporate legitimacy through the globalization of corporate imaginary

(Deephouse and Suchman 2008). Indeed, regulatory changes appear to be just the 'tip' of the political efforts deployed by the corporation. Imposing a dominant imaginary leads to a complex and partly overlapping ongoing process defining new rules and their crystallization by regulation practices in order to shape the way actions and behaviors are organized in specific institutional fields (Caronna 2004; Wicks 2001). However, the resistance against vaccine and vaccination expressed by some individuals demonstrated that the institutionalization processes at work are never complete (Lallement 2008). This appears because vaccine corporations by law do not have a direct access to individuals and because states are caught in the category of citizens, unable to grasp others. The incompleteness of institutions thus makes total hegemony unlikely, explaining, despite predation strategies, the difficulty for an institution, including the market, to secure its legitimacy in the long run. Legitimation processes will always be ongoing, and unfinished, leaving space for resistance and contestation.

In other words, we argue that becoming a dominant institution is a multidimensional phenomenon. It appears when necessary to link and align all the forms into one coherent framework or (predation) strategy to eventually dominate a sphere of activity, albeit temporally, in a continuously evolving process, until other actors manage to impose another imaginary.

NOTES

1. http://www.euripred.eu/news-events/news/news-message/vaccinology-in-africa-a-five-day-masters-level-course.html. Accessed 12 December 2014.
2. http://www.who.int/about/en/. Accessed 12 December 2014.
3. http://www.fda.gov/AboutFDA/WhatWeDo/default.htm. Accessed 12 December 2014.
4. http://www.cdc.gov/. Accessed 12 December 2014.
5. http://www.gavi.org/library/audio-visual/saving-childrens-lives-pledging-conference/. Accessed 13 December 2014.
6. http://www.fda.gov/newsevents/newsroom/pressannouncements/ucm416738.htm. Accessed 13 December 2014.

REFERENCES

Barley, S.R. (2007), 'Corporations, democracy, and the public good', *Journal of Management Inquiry*, **16** (3), 201–15.

Barley, S.R. (2010), 'Building an institutional field to corral a government: a case to set an agenda for organization studies', *Organization Studies*, **31**, 777–805.

Barley, S.R. and P.S. Tolbert (1997), 'Institutionalization and structuration: studying the links between action and institution', *Organization Studies*, **18** (1), 93–117.

Boddewyn, J.J. and J. Doh (2011), 'Global strategy and the collaboration of MNEs, NGOs and the provisioning of collective goods in emerging markets', *Global Strategy Journal*, **1**, 345–61.
Bonardi, J.P., G.L.F. Holburn and R.G. Vanden Bergh (2006), 'Nonmarket strategy performance: evidence from U.S. electric utilities', *Academy of Management Journal*, **38**, 288–303.
Calderón, R., J.L. Álvarez-Arce and S. Mayoral (2009), 'Corruption as a crucial ally against corruption', *Journal of Business Ethics*, **87**, 319–32.
Caronna, C.A. (2004), 'The misalignment of institutional "pillars": consequences for the US health care field', *Journal of Health and Social Behavior*, 45–58.
Castoriadis, C. (eds) (1975), *L'institution imaginaire de la société*. Paris: Seuil.
Crane, A., D. Matten and J. Moon (eds) (2008), *Corporations and Citizenship*, New York: Cambridge University Press.
Crouch, C. (2011), *The Strange Non-Death of Neoliberalism*, Cambridge: Polity.
Deephouse, D.L. and M. Suchman (2008), 'Legitimacy in organizational institutionalism', in R. Greenwood, C. Oliver, R. Suddaby and K. Sahlin-Andersson (eds), *The Sage Handbook of Organizational Institutionalism*. London: Sage Publications, pp. 49–77.
Dieleman, M. and J.J. Boddewyn (2012), 'Using organization structure to buffer political ties in emerging markets: a case study', *Organization Studies*, **33** (1), 71–95.
Djelic, M.L., B. Nooteboom and R. Whitley (2005), 'Introduction: dynamics of interaction between institutions, markets and organizations', *Organization Studies*, **26**, 1733–41.
Djelic, M.L. and S. Quack (eds) (2010), *Transnational Communities: Shaping Global Economic Governance*, Cambridge: Cambridge University Press.
Glaser, B.G. and A.L. Strauss (1967), *The Discovery of Grounded Theory: Strategies for Qualitative Research*, Chicago, IL: Aldin.
Gramsci, A. (1971), *Selections from the Prison Notebooks*, New York, NY: International Publishers.
Hay, C. and D. Wincott (1998), 'Structure, agency and historical institutionalism', *Political Studies*, **46** (5), 951–57.
Hickson, D., F. Agersnap, F. Ferraresi, G. Hofstede, A. Kieser, and C.T.J. Lammers (1980), 'Editorial', *Organization Studies*, **1**, 1–2.
Hillman, A.J. and M.A. Hitt (1999), 'Corporate political strategy formulation: a model of approach, participation, and strategy decisions', *Academy of Management Review*, **24**, 825–42.
Hillman, A.J., G. Keim and D. Schuler (2004), 'Corporate political activity: a review and research agenda', *Journal of Management*, **30**, 837–57.
Khanna, T. and K. Palepu (2005), 'Spotting institutional voids in emerging markets', *Harvard Business School Teaching Note* 106014.
Lallement, M. (2008), 'L'entreprise est-elle une institution? Le cas du Familistère de Guise', *Revue Française de Socio-Economie*, **1**, 67–87.
Lawrence, T.B. and R. Suddaby (2006), 'Institutions and institutional work', in S. Clegg, C. Hardy, T.B. Lawrence and W.B. Nord (eds), *The Sage Handbook of Organization Studies*, London: Sage, pp. 215–54.
Lawton, T., S. McGuire and T. Rajwani (2013), 'Corporate political activity: a literature review and research agenda', *International Journal of Management Reviews*, **15** (1), 86–105.
Levenstein, M.C. (2004), 'Review of *Organizing America: Wealth, Power, and the*

Origins of Corporate Capitalism by Charles Perrow', *Business History*, **46** (2), 661–3.
Levy, D.L. (2008), 'Political contestation in global production networks', *Academy of Management Review*, **33** (4), 943–62.
Moulin, A-M. (1996), *L'aventure de la vaccination*, Paris: Fayard.
Nyberg, D., A. Spicer and C. Wright (2013), 'Incorporating citizens: corporate engagement with climate change in Australia', *Organization*, **20**, 443–53.
Palazzo, G. and A.G. Scherer (2008), 'Towards a new theory of the firm as a political actor', in A.G. Scherer and G. Palazzo (eds) (2008), *The Handbook of Research on Global Corporate Citizenship*, Cheltenham: Edward Elgar Publishing, pp. 577–90.
Pérezts, M. and S. Picard (2015), 'Compliance or comfort zone? The work of embedded ethics in performing regulation', *Journal of Business Ethics*, **131** (4), 833–52.
Scherer, A.G. and G. Palazzo (2011), 'The new political role of business in a globalised world: a review of a new perspective on CSR and its implications for the firm, governance and democracy', *Journal of Management Studies*, **48**, 899–931.
Scott, W.R. (2008), *Institutions and Organizations*, London: Sage Publications.
Steyer, V. and C. Gilbert (2013), 'Exploring the ambiguous consensus on public–private partnerships in collective risk preparation', *Sociology of Health & Illness*, **35** (2), 292–303.
Suddaby, R. and R. Greenwood (2009), 'Methodological issues in researching institutional change', in D. Buchanan and A. Bryman (eds), *The Sage Handbook of Organizational Research Methods*, London: Sage Publications, pp. 177–95.
Walker, E.T. and C.M. Rea (2014), 'The political mobilization of firms and industries', *Annual Review of Sociology*, **40** (1), 281–304.
Wicks, D. (2001), 'Institutionalized mindsets of invulnerability: differentiated institutional fields and the antecedents of organizational crisis', *Organization Studies*, **22**, 659–92.
Wright, C. and D. Nyberg (2014), 'Creative self-destruction: corporate responses to climate change as political myths', *Environmental Politics*, **23** (2), 205–23.
Yin, R.K. (2003), *Case Study Research: Designs and Methods*, California: Sage Publications.
Young, I.M. (2004), 'Responsibility and global labor justice', *The Journal of Political Philosophy*, **12**, 365–88.

9. Political chocolate: branding it fairtrade

Renita Thedvall

INTRODUCTION: THE DYNAMICS OF STANDARDIZATION

The purchasing and logistics manager, Tom, and I meet the production manager, Lars, in the Chocolate Hall. It is in the older part of the building and the hall smells of chocolate. It is bright with beige/white machines and walls. Here, the cocoa butter, cocoa mass, sugar and other ingredients are mixed into chocolate. The mixed ingredients are transported on a long conveyer belt that takes up a large part of the room. There are two workers in the room. One of them is sitting in the control room in the Chocolate Hall making sure that the right recipe is mixed. The other moves along the conveyor belt checking the mixed ingredients. On the conveyer belt, the ingredients are milled to get rid of the grittiness. The goal is to get the grain size down to between 20 and 22 μm.[1] If it is 24 it gets too dry and if its lower it gets too wet. The milled chocolate is then transported on another conveyer belt to the so-called conch. The conches in the factory are six-ton tanks with a big dough mixer inside. In the conch, the rest of the cocoa butter is added (40 per cent), as well as fat and flavouring. The main purpose of the conch, however, is to get rid of water. The chocolate is conched for five hours and then transported to a tank for storage before it is pumped to the Chocolate Moulding.

The Chocolate Moulding is in the new part of the building, with stainless steel machines, white walls and a conveyor belt that takes up most of the room. In the Chocolate Moulding, the chocolate is moulded into a chocolate bar. Before the actual moulding, ingredients are added to the chocolate. Axel, one of the workers in the factory oversees the moulding machine and pours additional ingredients into the batch of chocolate, in this case cashew nuts. When it is properly mixed the chocolate is poured into the mould and then transported on the conveyer belt into the vibrator and cooling tunnel, to vibrate the chocolate into the mould and cool it to make it solid. After, it is released from the mould and moved on a conveyor belt to the wrapping and packeting downstairs. Here, we find Stefan who oversees the final step of the production process. The chocolate bars continue on the conveyor belt and go through a metal detector to make sure that there are no unwanted materials in them, before they are neatly separated and move into the flowpack machine to be covered by the carefully chosen branded wrapping, including the fairtrade label, around the chocolate bar.

A description of a production process of conventional chocolate would be identical. It would seem a simple affair to turn a conventional chocolate bar into fairtraded. According to the trade standards by Fairtrade International, which qualified the Swedish chocolate factory to use the faritrade mark on their chocolate bar, they only had to exchange conventional cocoa and sugar with fairtraded in the production process. On the factory floor, however, this process did not turn out simple at all and it brought a number of political concerns to the surface. In fact, the chocolate factory's choice to use an ethical label on one of its products brought a whole set of political discussions, as well as new priorities within the factory. The political in this context was not primarily the words and values in the fairtrade standards documents and certification criteria being implemented as part of the CSR strategy of the chocolate factory, but the fact that the fairtrade label, and its standards and compliance criteria, opened a space for politics in the chocolate factory, where issues of marketability and political ideals within the factory and ideals of fairtrade became intertwined, negotiated and navigated. The purpose of this chapter is to demonstrate the dynamics of standardization (Brunsson et al. 2012) when implementing fairtrade standards in a chocolate factory. What world views and ideals are embedded in Fairtrade International's fairtrade standards? How are these world views and ideals negotiated and navigated in relation to economic issues of marketability as well as other political ideals present in the factory?

During the last decades, we have seen an accelerating number of social and environmental labels on consumer products mediating political ideals of global solidarity and sustainable development through market mechanisms. The circulation of products with political language in the form of standards and compliance criteria is a vital part of today's global markets (Brunsson and Jacobsson 2000). These neoliberal forms of capitalism, with reduced role of states in transnational governance issues, the deregulation of markets and the increased role for the private sector to bring solutions, make room for standard-setting organizations such as Fairtrade International (Harvey 2005; Jaffee 2007; West 2012). Labelling is in line with global trends of non-governmental organizations regulating more and more areas, every so often formerly regulated by states or international agreements (for example Besky 2014; West 2012).

The label focused on in this chapter is the fairtrade mark defined by Fairtrade International. Fairtrade International is a multi-stakeholder organization made up of national labelling organizations, producer networks and so-called experts. Fairtrade International writes standards for fairtrade, which are audited and certified by FLOCERT. It is the words written, and the values they embody, as evinced in Fairtrade International's fairtrade standards documents and FLOCERT's compliance criteria documents, that make fairtrade labelled products into a political affair. Still, the circulation of words and values in the standards and certification criteria are never complete or unproblematic. As has been pointed out by scholars, the implementation of standards by audits and certification processes are often a result of translation and adjustment to local rule (Brunsson and Jacobsson 2000; Czarniawska and Sevon 1996). Brunsson et al. (2012) point to the fact that standards may appear stable, but that the adoption of standards is often a dynamic process. In the case studied here, it involves adjustments and negotiations of the fairtrade standards in relation to both economic and political concerns in the factory.

The chapter is based on three occasions of participant observation in the chocolate factory as well as six interviews, of which four are with management and two with factory workers. In addition, document studies of Fairtrade International's standards documents and FLOCERT's compliance criteria documents are used.[2] In the interviews I asked questions such as why the chocolate factory decided to use the fairtrade label, if it was important that it was fairtrade labelled or if it was sufficient that it was fairtrade, how they saw the market for fairtraded chocolate and if there was difference in the manufacturing of fairtrade labelled products and conventional products. The participant observation was performed in the chocolate factory by following the production of chocolate bars through the production line from the arrival of raw material to the finished chocolate bar. This was done at three occasions. The first occasion was in the production of conventional chocolate bars. The following two were when fairtrade labelled chocolate bars were manufactured. To complement the study I have also completed six interviews – in relation to the standard and compliance criteria documents – with employees at Fairtrade International and five interviews at FLOCERT in 2009 and 2011.

In the following sections, I first describe Fairtrade International and its labelling scheme in relation to the chocolate factory. Second, I show the world views and ideals that are embedded in Fairtrade International's fairtrade standards documents and what political message the label conveys. In the main part of the chapter, I present how the chocolate factory's management discuss and negotiate the ideals embedded in the fairtrade label with their own political and economic concerns as well as how these ideals are navigated on the factory floor. Finally, I conclude by discussing how the factory ended up with its own position on how to standardize and how that came to affect the business of producing political chocolate.

FAIRTRADE INTERNATIONAL AND THE FAIRTRADE LABEL

Characteristic of labelling schemes is that they are voluntary, but binding for those who decide to join. As Brunsson et al. (2012) write: 'A standard can be defined as a rule for common and voluntary use, decided by one or several people or organizations' (2012 p. 616). In the case of Fairtrade International, its aim is to regulate the production processes of producers in the Global South through standards-setting and audit processes based on Fairtrade International's world view regarding acceptable working conditions and development. In this way, the standards serve as a regulatory method – as legal documents within the framework of Fairtrade International's members (compare Brunsson and Jacobsson 2000; Lampland and Star 2009; Tamm Hallström 2004). This regulatory method is also known as soft law (Mörth 2004), which in contrast to hard law is only binding for its voluntary members and there is often no possibility of sanctions other than exclusion (Besky 2014; Jaffee 2007). Instead, there is a need for proof of compliance beforehand through audits rather than trusting producers to follow the law; what Snyder describes as regulation by publication (1994 p.199).

In these regulation by publication processes, working conditions, participation, transparency and environment, to mention a few of the wordings in the Fairtrade International's standards, are classified and made measurable by compliance criteria to show compliance and performance – the bureaucratic heart of neoliberalism (Power 1997; Rose and Miller 1992; Shore and Wright 2000). The language of compliance and performance is based on the logic presented by Power (1997) and Strathern (2000) two decades ago, in their descriptions of the audit society and audit cultures. As both authors noted, the need for auditing is based on a lack of trust in the production process, in this case keeping to the fairtrade standards, and a tendency to place trust in evaluations, preferably in the form of seemingly objective and politically neutral compliance criteria, in this case numbered 1–5. On the other hand, there is an integrated distrust in these verification markets (Tamm Hallström and Gustafsson 2014) where certifiers such as FLOCERT tend to seek accreditation from accreditors, which lays the ground for the 'governance spirals' that now have become the norm in the management of state bureaucracies as well as in international, non-governmental and transnational organizations (Botzem and Hofmann 2010; Djelic and Sahlin-Andersson 2006; Power 1997). This is also the case for FLOCERT's certification, which became ISO 65 accredited by the International Organization for Standardization (ISO) in 2004 in order to create trust in its certification.

The fairtrade movement has been active since the 1940s, but it was not until 1988 that the first fairtrade label was introduced, in the format of the Max Havelaar label (Netherlands). This change is in the literature referred to as the shift from the alternative trade-dominant movement to the certification/labelling-dominant movement when social movements became engaged in markets by developing labels, standards and audit criteria rather than working against the market (see Raynolds et al. 2007). Many of the national fairtrade labelling organizations of the Global North, such as Rättvisemärkt in Sweden, Transfair in Italy and Max Havelaar began to cooperate, and in 1997 the cooperation was formalized into the Fairtrade Labelling Organization International (FLO), or, as it is now referred to, Fairtrade International. In the beginning, the membership constituted only the national fairtrade labelling organizations of the Global North, but in 2007 the producers of the Global South also became members of Fairtrade International. They organized themselves into three producer networks according to region: Africa, Asia and Latin America. It is only countries in these regions, which are also included on the OECD's DAC list[3] that are part of Fairtrade International's geographical scope. In other words, it is only products from these regions and countries that may be fairtrade labelled.

In 2002, Fairtrade International developed its own fairtrade label,[4] which most national fairtrade labelling organizations now use, especially since 2011 when the newly designed fairtrade label provided Fairtrade International with its current brand mark. The fairtrade label, or fairtrade mark[5] as it is officially referred to within Fairtrade International, is licensed to producers and traders. With the launch of the label in 2002, Fairtrade International began to write fairtrade standards and compliance criteria used to certify producers and traders. In 2004, however, the organization divided Fairtrade International into the standard-setting body, Fairtrade International and the certification body, FLOCERT. As mentioned, this change occurred partly because FLOCERT became ISO 65 accredited, an accreditation that requires standard-setting and certifying organizations to be separated. FLOCERT thus became an independent ISO accredited profit-making organization that certifies producers and traders according to Fairtrade International's fairtrade standards.

FLOCERT audits the product of a producer and/or trader, and measures compliance[6] by translating the standards into measurable categories and determining a grade average for each standard. This translation process is made by FLOCERT and is the product of FLOCERT, but with input from Fairtrade International, for example through their mutual observation status in Fairtrade International's Standard Committee and FLOCERT's Certification Committee. Compliance and performance is measured on a scale from 1 to 5. For the core principles of the standards the organizations must receive a grade of at least 3.0 on each standard and core principles must be met from year zero. A grade average of at least 3.0 is required on the development principles, and some of these principles must be fulfilled within three years and some within six years.

Through the entire commodity chain, FLOCERT handles the certification process by way of measuring compliance, in both the Global North and Global South. The idea is that the product is certified according to the standards that apply throughout the whole chain, from producer to consumer. If a chocolate factory in the Global North wants a fairtrade label for its products it must use fairtrade labelled ingredients. For the chocolate bars to be fairtrade labelled, the cocoa and sugar – as well as cashew nuts in one of the chocolate bars – must be produced by a farm in the Global South (within Fairtrade International's geographical scope) that is fairtrade certified according to the generic standards for small producer organizations and the specific product standards for cocoa, sugar and cashew nuts. A trader in the Global North that turns cocoa into cocoa butter and cocoa mass, must be certified by the trade standards, as do the refineries in the Global North that refine the sugar. The chocolate factory must also comply with the generic trade standards.

The certification is sold to producers and traders by FLOCERT, and there are different certification fees for producers and traders in the Global South versus the Global North. Traders and producers in the Global North are also required to pay a Fairtrade minimum price. It is a floor price that covers, or should cover, average production costs.[7] If the minimum price is higher than the market price, buyers of the fairtrade labelled product in question must pay the minimum price in order to be permitted to use the fairtrade label. Furthermore, traders and producers in the Global North are obliged to pay a Fairtrade Premium that producers in the Global South must invest in developing their business, workers, if any, and/or their local communities.

STANDARDIZING FAIRTRADE

The fairtrade standard is based on the idea that trade will bring development to producers in the Global South. They are expected to be entrepreneurial using the fairtrade brand to elevate themselves from poverty (Besky 2014; Fridell 2007). Compared to other social and environmental labels the concept of development is particularly pertinent for the fairtrade label. In Fairtrade International's view, poverty is understood as the 'lack of effective integration into the market economy' (Lyon 2011 p.15), and the organization trusts that production and trade will solve problems of poverty. Patrick at FLOCERT declared: 'It is not charity it's trade' (February 2009). The trade is, however, conditioned by setting up standards for what fair development is in the Global South.

According to Fairtrade International's standards, the cocoa farm, sugar plantation and/or cashew grower should, for example, have an employment policy, practice freedom of labour, freedom of association and collective bargaining, care for occupational health and safety, produce no genetically modified organisms, restrict the use of agrochemicals, prevent soil erosion and think of economically strengthening the organization (Fairtrade International 2009a). In addition, cashew growers need to be protected from cashew nut liquid, as written under the heading of occupational health and safety in the specific product standard (Fairtrade International 2009b). The wordings in Fairtrade International's standards documents necessarily involve comprehensive social simplifications, in Scott's (1998) terminology, in that they need to be transferrable into different contexts, may it be cocoa farmers in Ghana, a sugar plantation in Malawi or a cashew nut grower in Brazil. Words such as transparency or non-discrimination have a global quality to them, without fixed meaning, and seen as moveable across organizational contexts. There is also an assumption that producers in the Global North already have established national laws and regulations for transparency, democracy, non-discrimination, collective bargaining and so forth at their production sites, which is visible in the fact that producers in the Global North are mainly certified against traceability of ingredients.

In terms of fairtrade, average consumers in the Global North are unlikely to be concerned with the actual wording of fairtrade standards. Still, it is expected that consumers have an idea of what fairtrade could stand for. This is at least what Fairtrade International aim for when trying to attract activist or political consumers that use their buying power to try to affect global labour and trade relations (Fisher 2007; Micheletti 2003). For political consumers, the idea of sustainable development – the need to include the environmental, the social and the economic in development of economy, industry, energy, food security, ecosystems (WCED 1987) – is most likely taken for granted as a vision for the future. These consumers would presumably be familiar with and assume that most of the wordings in the table of contents are part of Fairtrade International's fairtrade standards (Fairtrade International 2009a), for instance, transparency, participation, democracy, non-discrimination, biodiversity, pest management, freedom of labour. The universalism of these global policy concepts is in many ways a prerequisite for the fairtrade label to operate in global markets, since most political consumers of fairtrade commodities are likely to associate the standards with these words or words like them, even if they do not know the exact wordings of the principles of the standard. The global policy concepts are also multivocal, allowing for a breadth of interpretations. This makes it possible to appeal to a wide range of political consumers.

The fact that the label could attract a wide range of political consumers was also a determining factor for the choice of using the fairtrade label on the chocolate bar at the chocolate factory. It was part of what made the fairtrade label economically attractive for a producer in the Global North. Still, it was not without negotiation. When the fairtrade standards entered the chocolate factory it opened a space for politics where the chocolate factory's political ideals and economic concerns were brought to the fore.

NEGOTIATING FAIRTRADE IDEALS IN THE CHOCOLATE FACTORY

The decision to use the fairtrade label for one of its chocolate bars had been the subject of long discussions among the managers at the chocolate factory in question. The management of the factory understood itself as having been in the business of CSR for a long time. As many other factories during the turn of the twentieth century they built a whole industrial community around the factory. Houses for employees were erected. The industrial community had their own bus and bank. As Carl, the CEO, said:

> So, there's a legacy in the company to take social responsibility, which at the time was taken in all the locations [in which there were factories], but has since expanded to the province, to Sweden and Europe and in the end the World. So these CSR issues, what we internally call *corporate responsibility* are something that we have worked hard on and we think it's an important part of what the factory stands for. We want to build our business on values. (Interview, May 2010)

Still, it was not the CSR issues that were the crucial factor for choosing to use the fairtrade label on one of its products. The chocolate factory was in the process of developing a new milk chocolate bar. It was a difficult segment, Carl, the CEO, and Tom, the purchasing and logistics manager, explained to me, since a competing factory had almost a monopoly, like a patent on milk chocolate bars. To carve a space for themselves within this segment they had to do something special, they thought. First, they had had other ideas like building on their history and heritage and using old recipes from the nineteenth century, but finally they decided to go for a CSR label. Most of the CSR labelled chocolate bars belonged to the so-called premium section, so they were made with dark chocolate. There was no fairtrade labelled milk chocolate bar in Sweden and this could make it possible to break into this segment of the market, they thought. At first they had an idea of making their own CSR label, but abandoned it. Carl, the CEO, clarified:

> And then there were some wild ideas to do a label of our own called 'fair worlds' or something like that. Then we pretty soon realized that we would never be able to market the Chocolate Bar *and* our own label. Then, we looked at some other international labelling systems: Rainforest Alliance and UTZ. We were thinking of the green issues. We wanted to work to improve farming conditions. These types of issues, environmental issues, the working conditions for farmers in poor countries. It's difficult to choose and say that this is more important than the other. But I think the deciding factor in the end was the cocoa bean and cocoa farmers' working conditions, since it's in some way the heart of our business. (Interview, May 2010)

Carl and Tom spoke lovingly about the cocoa bean and showed a genuine interest in the working conditions on the cocoa bean farms. They did, however, have some difficulties attending to the other demands that using the fairtrade label would bring, such as the need to use sugar from the Global South. Most sugar in the Global South comes from sugar canes, while the chocolate factory got its sugar from locally produced sugar beets. Carl, the CEO, was irritated when he said:

> We had a discussion about this sugar cane issue. We had a hard time accepting that we should buy sugar canes from Brazil when the whole county is full of sugar. From an environmental point of view one can also ask oneself: Is it so wise to transport sugar across the globe? (Interview, May 2010)

For this reason, they considered using the UTZ label, because it was possible to become UTZ certified with regards only to cocoa. But UTZ was not as well known as fairtrade and that became the deciding factor. Some of the political concerns they had with fairtrade had to give way to economic interests and marketing strategies. The fairtrade label was, in this way, used as a brand to promote a new product, to make their way into a difficult segment, while at the same time highlighting the factory's political concern for the cocoa bean growers. The fact that they also had to use sugar canes from the Global South had to be handled. The fairtrade ideals needed to be adjusted into the production process on the factory floor to suit the ideals that the factory wanted to support.

NAVIGATING FAIRTRADE IDEALS ON THE FACTORY FLOOR

Tom, the purchasing and logistics manager, and I walked to the entrance of the factory. It consisted of a brass fence decorated with cocoa beans in natural size. Outside, there was a changing room that included blue protective coats and disposable hats for guests. I put on a coat, removed my jewellery, putting it in a locker and hid my hair in a combined white hat and hairnet. Right at the entrance there were blue plastic socks to put on shoes. Tom put his card on the card machine and entered a code to get in. As we walked along what the workers called 'the walkway of sighs', I noticed the Lean whiteboard on the side where the staff met every morning to go through what had happened in the production lines during the last 24 hours. At the end of the corridor we washed our hands before we entered through a white door into heart of the factory where the chocolate bars were being produced.

It was in the production line, in the raw material supply storage area, the Chocolate Hall, the Chocolate Moulding and the wrapping and packeting that fairtrade ideals had to be navigated in relation to economic concerns and the political ideals that the factory wanted to uphold. The chocolate factory's fairtrade chocolate bars were certified according to the trade standards of 2010 and the main focus of FLOCERT's auditors was the traceability of cocoa, sugar and cashew nuts. There needed to be physical traceability of the cashew nuts in the production line, while this was not needed in regards to cocoa and sugar. The traceability of cocoa had an exception for physical traceability. The standards document read:

> During the first year of application of this standard further research will ascertain whether or to what degree the principle of physical traceability is achievable. Until a decision is taken on the outcome of this research, operators are exempt from physical traceability requirements. Requirements on traceability through documentation must still be complied with. (Fairtrade International 2009d)

From the perspective of FLOCERT's auditors then, it was initially not important if the cocoa in the fairtrade chocolate bars was fairtraded as long as the amount of fairtrade cocoa that entered into production corresponded to the amount of cocoa that was needed to produce the actual fairtrade chocolate bar. Thus, Fairtrade International did not demand physical traceability though they wanted the manufacturers and producers in the Global North to aim for it. Yet, the chocolate factory's management found it difficult both in relation to consumers and staff not to aim for physical traceability of cocoa. The political ideals regarding cocoa and the factory's concern for the working conditions on cocoa farms made it difficult not to ascertain physical traceability of cocoa, the soul of chocolate bar production. They did not have the same concerns for sugar, which as explained earlier did not go as well with the ideals already present in the factory when they decided to use fairtrade.

Nevertheless, the physical traceability of cocoa did create some difficulties in the production process. In the conventional production of chocolate bars, the cocoa butter and cocoa mass were pumped into the 30-ton tanks directly from a bulk truck. This would not be possible with regard to the fairtrade chocolate because of the small production. Tom, the purchasing and logistics manager, said: 'Our process is designed for cocoa being pumped into large tanks by bulk trucks. The fairtrade production we do here is relatively small and that means we can't take it in liquid form' (Interview, May 2010).

Tom continued and explained that the bulk truck could not deliver small volumes of cocoa mass and cocoa butter since it needed to fill its tanks in order to create stability. Instead, they had to buy the fairtrade cocoa butter in 25-kilo stocks, and the cocoa mass in pellets and melt it in the factory. Returning to the factory, when Tom and I toured the factory floor, we situated ourselves on the loading dock. In comparison to the brightness of the Chocolate Hall, the loading dock was dark. There were seven one-ton tanks scattered on the dock crowding the place. Peter, one of the workers at the chocolate factory, had started to fill a tank with cocoa mass pellets and had already filled five of them. He was standing on a tray turned upside down trying to reach the hole in which to direct the big hose attached to the truck outside. He was bent over, looking down the hole to make sure that it was completely filled before he closed the hose, sealed the tank and moved to the next one. Tom explained to me that they would only use three of these tanks for this round of producing fairtrade chocolate bars. The rest would be saved for a later occasion. The three-ton tanks would be heated and it would take about three days before they could be used.

A few days later it was time to make fairtrade chocolate bars. I met Lars, one of the workers, in the Chocolate Hall in the older part of the building smelling like chocolate. The beige/white machines were set to mix the cocoa butter, cocoa mass, sugar and other ingredients into chocolate. The cocoa butter and the cocoa mass was fairtrade labelled. The sugar, however, should have been fairtrade labelled but was not.

Fairtrade labelled sugar needed be farmed in an area that was within Fairtrade International's geographical scope, in this case mainly the Global South. As mentioned, the managers at the chocolate factory were for a while thinking of creating their own label named 'fair worlds' or 'fair and close by', for this reason. It was not just because of the geographical distance, but also because it was difficult to get a hold of sugar in the right colour – it was too yellow – and with the right bacteriological requirements. Tom explained to me why they had not been able to find fairtrade labelled sugar:

> It's a combination of bacteriological requirements and particle size or granulation size on sugar. And also the manner in which the sugar is delivered to us. We have a production system that's adapted to sugar supplies in bulk. There comes a truck with sugar and then the sugar is blown into our silos. Most of the fairtrade sugar today comes in small bags, 25 kg. It's possible to get one-ton bags, but our production doesn't support these bag sizes. We have to get supplies in a bulk truck for it to work. So based on these three parameters, the way it gets here, bacteriological problems and granulation size we can't find a fairtraded sugar. And we have really looked properly. We have probably asked all sugar producers in Europe as well as sugar producers outside Europe, and haven't found anything that matches our need. (Interview, May 2010)

While the chocolate factory aimed for physical traceability on cocoa they did not regarding sugar. There was not the same affection for or understanding of sugar as for cocoa. The politics around sugar had more to do with the idea of transporting sugar long distances. They advocated using local sugar from beets grown in Sweden rather than sugar canes transported from the Global South. Also, the fact that they did not aim for physical traceability on sugar made it even more important to have the right colour of sugar. Sugar was transported from a silo and pumped into different production lines, and it was important not to have yellow candy foam when they wanted it to be white, as explained by Tom.

The chocolate factory had been given an exemption and as compensation they had to pay a Fairtrade Premium to a sugar cane cooperative in Malawi, but they were worried what would happen if the exemption were not to be continued. The only refinery in Europe that refined sugar canes was located in the United Kingdom. Tom, the purchasing and logistics manager continued by saying that the refineries in the United Kingdom handled sugar canes by tradition, because of their colonial history importing from the colonies (Interview, September 2010). The consensus at the factory seemed to be that the sugar refineries did not want to move into each other's markets, and Nordic Sugar had no interest in refining sugar canes if the demand did not increase considerably. At the factory they were not sure what to do. Carl, the CEO, exclaimed with a dejected voice: 'We don't really know what to do at all with fairtrade. It's this sugar cane issue. If there's no solution, then we don't know . . .' (Interview, May 2010).

The solution proposed by Fairtrade International was to produce more fairtrade labelled products. In response to this Carl, the CEO, said that if they would change their whole production into fairtrade then Nordic

Sugar would happily deliver refined fairtrade sugar canes, but he added that there was no market for such a change. He said:

> But it's a decision that can't be made, because there's no market, no demand. There's no price acceptance from customers and if we don't raise the price then there's no factory anymore. Fairtrade is, after all, still a niche in our segment. Chocolate is still pretty small. This is the first milk chocolate bar of significant size that is fairtrade labelled. (Interview, May 2010)

For the fairtrade auditors from FLOCERT, it was important that the amount of cocoa in the fairtrade chocolate bars that were manufactured and sold should not exceed the amount of fairtrade cocoa that goes into the factory. This would certainly not be the case at the time when I was there, because of the 17000 chocolate bars ordered from sales they were only able to manufacture 15049. Some of the fairtrade chocolate was left in the tank and in the pipes that transported the chocolate from storage, which meant that there was not enough chocolate to make 17000 chocolate bars. The fairtrade chocolate left in the tanks and pipes would thus be sold as conventional chocolate.

Furthermore, the response from customers was not what the chocolate factory had hoped for, both Carl, the CEO, and Tom, the purchasing and logistics manager stated. Within the walls of the factory this was also a story I heard several times. The retailers wanted it, the customers said they wanted it, but at the moment of buying they did not buy it. Stefan, one of the workers on the factory floor, sighed and said that he was informed to produce 17000 and at first he thought it was 17000 cartons, but soon realized that it was only 17000 chocolate bars. In the end, the chocolate factory stopped their production of fairtrade milk chocolate bars. In 2012, the chocolate bar had disappeared from the production line and was no longer present in the organizational story on the chocolate factory's website. The market for fairtrade chocolate was not what the factory had hoped for. In addition, the complicated political navigations due to the factory's focus on traceability of cocoa and the conversion costs they created both in terms of damaging working conditions for people, such as Peter at the loading dock, and the production loss it created when resetting production strained the business of political chocolate.

CONCLUSION: THE POLITICS OF FAIRTRADE STANDARDS IN THE BUSINESS OF CHOCOLATE

The chapter has shown the dynamics of standardization by bringing to the fore the politics of fairtrade standards, not only in the standards themselves, but also on the factory floor of a Swedish chocolate factory producing fairtrade chocolate bars. The business of complying with the standards opened a space for politics in the chocolate factory where issues of marketability and political ideals of fairtrade and ideals within the factory became intertwined, negotiated and navigated. In this way, the adoption of the standards became a dynamic process where the label created a whole range of political discussions that pertained to marketability, the factory's focus on the working conditions of the cocoa bean growers and the reality that the fairtrade label also brought the need to use fairtraded sugar. In fact, through the adjustment and negotiation process in relation to both economic and political concerns the factory ended up with its own take on how to standardize according to the fairtrade standards.

The political focus on the cocoa and the cocoa bean, for instance, meant that the factory wanted to have traceability that is the fairtrade labelled chocolate bars should include actual fairtrade labelled cocoa butter and cocoa mass. This was not necessary according to the standard or to the compliance criteria, but it was against their political ideals not to aim for traceability. This priority had to be navigated on the factory floor where the production line had to reset for the fairtrade label chocolate bars so that they would only include fairtrade labelled chocolate, in turn contributing to high conversion costs both because of the uncomfortable working conditions it created and the additional staff needed to convert production.

Sugar, on the other hand, was not as close to their hearts. The issue of sugar brought to the fore the fact that the sugar had to be produced in the Global South in order to be fairtrade labelled. It was against their ideals, which prescribed locally produced products such as sugar from Swedish sugar beets. Still, the exception negotiated due to colour and bacteriological conditions and the difficulty of finding a supplier made it possible to retain their ideal of locally produced Swedish sugar and use the existing production unit when pumping sugar into the production line.

In this way, the words and the values in the standards documents and compliance criteria were translated and adjusted turning the fairtrade labelled products into a political affair matching the chocolate factory's political ideals. Still, the negotiated fairtrade ideals did not carve out a space for them in the milk chocolate segment. Balancing business and politics on the factory floor, navigating fairtrade ideals in relation to their own political concerns regarding traceability of cocoa and sugar canes versus sugar beets proved to be overly complicated in relation to sales. Thus, making a business out of being fairtrade opened a space for politics within the factory but not for business and the carefully chosen chocolate bar wrapping including the fairtrade label was discarded and wrapping papers without fairtrade labels were put in the flowpack machine.

NOTES

1. μm may also be referred to as micrometre. One millimetre is 1000 micrometre.
2. Research underpinning this chapter was made possible by a research programme grant from Riksbankens Jubileumsfond. The Swedish Foundation for Humanities and Social Sciences, Organizing Markets, coordinated by Nils Brunsson.
3. The DAC list is developed by the Development Assistance Committee of OECD and they write on their website that the countries eligible for official development assistance are: '. . . all low and middle income countries based on gross national income (GNI) per capita as published by the World Bank, with the exception of G8 members, EU members and countries with a firm date for entry into the EU. The list also includes all of the Least Developed Countries (LDCs) as defined by the United Nations (UN)' (http://www.oecd.org/dac/stats/daclist.htm. Accessed 9 May 2017).
4. The national labelling organizations such as Max Havelaar in the Netherlands or Rättvisemärkt in Sweden first had their own labels. Now, they license Fairtrade International's fairtrade label to corporations that want to label their products fairtrade.
5. Fairtrade International has the 'Fairtrade Mark' to which the standards and compliance criteria refer to in this chapter. They also have the 'Fairtrade Programme Mark' that can be used when companies in the Global North only use, for example, one of the ingredients that is fairtrade labelled in their products. The Programme Mark is a new mark that was introduced in 2014.
6. The standards change regularly. In the chapter I refer to the standards that were valid at the time of fieldwork.
7. The floor price should cover the average cost but the prices sometimes fluctuate in an unexpected manner and Fairtrade International sometimes lags behind in its decision making on higher or lowering the floor price.

REFERENCES

Besky, S. (2014), *The Darjeeling Distinction. Labor and Justice on Fair-Trade Tea Plantations in India*, Berkeley: University of California Press.

Botzem, S. and J. Hofmann (2010), 'Transnational governance spirals: the transformation of rule-making authority in internet regulation and corporate financial reporting', *Critical Policy Studies* **4** (1), 18–37.

Brunsson, N. and B. Jacobsson with associates (2000), *A World of Standards*, Oxford: Oxford University Press.

Brunsson, N., A. Rasche and D. Seidl (2012), 'The dynamics of standardization. Three perspectives on standards in organization studies', *Organization Studies* **33** (5–6), 613–32.

Czarniawska, B. and G. Sevon (1996), *Translating Organizational Change*, Berlin: Walter de Gruyter.

Djelic, M.L. and K. Sahlin-Andersson (2006), *Transnational Governance: Institutional Dynamics of Regulation*, Cambridge, UK: Cambridge University Press.

Fairtrade International (2009a), *Generic Fairtrade Standards for Small Producers' Organizations. Current version 15.08.2009*, Bonn: Fairtrade Labelling Organizations International (now Fairtrade International).

Fairtrade International (2009b), *Fairtrade Standards for Nuts and Oilseeds for Small Producer Organizations. Current version 16.02.2009*, Bonn: Fairtrade Labelling Organizations International.

Fairtrade International (2009c), *Generic Fairtrade Trade Standards. Current version 15.08.2009*, Bonn: Fairtrade Labelling Organizations International.
Fairtrade International (2009d), *Fairtrade Standards for Cocoa for Small Producer Organizations. Current version 16.02.2009*, Bonn: Fairtrade Labelling Organizations International.
Fisher, C. (2007), 'Selling coffee, or selling out?: Evaluating different ways to analyze the fair-trade system', *Culture & Agriculture* **29** (2), 78–88.
Fridell, G. (2007), *Fair Trade Coffee. The Prospect and Pitfalls of Market-Driven Social Justice*, Toronto: Toronto University Press.
Harvey, D. (2005), *A Brief History of Neoliberalism*, Oxford: Oxford University Press.
Jaffee, D. (2007), *Brewing Justice. Fair Trade Coffee, Sustainability, and Survival*, Berkeley: University of California Press.
Lampland, M. and S.L. Star (eds) (2009), *Standards and their Stories. How Quantifying, Classifying and Formalizing Practices Shape Everyday Life*, London: Cornell University Press.
Lyon, S. (2011), *Coffee and Community. Maya Farmers and the Fair-trade Markets*, Boulder: University of Colorado Press.
Micheletti, M. (2003), *Political Virtue and Shopping: Individuals, Consumerism, and Collective Action*, New York: Palgrave.
Mörth, U. (ed.) (2004), *Soft Law in Governance and Regulation. An Interdisciplinary Analysis*, Cheltenham, UK and Northampton, MA, USA: Edward Elgar Publishing.
Power, M. (1997), *The Audit Society. Rituals of Verification*, Oxford: Oxford University Press.
Raynolds, L., D. Murray and J. Wilkinson (2007), *Fair Trade. The Challenges of Transforming Globalisation*, London: Routledge.
Rose, N. and P. Miller (1992), 'Political power beyond the state. Problematics of government', *British Journal of Sociology*, **43** (2), 173–205.
Scott, J.C. (1998), *Seeing Like a State. How Certain Schemes to Improve the Human Condition Have Failed*, New Haven, CT: Yale University Press.
Shore, C. and S. Wright (2000), 'Coercive accountability: the rise of audit culture in higher education', in M. Strathern (ed.), *Audit Cultures. Anthropological Studies in Accountability, Ethics and the Academy*, London: Routledge, pp. 57–89.
Snyder, F. (1994), 'Soft law and institutional practice in the European community', in S. Martin (ed.), *The Construction of Europe. Essays in Honour of Emile Noël*, London: Kluwer Academic Publishers, pp. 198–225.
Strathern, M. (ed.) (2000), *Audit Cultures. Anthropological Studies in Accountability, Ethics and the Academy*, London: Routledge.
Tamm Hallström, K. (2004), *Organizing International Standardization*, Cheltenham, UK and Northampton, MA, USA: Edward Elgar Publishing.
Tamm Hallström, K. and I. Gustafsson (2014), 'Value-neutralizing in verification markets. Organizing for independence through accreditation', in S. Alexius and K. Tamm Hallström (eds), *Configuring Value Conflicts in Markets*, Cheltenham, UK and Northampton, MA, USA: Edward Elgar Publishing.
WCED (1987), *Our Common Future*, Oxford: Oxford University Press.
West, P. (2012), *From Modern Production to Imagined Primitive. The Social World of Coffee from Papua New Guinea*, Durham: Duke University Press.

10. Preventing markets from self-destruction[1]

Bo Rothstein

IS THERE SUCH A THING AS LEGAL CORRUPTION?

In his 'farewell lecture' on 9 December 2008, former leading World Bank economist Daniel Kaufmann introduced the concept of *legal corruption*. The term certainly seems like an oxymoron, but Kaufmann motivates it by arguing for the need to redefine corruption to include 'how elites collude and purchase, or unduly influence the rules of the game, shape the institutions, the policies and regulations and the laws for their own private benefits'. If this is done illegally, as in the traditional use of the term corruption, or legally, is according to Kaufmann of minor interest from the viewpoint of economic and social efficiency. The term 'legal corruption' covers processes when public policy is thwarted or 'captured' by various private interests instead of serving the common/public interests, thus all forms of 'privatization of public policy'. Kaufmann's case in point is the background to the current financial and economic crisis and he points out how powerful agents in the financial sector used their influence to 'relax regulatory oversight and capital requirements'. Kaufmann specifically points to a meeting held in April 2004 when the CEOs of the (then) five big investment banks on Wall Street persuaded the US Securities and Exchange Commission to relax regulation that stipulated their need for financial reserves.[2]

By introducing the idea of 'legal corruption', Kaufmann makes it possible to connect the study of corruption to the analysis of the power of special interests groups in politics, not least in economic issues (see also Geddes 1994; Johnson 2009; Johnson and Kwak 2010; Olson 1982, 2000). It should be underlined that the issue here is not related to the standard 'principal-agent' theory where the problem is how the (honest) principal can use various incentives to control the (corrupt) agents. Instead, 'legal corruption' is to be understood as a problem of collective action leading to a social trap situation in the following sense. The agents may all know that they all as a group would benefit from a certain set of regulations, but not knowing if the other agents will 'play by the rules' it makes no sense to be the only agent that refrains from undermining them by opportunistic (that is self-interested) actions. The current financial crisis leads, according to Kaufmann, to the following conclusion, 'If anybody thought that the governance and corruption challenge was a monopoly of the developing world . . . that notion has been disposed completely'.[3] Another well-known economist, Simon Johnson (2009), writes about the corrupting influence from Wall Street to the US government as a 'quiet coup'. As Claude Rochet (2008) has argued, this line of reasoning can be traced all the way back to Machiavelli's argument of how easily the 'common good' can be undermined by corrupt practices from opportunistic agents and that this is an argument for strong (and ruthless) leadership. The problem with this argument is that in a corrupt setting, the leaders can be expected to get most of the rents from the corrupt practices and so have no incentive to change the system (Rothstein 2011).

There are now a great many explanations for the financial crises that erupted in 2008 of which most have to do either with moral condemnations of excessive greed or lack of foresight among central agents. My argument is that, while valuable, these explanations do not touch the root cause of why the financial markets collapsed in the fall of 2008. The main goal of this chapter is to provide such an explanation based primarily on insights from theories about corruption and the provision of public goods that has emanated from theories about the importance of institutions for understanding the variation in valued social outcomes. About the causes of the financial crises, the well-known financial speculator and philanthropist George Soros, has stated the following:

> There are two features that I think deserve to be pointed out. One is that the financial system as we know it actually collapsed . . . The other feature is that the financial system collapsed of its own weight. That contradicted the prevailing view about financial markets, namely that they tend toward equilibrium, and that equilibrium is disturbed by extraneous forces, outside shocks. Those disturbances were supposed to occur in a random fashion. Markets were seen basically as self-correcting. That paradigm has proven to be false. So we are dealing not only with a collapse of a financial system, but also with the collapse of a world view.[4]

If, as Soros points out, we have to deal with the breakdown of a dominant ideology that markets are self-correcting, this would entail a change in how social scientists think about the supply of regulations. The two major questions are: Can market agents as they are portrayed in neoclassical economics provide the type of regulations markets need and if so, can they sustain them?

In this chapter I will present four interrelated arguments that sum up to a theory about the relation between the logic of markets, regulation and social efficiency. The first, and least controversial, is that competitive markets are, at least so far in human history, the most efficient organizational form of creating a utilitarian-based economic efficiency for the production of most goods and services. Such markets are characterized by free entry, low transaction costs, reasonably good and freely available information, goods that are not by their very nature collective, low external effects and efficient protection of property rights. The second argument is that in order to reach this utilitarian based (also know as 'Pareto', but henceforth social) efficiency, markets need a large and complicated set of institutions, which are both formal as well as informal (North 1998a; North 1998b). Since such institutions will in the long run make all market agents better off, they can be called *efficient institutions*. The third argument is that we have little reason to expect that agents acting from the standard self-interested utility-maximization template will create such institutions endogenously. This is because such efficient institutions are genuine public goods and are therefore prone to the well-known problem of collective action.

The implication is that, contrary to what has been taken for granted by most policymakers in the area of financial regulation (see for example Johnson and Kwak 2010), we should expect market agents to act in a way that either will prevent efficient institutions to be established, or if they are established, will try to destroy them by various forms of 'free riding'. To use a metaphor from evolutionary biology, we have no reason to expect that efficient institutions will evolve by any selection mechanism that is generated from the sum of agency that operates on markets. Instead, my argument is that if the agents act from the standard template in neoclassical economics, markets are endogenously self-destructive leading to a social trap type of situation. The fourth argument is that markets can only reach social efficiency if the agents that have the responsibility to produce and reproduce the necessary institutions act according to a logic different from the logic that market agents use when operating in the market. In short, my ambition is to make the case for the existence of a paradox in social organization, namely that *you can have a market about anything as long as you don't have a market about everything.*

Institutional economists working with these problems in developing countries have emphasized the need for efficient informal and formal institutions. One example among many is Dani Rodrik who writes that 'the encounter between neo-classical economics and developing societies served to reveal the institutional underpinnings of market economies'. Among such institutional underpinnings Rodrik lists a well-specified system of property rights, effective regulation that hinders monopolies to dominate markets, uncorrupted governments, the rule of law and social welfare systems that can accommodate risks. Interestingly enough, Rodrik also mentions the importance of informal societal institutions that foster social cohesion, social trust and cooperation. Most important, he criticizes neoclassical economics by arguing that 'these are social arrangements that economists usually take for granted, but which are conspicuous by their absence in poor countries' (Rodrik 2007, p. 153, see also Geddes 1994).

If this is the case, the question of how such institutions can be established and maintained should be a top priority for the social sciences, especially if Daron Acemoglu and James Robinson are right when they state that 'differences in economic institutions are the major source of cross-country differences in economic growth and prosperity' (Acemoglu and Robinson 2006, p. 674). As I will argue further on, so far the question of how such efficient institutions can be established and reproduced has attracted surprisingly little attention both in economics, political science and in economic sociology (Rothstein 2011).

MARKETS, SOCIAL EFFICIENCY AND DEMOCRACY

The argument about the social efficiency of markets should not be understood in an absolute, but in a relative sense. The reason that markets cannot be seen as efficient in an absolute sense is that market agents cannot be presumed to be in possession of anything close to perfect information or be unboundedly rational or that transaction costs are instantaneous and costless (Menard and Shirley 2005). On the contrary, empirical research about how market agents act shows the opposite. Agents are often myopic, they rarely have perfect information, they make computational mistakes when calculating costs versus benefits, even if the value/risk is the same they are more likely to avoid losses than opt for gains, their beliefs can often be manipulated, transactions have sometimes large costs, and so on (Frohlich and Oppenheimer 2006; Loewenstein et al. 2004; Ostrom 1998). It is only in very rare cases that markets can be expected to reach what economists call Pareto-efficiency, because agents cannot be expected to meet the assumptions made in the standard welfare economics theorem. As stated by Joseph Stiglitz, 'a closer look at those assumptions, however, suggests that the theorem is of limited relevance to modern industrial economics' (Stiglitz 2002, p. 43). My argument for markets as efficient is based on the much more mundane argument that so far, for most goods and services, the alternatives to democratically regulated competitive markets have not delivered. Neither systems of central planning nor 'market socialism' have lived up to expectations of creating a reasonable degree of efficiency or anything close to social or economic equality (Wright 2006). For most goods and services, competitive markets are more efficient than known or tried alternative forms of production. This is also a central lesson from much of development studies (Bigsten and Fosu 2004). In addition, markets seem to have important advantages when it comes to innovation and in furthering a Schumpeterian 'creative destruction' (Olson 1982).

While economists deal with aggregate individual-based utilitarian efficiency, political scientists are engaged in understanding power and what can be considered as ways to make the use of political power legitimate. The standard argument from most political scientists is that for large groups (cities, regions, states), the best way to make power legitimate is through some form of electoral-representative democracy. Such a system can in many cases solve the problem of power for macro-decisions like tax laws or social security schemes. The reason is that such laws or policies are mostly universal and can be applied according to an 'equality before the law' principle, without involving much (or any) micro-level discretion at the point of delivery. In other cases, research on the implementation of public policies has clearly shown that such micro-level discretion cannot be avoided (Smith 2003). This problem is especially acute in service delivery – for example in health – or elderly care, care of disabled persons, but also for example in preschools and schools. What takes place between the public employee(s) that delivers the service and the citizen in such areas is problematic from a micro-power approach, since the citizen/client is often in a situation of dependence.

These are situations where the electoral-representative system for making the use of public power legitimate reaches a limit because 1) laws can not be made with the required precision to account for all possible variations and 2) there is often a need to let professionals have discretion because they have the knowledge that is needed for how to handle different situations/cases (Rothstein 2005). From this perspective, a right for the citizen to 'exit' and opt for another service provider is likely to increase his or her power, either directly by actually exiting or by the fact that the service providing organization anticipates that the citizen/client may exit and that such an exit will carry losses for the organization (Besley and Ghatak 2007). This will of course happen if the service in question is provided on a 'pure' market system where the client pays directly for the service. However, the same effect can apply if the government provides the service and it is paid for by taxes by using some form of voucher system. Such a system may, as is the case with pure markets, give the service providing organization (for example, the nursing home or the preschool) an incentive to improve the service production and thus increase the overall efficiency of the policy in question. Thus, markets could be favoured not only from an efficiency point of view, but also from a 'making power legitimate' point of view (Besley and Ghatak 2007).

INSTITUTIONS – THE TWO MAIN TYPES AND THE TWO MAIN FORMS

According to the 'New Institutional Economics' (henceforth NIE), 'institutions are the written and unwritten rules, norms and constraints that humans devise to reduce uncertainty and control the environment' (Menard and Shirley 2005, p. 1). The implication of such a broad definition is that institutions can come in many *forms* – from constitutional laws to what has become known as 'standard operating procedures' or 'work rules' (Ostrom 1990), which are known and generally agreed upon but that are unwritten. The idea that institutions include not only formal but also informal rules means that it is difficult to distinguish them from a society's basic cultural traits. From a policy perspective this is problematic because, while it is possible to change written rules and 'standard operating procedures/work rules' through for example a democratic process, this is much more difficult with things like 'shared mental models' (Denzau and North 1994) and other such generally held basic beliefs which are rooted in a society's historically established culture (Rothstein 2005). In any case, as a first distinction, we can differentiate between two basic forms of institutions, namely formal and informal.

Institutions can of course have many functions and roles. George Tsebelis (1990) has made a valuable distinction between 'redistributive' and 'efficient' institutions. The former is simply a rule that moves resources or power from one group of agents to another. A familiar example of such a formal redistributive institution would be most social insurance and tax systems. Informal redistributive institutions would be systems known as tribalism, clan-based societies and societies characterized by what has been termed 'amoral familism' (Banfield 1958). In such societies, economic agents are reluctant to deal with agents outside their clan, tribe or extended family because they distrust such agents. On the other hand, they would give favourable treatments to agents within this type of circle. Other normatively more problematic examples of redistributive institutions are the type of extortion used by organized crime against small- and medium-sized businesses (Varese 2001).

The existence of *redistributive institutions* is in general not difficult to explain using standard assumptions about the consequences of the allocation of various power resources in a society. For example, variation in the extension and coverage of different social insurance systems has been explained by the variation in class-based power resources (Korpi and Palme 2003). One can generally expect that those with lots of power resources will establish institutions that make it easier to dominate those that have fewer resources. As I will argue further on, we should expect market agents with lots of resources to try to establish institutions that will limit the possibilities for competition from other agents in their market with fewer resources. There are, however, also instances when social norms about decency and appropriateness play a role (Elster 1991; March and Olsen 1989). One example is the strengthening of legal norms in many Western countries about how to treat and take care of animals. However, the general assumption here is that market agents, when trying to establish or change institutions, will act according to a 'logic of exchange' and maximize their material gains.

Efficient institutions, on the other hand, have quite the opposite character since their effect is to improve the welfare of all actors in a specific system of exchange. As such, they are genuine collective (or public) goods and are therefore, as will be discussed further below, difficult to explain from standard assumptions about human behaviour in economics. Seen in the light of non-cooperative game theory, these are institutions that make it possible to avoid situations such as suboptimal outcomes in n-persons prisoners' dilemma type of games. In the closely related social dilemma theory, efficient institutions make it possible for agents to avoid ending up in situations known as social traps. Such formal efficient institutions have also been described as 'universal' (Rothstein 2005; Mungiu-Pippidi 2006), 'impartial' (Rothstein and Teorell 2008) or 'impersonal' (North et al. 2009). For market agents, this would be institutions that secure property rights, that produce reliable information about the solvency and credit record of firms, as well as an incorrupt and impartial judiciary, a state government operating by the 'rule of law' principles, and anti-trust legislation that can secure 'fair competition' by ruling out cartels or other forms of blockades against new agents entering the market. For most citizens, an honest, impartial and reasonably efficient public administration would also be counted into this category of efficient institutions. On the labour market, this can be general agreements between trade unions and employers' federations that facilitate the possibilities of solving wage negotiations without having to resort to costly open conflicts.

The most well-known example of informal efficient institutions is when generalized trust and social capital are widespread in the population. Institutions like this increase the likelihood that other market agents will not use opportunistic or treacherous strategies but instead follow contracts in a benevolent way. Generalized trust and other forms of social capital thereby decrease transaction costs (Keefer and Knack 2005). Theoretically,

Table 10.1 Institutional forms and functions: examples

		Type of institution	
		Formal	Informal
Function	Efficient	Rule of Law	Generalized trust
		Impartial admin.	Social capital
		Audit systems	Public service ethics
	Redistributive	Progressive taxes	Familism
		Welfare policies	Corruption
		Industrial rel. laws	Lobbying

what efficient institutions do is to increase the likelihood that agents that are exchanging values will trust that the other agents will not behave in a treacherous way (Levi 2006). Thus, efficient institutions induce change in agents' choice of strategy by increasing the likelihood that most agents will believe that most other agents cooperate honestly, which in turn will make it more rational for the individual agent to behave honestly. It should be added that the distinction between 'efficient' and 'redistributive' institutions is a theoretical ideal-type construct. In real life, many efficient institutions have some redistributive effects and vice versa (Tsebelis 1990). However, for the sake of theoretical simplifications, we will distinguish between these two *types* of institutions (redistributive and effective) and forms of institutions (informal and formal). If the two institutional forms and the two institutional types we have identified are cross-tabulated, the following typology and examples come out (Table 10.1).

It should be added that these forms and types empirically are strongly correlated. For example, high levels of corruption correlate with low levels of generalized trust, and high levels of 'rule of law' correlates with high levels of generalized trust (Rothstein and Stolle 2008; Rothstein and Uslaner 2005). However, while correlations in general are strong between formal and informal institutions in both cases, how the causality works between them is a very complicated and mostly unresolved matter. The most plausible explanation is that formal and informal efficient institutions are mutually reinforcing entities in which causality operates with lots of feedback mechanisms over time. A good example of this is the analysis by Farrell and Knight of how firms in a certain district in Northern Italy use trust-based collaboration to strengthen their market position as a collective, while also being competitors in the very same market segment. What they show is that the formal efficient types of institutions work, so to say, behind the scene as a last resort possibility for agents to deal with opportunistic/treacherous behaviour, while it is the informal trust-based relations that create the system of mutually beneficial cooperation (Farrell and Knight 2003). Other studies show that informal and formal efficient institutions can be functional substitutes (Simon 2010; Widmalm 2008). A case in point is China that has experienced high levels of growth despite having mainly redistributive (in many cases outright corrupt) formal institutions.

THE DIFFICULT ART OF SUPPLYING EFFICIENT INSTITUTIONS

The central claim from the NIE approach is that efficient formal institutions are necessary for creating economic efficiency and economic growth, especially in poverty stricken Third World countries (North 2006; Rodrik 2007; Shirley 2005). It has also been claimed that such institutions explain the 'miraculous' economic growth in Western Europe that started in the late seventeenth century (North 1990). While most scholars in the NIE approach concentrate on formal institutions, Douglass North has again and again emphasized the importance of the informal ones with concepts such as 'shared mental models' and 'norms of behavior, conventions, and internally imposed codes of conduct' (Denzau and North 1994; North 1998a, 1998b).

The problem is often labelled as that of creating 'credible commitments' between agents when they enter into contracts in a market (Keefer and Knack 2005). Without institutions that establish credible assurances that treacherous[5] agents who renege on or violate contracts will be punished (or ostracized), so as to establish a general belief among most agents that such behaviour is uncommon, transaction costs will skyrocket and people will be disinclined to make productive investments. The result is that many otherwise profitable economic exchanges or investments will not come about because the agents will distrust one another to fulfil the contract. If dishonest and treacherous behaviour becomes what is generally expected (also known as 'common knowledge'), almost all agents on the market will be losers and the market will not produce a socially efficient outcome. Such a situation is also known as a 'suboptimal equilibrium' because it is self-reinforcing, as the existence of repeated and widespread dishonest behaviour establishes mutual distrust (Bardhan 1997). Moreover, once generalized trust is broken, it becomes for a number of psychological reasons hard to mend. Because of this, agents can be 'trapped' in a situation of mutual distrust. The efficiency that markets are supposed to generate is thus threatened by what has been called a 'social trap' type of situation in which mutual distrust makes all agents worse off (Rothstein

2005). A social trap is a situation in which all agents know that they will all in the long run be better off if they can be trusted to follow the rules emanating from the efficient institutions and thus compete on the market in an honest and fair way. However, this only makes sense if they can trust that (almost) all the other agents adhere to such a standard of behaviour. What is 'rational' for the individual agent is thus not primarily given by any cost/benefit calculation over the transaction(s) as such, but instead by what the agents think about the other agents' beliefs about the strategy/trustworthiness of all other agents, including herself. Robert Aumann and Jacques Dreze have called this 'interactive rationality'. Seeing rationality in this social perspective has important implications because it shows the indeterminate nature of standard neoclassical theory and standard game theory that solely build on the idea that individuals will act so as to maximize their own pay-offs. Aumann and Dreze have formulated the implication in the following way:

> if one is given only the abstract formulation of a game, one cannot reasonably hope for an expectation and optimal strategies. Somehow, the real-life context in which the game is played must be taken into account. The essential element in the notion of context is the mutual expectations of the players about the actions and expectations of the other players. (Aumann and Dreze 2005, p. 9)

Thus, the outcome of social and economic interactions depends on how the 'real-life context' has constructed the 'mutual expectations', such as whether the other agents can be trusted or not. In, sum, the argument is that this 'real-life context' to a large extent consists of historically established and 'often taken for granted' formal and informal institutions. Corruption and its related problems should thus according to this perspective not be seen as a 'principal-agent' problem but a 'collective action' type of problem (Rothstein 2011).

For example, if institutions that would make treacherous behaviour the exception are lacking, market agents would come to believe that most other players cannot be trusted in economic transactions. If such trust is lacking, it makes no sense to be the only honest player in a 'rotten game'. Instead, it makes more sense to try to change the 'efficient' institutions to become 'redistributive' so that they will support the specific agents' (or, more likely, group of agents') position on the market. This can be done in numerous ways by means of corruption, secret price negotiations, political lobbying, clientelistic networks, patrimonialism, organized crime, civil wars about the control of economic resources and other sorts of violence. If a majority of the agents, because of the lack of trust in the honesty of the generalized 'other agent', act in these ways, the market will not deliver anything that can be expected to come even close to a socially efficient outcome. In sum, we face two interrelated problems. The first is that efficient institutions as they have been defined here are a genuine public good and, as with all such goods, they are collectively rational but it is in many cases irrational for the individual agent to contribute to them or respect them. As will be shown further on, given standard assumptions about the operational logic of market agents, we cannot assume that such institutions will be provided by them in any organic or functionalist way.

Second, if efficient institutions have been established, we should expect market agents to try to change them to become redistributive. When it comes to formal institutions, they are likely to use various forms of lobbying to change the general rules (laws, regulations) so that they will be favoured at the expense of their competitors (Olson 1982).[6] When it comes to the specific implementation of general rules, they are likely to use bribes or take part in other similar forms of corruption. One need only take a quick look at many of the different indexes of corruption that are provided by organizations such as Transparency International and the World Bank Research Institute to conclude that systemic or semi-systemic corruption is the rule around the world, not the exception. As stated in a chapter in the *Handbook of Institutional Economics*, 'The vast majority of humans today live in countries that have failed to create or sustain strong institutions to foster exchange and protect persons and property' (Shirley 2005, p. 612). Another example of means to destroy well-known efficient institutions is when powerful economic networks establish systems of organized collaboration with government agencies to further their specific interests against their competitors. Such networks, also known as neo-corporatist systems of exchange, have been, and are still, very common in many Western European countries (Lindvall and Sebring 2005). One can add other forms for destroying universal/efficient institutions such as clientilistic networks (Roninger 2004), powerful political-industrial complexes (Hossein-Zadeh 2006) or organized crime (Varese 2001). As Douglass North has put it, 'institutions are not necessarily or even usually created to be socially efficient' (North 1998a, p. 249). The earlier idea in economics that market agents would in a sort of functionalist trial-and-error fashion be able to create efficient institutions is simply not credible given the known historical record (North 1998b).

THE PROBLEM IS FAILURES IN CREATING AND SUSTAINING MARKETS, NOT MARKET FAILURES

The argument presented here is different from the standard 'market failure' argument in neoclassical economics which has a long history dating back to Adam Smith's famous statement that 'people of the same trade seldom meet together, even for merriment and diversion, but the conversation ends in a conspiracy against the public, or in some contrivance to raise prices' (see also Cowen and Crampton 1988). The standard 'market failure' theory proposes that there are a number of specific situations or a certain type of goods for which markets can not attain social efficiency, such as when the goods have large costs that are not reflected in the price, when the consumption of the good is not exclusive, when the production of the good has large social benefits, or when information problems become too extensive. In such cases, most neoclassical economists argue that there is a need for some form of government intervention or regulation.[7] The argument from neoclassical economics is, thus, that in general markets will create efficiency if left to themselves but that there are a number of special or exceptional circumstances that call for external government intervention. In contrast, my argument is that also for 'perfect market goods' with low externalities and when consumption is exclusive and information is (almost) free and perfect, market agents behaving like market agents can generally not be expected to generate efficiency because we have very little reason to believe that such agents will create the necessary type of what has been defined earlier as efficient institutions. This is slowly becoming clear from the NIE research programme. For example, Avner Greif argues that such institutions exist only 'in a few advanced contemporary countries and only in recent times' (Greif 2005, p. 737; see also North et al. 2009). As Acemoglu and Robinson have put it, 'An agreement on the efficient set of institutions is often not forthcoming because . . . groups with political power can not commit to not using their power to change the distribution of resources in their favour' (Acemoglu and Robinson 2008, p. 8).

Why can market agents not be expected to create the efficient institutions that they need in order to create an efficient market?[8] North states the problem as follows, 'Neoclassical theory is simply an inappropriate tool to analyse and prescribe policies that will induce development. It is concerned with markets, not with how markets develop' (North 1998a, p. 247). One problem is that if political leaders successfully create a state that is administratively strong enough to protect property rights, they will also have access to an administrative machine that can violate those rights (North 1990, p. 59). If those in control of the state are the type of actors assumed by the utility maximizing model, they will also exploit that power to enrich themselves at the expense of the people's rights (Weingast 1993, p. 287). As the situation in the many so-called failed states in Africa has been described by Robert Bates, 'The civil service assumes the role of a specialist in violence, using its command over the bureaucracy to redistribute income from the citizens to themselves' (Bates 2008, p 29). In so doing, they inevitably create distrust of the state as an institution, which is a barrier to the willingness to invest or take other economic risks.

A second problem has its background in the fact that creating efficient institutions is a large, complicated and costly enterprise. As Hernando de Soto has shown, it took centuries for the efficient type of institutions upon which modern Western market economies are based to emerge (de Soto 2000). The jurisprudential regulations are complicated; the institutions required are many, costly and comprehensive (Greif 2005). It is not solely a matter of police and public courts, but also of institutions like registrar offices that establish ownership rights to real property, a working land survey office, receivers, official agencies for the collection of debts, taxation and numerous inspection authorities and so on. Precisely because it is a large and costly enterprise, the creation and reproduction of such institutions must be seen as a classic collective action problem and, as such, it is impregnated with all sorts of freeriding problems (Sened 1997). In addition, there is ample empirical support for the claim that even if such institutions are created, individual market agents have strong reasons to try to bend them to become redistributive so to work in their favour (Malaquias 2007; Olson 1982). These three problems – the strong state problem and the two collective action problems – should be seen as the general rule for what to expect.

One main exception from the general rule that market agents are generally unable to create efficient institutions is the work on 'common pool resource problems' by Elinor Ostrom. She has shown that groups of economic agents who are all dependent on a local natural resource can create (efficient) institutions that prevent freeriding types of extraction that would be detrimental to the sustainability of the resource in question. Finding out that economic agents, if left to themselves without government interference, can overcome the famous 'tragedy of the commons' problem is a major achievement and her research has rightfully gained a lot of attention (Ostrom 1990). Other studies, for example of water control systems, have confirmed her results (Kaijser 2002).

However, there are a number of arguments for why her findings are not generalizable to modern competitive markets. First, all her cases are local groups in which the agents in question have been able to develop strong social bonds and mutual trust over a very long time. Second, the groups are socially and ethnically homogeneous, something that other scholars have put forward as critical. For example, a review of the literature concludes that 'the negative association between ethnic heterogeneity and public goods provision is widely accepted' (Habyarimana et al. 2006). Other scholars contend that the negative relation between ethnic heterogeneity and public goods production is 'one of the most powerful hypotheses in political economy' (Banerjee et al. 2005). They add that this is not only the case in such obvious and extreme cases like civil wars, but also under 'normal' times.

Third, success depends on the opportunity for the group to enforce strict rules about who has the right to use the resource in question, which implies that a cartel-like situation already exists. Fourth, she reports a number of cases where such local regulations have failed due to a number reasons, most of them related to the failure of the agents to enter into what should be called a deliberative democratic process. Lastly, while the state is far away, it seems to be present in the shadow. For example, in her famous case about water regulation in Southern California, it is government institutions that provide the forum for discussions and decisions. In her conclusion, Ostrom states that 'most of the institutional arrangements used in the success stories were rich mixtures of public and private instrumentalities' (Ostrom 1990, p. 182).

Milgrom et al. (1990) in an oft-quoted paper have examined another well-known historical case dealing with the problem of producing efficient institutions. Their example illuminates how merchants of a certain region in fourteenth-century Europe could develop legal praxis that greased the wheels of trade despite the lack of credible state institutions. The problem they were facing was that of managing situations in which contractual disputes arose between two merchants, that is, how they should handle the deceptive behaviour of certain merchants in terms of various kinds of breach of contract. The situation may be likened to a classic social trap – all merchants have a vested interest in everyone behaving honestly, but there is no point in being the only honest actor if everyone else is engaged in trickery and deceit of one kind or another. If 'everyone does it', the financial gains to be had from trade decline substantially, in part because fewer transactions are completed and in part because the actors are forced to devote considerable resources to protecting themselves from the deceptive actions of others. The costs incurred by merchant A to enter into a financial contract with merchant B, who intends to swindle A, are substantial. Even if the wronged A spreads information that the dishonest merchant B is not to be trusted, B could of course counter that information with contrary disclosures. Absent credible information institutions, other merchants have little or no means of determining who is in the right.

Milgrom et al. claim that the merchants' guilds of fourteenth-century France appointed 'law merchants'. The law merchants were empowered to act as judges in disputes between merchants and to publicize information about merchants that refused to voluntarily accept the verdicts of their deliberations (for example, by paying compensation to the wronged party). This made deceptive behaviour and refusal to comply with the verdicts of the law merchants an expensive business, since merchants who did so gained a reputation for lacking credibility and for being unreliable trading partners. This led to a strong decline in deceptive behaviour, because it was in the merchants' own interest to avoid getting such a reputation (in these contexts, the appearance of credibility is a vital asset). Therewith, according to these authors, an institution for solving the problem of the social trap had blossomed from the market's own inherent logic. The actors had a self-interest both in establishing the institution and in obeying the verdicts of the law merchants, which made the institution as such self-reinforcing. According to this analysis, a type of society under the rule of law had sprung up by itself, the problem of the social trap had been resolved by the self-interested utility maximizing actors of their own volition and with no outside involvement by something like a state or some form of social norms.

This is a neat and very appealing historical case. However, to generalize from this single case to the universe of the problems of supplying market with efficient institutions is in my view somewhat idealistic, if not to say naive, given what we now know about the pervasiveness of (legal or illegal) corruption, clientelism and patronage in most countries. For one thing, merchants and trading companies are not homogeneous quantities. The logic of the market dictates that some will eventually become much more financially strong than others. If they are economic rationalists, the large trading houses will use their financial strength to bribe or corrupt the law merchants in one way or another to gain economic advantages. They will also try to get their confidants in corruption installed in those positions in order to render verdicts in their own trading house's favour. And if the law merchants are also economic rationalists, their integrity will be for sale as long as the price is right and the transaction can be kept secret. Secret interactions are the hallmark of corruption. Such a scenario is a rather apt description of events in Russia after the privatizations of the 1990s. The economic oligarchs seem to have become so strong that they have managed to buy attempts to build universal legal institutions out of existence (Hedlund 1999; Ledeneva 2006).

As I have shown elsewhere, when well-known scholars in this tradition try to solve the problem of how efficient institutions can be created, they introduce a number of non-economic explanations such as 'beliefs', 'norms', 'legitimacy', 'altruistic actors' and so on (Rothstein 2005, Chapter 6). This may very well be true, but in light of their utility-based rationalistic models, these are all ad hoc explanations and are thereby outside the reach of their theory. As Mark Irving Lichbach (1997) as well as Dino Falaschetti and Gary Miller (2001) have shown, within the rationalistic paradigm there is no solution to the problem of creating efficient institutions.

An alternative and in many ways more promising approach to the problem of markets and institutions can be found in the economic sociology literature. The main claim from this approach is that markets are always socially embedded. (Block 2007; Dobbin 2004). This approach entails a very relevant critique of the neoclassical models of how markets operate since it shows that markets are almost never based on a pure utility-maximizing logic but depend on historically established and often 'taken-for-granted' formal and informal institutions that can vary a lot between different settings (Fligstein and Dauter 2007). A part of this literature is inspired by Karl Polanyi's theoretical framework developed in his well-known book *The Great Transformation* published in 1944. Central to Polanyi's claim is also a strong critique of the idea of the possibility of a 'self-adjusting market' (cited in Block 2007, p.5). However, the problem with this approach – within the context of this discussion – is that there is no such thing as 'efficient' institutions in economic sociology, only different types of what here has been labelled redistributive institutions (Block 2007). Second, the concept of embeddedness lacks precision, since it can be almost anything that surrounds a market. Third, the approach is not well suited to handle variations across time and space since it does not entail a well-specified theory of why embeddedness differs.

Overall, the results that come out from economic research about how to minimize corruption also seem to be contradictory. On the one hand, there are well-known economists, such as Alberto Alesina, who concludes that 'a large government increases corruption and rent-seeking' (Alesina and Angeletos 2005, p. 18). The problem with this result is that it flies in the face of almost all empirical measures of corruption, which indicate that among the least corrupt countries in the world are the Nordic countries, which are well-known for having huge public sectors (Persson and Rothstein 2015). Thus, an equally well-known and highly respected economist, Timothy Besley, states that:

> There is a section of opinion that equates good government to small government. Moreover, this has been a dominant tradition in political economy in the past. However, there is nothing in modern political economics to support this claim. (Besley 2007, p. 233)

This type of contradiction from leading scholars in the social sciences on a crucial topic like this is, to put it mildly, not very reassuring. In sum, if the provision of efficient institutions is to be understood as a genuine collective action/public goods problem, and given what is known about this type of problem, it will be very difficult to solve in large-n settings. Shifting from a suboptimal equilibrium by providing a large-enough set of efficient institutions may demand a 'big bang' type of change (Rothstein 2011).

A CONCLUDING ILLUSTRATIVE STORY

The main point in this chapter is that modern liberal societies face a behavioural paradox. On the one hand, markets based on utility maximization have been shown to create unsurpassed economic efficiency. On the other hand, in order to remain efficient, markets require a large set of agency that is not driven by utility maximization but instead by a concern for establishing and sustaining institutions that operate for the common good. How to reconcile both these types of agency is an important and difficult challenge for our type of societies, especially if we preach to future elites that utility maximization is the only game in town (Ostrom 1998, p. 20).

The ever-so popular HBO TV show *The Sopranos* contains a scene that speaks to the problem of legal corruption and the supply of efficient institutions. In a state of rage, the mob leader himself, Tony Soprano, with a gun in his hand goes after a low-level gang member that has betrayed him and kills him. Usually, he would of course have used an underling for an operation like this, but this time (due to his mental instability that is a central theme of the series) he is so overtaken by emotions that he forgets the golden rule that mafia bosses should never do any of the dirty work themselves. As it happens, an 'ordinary citizen' sees him chasing after the victim. This eyewitness goes to the police, not knowing that it is the local mafia leader that he has seen. The 'ordinary Joe' tells the police that he is just sick and tired of all the violence in his neighbourhood and that he as a law-abiding citizen wants to help the police to clean up the neighbourhood. When the police commissars show him a bunch of photos of known criminals, he directly identifies the perpetrator – still not knowing who the person he identifies is. After he has left the police station, the police commissars are in a state of joy since they now seem to have what they need to put Tony Soprano behind bars. In the next scene, the eyewitness is sitting comfortably in what seems to be a middle-class home listening to classical music. A woman his age, probably his wife, is sitting close to him reading the newspaper. Suddenly, she starts screaming and then shouts at him to read an article in the paper. The article makes it clear to this honest and law-abiding citizen that the person he has identified at the police station as the perpetrator is the well-known local mafia leader Tony Soprano. The law-abiding citizen then throws himself at the phone, calls the police commissar whose direct number he has, and in a terrified voice says that he did not see anything and that he will not serve as a witness. The interesting detail here is the book our law-abiding citizen was reading before his wife showed him the newspaper article. An observant spectator has about one second to see that it is the philosopher Robert Nozick's modern classic *Anarchy, State and Utopia* – an icon for all ultra-liberal, anti-government and free-market proponents ever since it was published (Nozick 1974). The message from the people behind *The Sopranos* seems clear: in a 'stateless' Robert Nozick type of society, where everything should be arranged by individual, freely entered contracts, markets will deteriorate into organized crime. The conclusion is again, that there can be a market for anything as long as there is not a market for everything. Or in other words, if everything is for sale, markets will not come close to what should count as social efficiency.

NOTES

1. This chapter is a revised version of an article titled 'Can markets be expected to prevent themselves from self-destruction' published in *Regulation & Governance*, 2011, 5(4): 387–500. The permission to reprint is gratefully acknowledged.
2. See article in *New York Times*, 3 October 2008, 'Agency's '04 rule let banks pile up new debt' by Stephen Labaton that gives a vivid description of what happened.
3. Kaufmann has led the World Bank Institute's work on 'Governance Issues'. His farewell lecture can be found at http: //info.worldbank.org/etools/bspan/PresentationView.asp?PID=2363&EID=1056. Accessed 3 March 2015.
4. George Soros, *New York Review of Books*, 11 June 2009.
5. Economists often use the term 'opportunistic' to describe such behaviour, which I think is too nice a term for this type of agency. However, to keep with established vocabulary, I limit myself to this endnote protest.
6. Joseph Stiglitz, winner of the Prize in Economics to the memory of Alfred Nobel, recalls that when he was chair of the Council of Economic Advisors under former US President Bill Clinton, CEOs of major US companies regularly came to his office stating their support for the free-market principle that governments should not interfere in the market. However, as a rule they told Stiglitz that their particular industry was a special case that needed strong support from the US government (from Block 2007, p. 12).
7. It should however be noted that many neoclassical economists also warn that the effects of such government intervention could worsen the situation, see many of the chapters in Cowen and Crampton (1988).
8. Cowen and Crampton (1988) entails a number of chapters describing cases when economic agents have been able to overcome the collective action problem and produce public goods. The cases are all interesting but they are clear cases of exceptions bordering on the anecdotal. This is largely 'make believe' economics.

REFERENCES

Acemoglu, D. and J.A. Robinson (2006), 'Paths of economic and political development', in B. Weingast and D. Wittman (eds), *Handbook of Political Economy*, Oxford: Oxford University Press, pp. 673–92.

Acemoglu, D. and J.A. Robinson (2008), *The Role of Institutions in Growth and Development*, Washington, DC: The World Bank (On behalf of the Commission on Growth and Development).
Alesina, A. and G.M. Angeletos (2005), 'Corruption, inequality, and fairness', *Journal of Monetary Economics*, **52**, 1227–44.
Aumann, R.J. and J.H. Dreze (2005), 'When all is said and done, how should you play and what should you expect', Jerusalem: Hebrew University, Centre for the Study of Rationality.
Banerjee, A., R. Somanathan and L. Iyer (2005), 'History, social divisions and public goods in rural India', *Journal of the European Economic Association*, **3**, 639–47.
Banfield, E.C. (1958), *The Moral Basis of a Backward Society*, New York, NY: The Free Press.
Bardhan, P. (1997), 'Corruption and development: a review of the issues', *Journal of Economic Literature*, **35**, 1320–46.
Bates, R.H. (2008), *When Things Fell Apart: State Failure in Late Century Africa*, New York, NY: Cambridge University Press.
Besley, T. (2007), *Principled Agents? The Political Economy of Good Government*, Oxford: Oxford University Press.
Besley, T. and M. Ghatak (2007), 'Reforming public service delivery', *Journal of African Economies*, **16**, 127–56.
Bigsten, A. and A.K. Fosu (2004), 'Growth and poverty in Africa: an overview', *Journal of African Economies*, **13**, 1–15.
Block, F. (2007), 'Understanding the diverging trajectories of the United States and Western Europe: a neo-Polanyian analysis', *Politics & Society*, **35**, 3–33.
Collier, P. (2007), *The Bottom Billion. Why the Poorest Countries Are Failing and What Can Be Done About It*, Oxford: Oxford University Press.
Cowen, T. and E. Crampon (eds) (1988), *The Theory of Market Failure*, Fairfax: George Mason University Press.
de Soto, H. (2000), *The Mystery of Capital: Why Capitalism Triumphs in the West and Fails Everywhere Else*, London: Black Swan.
Denzau, A.T. and D.C. North (1994), 'Shared mental models, ideologies and institutions', *Kyklos*, **47**, 3–31.
Dobbin, F. (2004), *The Sociology of the Economy*, New York: Russell Sage Foundation.
Ellerman, D.P. (1992), *Property and Contract in Economics: The Case for Economic Democracy*, Oxford: Blackwell.
Elster, J. (1991), 'Rationality and social norms', *Archives Europennées de Sociologie*, **31**, 233–56.
Falaschetti, D. and G. Miller (2001), 'Constraining the Leviathan, moral Hazard and credible commitment in constitutional design', *Journal of Theoretical Politics*, **13**, 389–411.
Farrell, H. and J. Knight (2003), 'Trust, institutions, and institutional change: industrial districts and the social capital hypothesis', *Politics & Society*, **31**, 537–66.
Fligstein, N. and L. Dauter (2007), 'The sociology of markets', *Annual Review of Sociology*, **33**, 105–28.
Frohlich, N. and J.A. Oppenheimer (2006), 'Skating on thin ice: cracks in the public choice foundation', *Journal of Theoretical Politics*, **18**, 235–66.
Geddes, B. (1994), *Politician's Dilemma: Building State Capacity in Latin America*, Berkeley, CA: University of California Press.

Greif, A. (2005), 'Institutions and the path to the modern economy: lessons from medieval trade', in C. Ménard and M.M. Shirley (eds), *Handbook of Institutional Economics*, Amsterdam: Springer, pp. 727–86.
Habyarimana, J., M. Humphrey, D.N. Posner and J.M. Weinstein (2006), *Why Does Ethnic Diversity Undermine Public Goods Provision?*, Washington, DC: Centre for Global Development.
Hedlund, S. (1999), *Russia's Market Economy: A Bad Case of Predatory Capitalism*, London: UCL.
Hossein-Zadeh, I. (2006), *The Political Economy of U.S. Militarism*, Basingstoke: Palgrave Macmillan.
Johnson, S. (2009), 'The quiet coup', *The Atlantic* (May 2009 issue).
Johnson, S. and J. Kwak (2010), *13 Bankers, the Wall Street Takeover and the Next Financial Meltdown*, New York: Pantheon Books.
Kaijser, A. (2002), 'System building from below, institutional change in Dutch water control systems', *Technology and Culture*, **43**, 521–48.
Keefer, P. and S. Knack (2005), 'Social capital, social norms and the new institutional economics', in C. Ménard and M.M. Shirley (eds), *Handbook of Institutional Economics*, Amsterdam: Springer, pp. 701–35.
Korpi, W. and J. Palme (2003), 'New politics and class politics in the context of austerity and globalization, welfare state regress in 18 countries, 1975–95', *American Political Science Review*, **97**, 425–46.
La Porta R., F. Lopez-de-Silanes, A. Shleifer and R. Vishny (1999), 'The quality of government', *Journal of Law, Economics and Organization*, **15**, 222–79.
Ledeneva, A.V. (2006), *How Russia Really Works: The Informal Practices that Shaped Post-Soviet Politics and Business*, Ithaca: Cornell University Press.
Levi, M. (2006), 'Why we need a new theory of government', *Perspectives on Politics*, **4**, 5–19.
Lichbach, M.I. (1997), *The Co-operator's Dilemma*, Ann Arbor: University of Michigan Press.
Lindvall, J. and J. Sebring (2005), 'Policy reform and the decline of corporatism in Sweden', *West European Politics*, **28**, 1057–74.
Loewenstein, G., M. Rabin and C. Camerer (2004), *Advances in Behavioral Economics*, New York: Russell Sage Foundation.
Malaquias, A. (2007), *Rebels and Robbers: Violence in post-Colonial Angola*, Uppsala: Nordiska Afrikainstitutet.
March, J.B. and J.P. Olsen (1989), *Rediscovering Institutions: The Organizational Basis of Politics*, New York: Basic Books.
Menard, C. and M.M. Shirley (eds) (2005), *Handbook of New Institutional Economics*, Amsterdam: Springer.
Milgrom, P., D.C. North and B.R. Weingast (1990), 'The role of institutions in the revival of trade: the law merchant, private judges, and the champagne fairs', *Economics and Politics*, **2**, 1–23.
Miller, G. and T. Hammond (1994), 'Why politics is more fundamental than economics: incentive-compatible mechanisms are not credible', *Journal of Theoretical Politics*, **6**, 5–26.
Mungiu-Pippidi, A. (2006), 'Corruption, diagnosis and treatment', *Journal of Democracy*, **17**, 86–99.
North, D.C. (1998a), 'Economic performance through time', in M.C. Brinton and V. Nee (eds), *The New Institutionalism in Sociology*, New York: Russell Sage Foundation, pp. 247–57.

North, D.C. (1998b), 'Where have we been and where are we going?', in A. Ben-Ner and L. Putterman (eds), *Economics, Values and Organization*, Cambridge: Cambridge University Press, pp. 491–508.
North, D.C. (1990), *Institutions, Institutional Change and Economic Performance*, Cambridge: Cambridge University Press.
North, D.C. (2006), 'What is missing from political economy', in B. Weingast and D. Wittman (eds), *Handbook of Political Economy*, Oxford: Oxford University Press, pp. 1003–9.
North, D.C., J.J. Wallis and B.R. Weingast (2009), *Violence and Social Orders: A Conceptual Framework for Interpreting Recorded Human History*, Cambridge: Cambridge University Press.
Nozick, R. (1974), *Anarchy, State and Utopia*, Cambridge, MA: Harvard University Press.
Olson, M. (1982), *The Rise and Decline of Nations, Economic Growth, Stagflation, and Social Rigidities*, New Haven: Yale University Press.
Olson, M. (2000), *Power and Prosperity, Outgrowing Communist and Capitalist Dictatorships*, New York: Basic Books.
Ostrom, E. (1990), *Governing the Commons: The Evolution of Institutions for Collective Action*, New York: Cambridge University Press.
Ostrom, E. (1998), 'A Behavioral approach to the rational choice theory of collective action', *American Political Science Review*, **92**, 1–23.
Persson, A. and B. Rothstein (2015), 'It's my money. Why big government may be good government', *Comparative Politics*, **47**, 231–49.
Rochet, C. (2008), 'The common good as an invisible hand: Machiavelli's legacy to public management', *International Review of Administrative Sciences*, **74** (3), 497–521.
Rodrik, D. (2007), *One Economics, Many Recipes, Globalization, Institutions and Economic Growth*, Princeton: Princeton University Press.
Roninger, L. (2004), 'Political clientelism, democracy and market economy', *Comparative Politics*, **36**, 353–75.
Rothstein, B. (2005), *Social Traps and the Problem of Trust*, Cambridge: Cambridge University Press.
Rothstein, B. (2009), 'Creating political legitimacy, electoral democracy versus quality of government', *American Behavioral Scientist*, **53**, 311–30.
Rothstein, B. (2011), *The Quality of Government: Corruption, Social Trust and Inequality in Comparative Perspective*, Chicago: University of Chicago Press.
Rothstein, B. and D. Stolle (2008), 'The state and social capital: an institutional theory of generalized trust', *Comparative Politics*, **40**, 441–67.
Rothstein, B. and J. Teorell (2008), 'What is quality of government? A theory of impartial government institutions', *Governance*, **21**, 165–90.
Rothstein, B. and E.M. Uslaner (2005), 'All for all. Equality, corruption and social trust', *World Politics*, **58**, 41–73.
Sened, I. (1997), *The Political Institution of Private Property*, Cambridge, MA: Cambridge University Press.
Shirley, M.M. (2005), 'Institutions and development', in C. Ménard and M.M. Shirley (eds), *Handbook of Institutional Economics*, Amsterdam: Springer, pp. 611–38.
Simon, W.H. (2010), 'Optimization and its discontents in regulatory design, bank regulation as an example', *Regulation & Governance*, **4**, 3–21.
Smith, S.R. (2003), 'Street-level bureaucracy and public policy', in G.B. Peters and

J. Pierre (eds), *Handbook of Public Administration*, London: Sage Publications, pp. 354–65.

Stiglitz, J.E. (2002), 'Keynesian economics and critique of first fundamental theorem of welfare economics', in T. Cowen and E. Crampton (eds), *Market Failure or Success, The New Debate*, Cheltenham: Edward Elgar, pp. 41–59.

Tsebelis, G. (1990), *Nested Games: Rational Choice in a Comparative Perspective*, New York: Cambridge University Press.

Varese, F. (2001), *The Russian Mafia: Private Protection in a New market Economy*, Oxford: Oxford University Press.

Weingast, B.R. (1993), 'Constitutions as governance structures: The political foundations of secure markets', *Journal of Institutional and Theoretical Economics*, **149**, 286–311.

Werhane, P. (1994), *Adam Smith and his Legacy for Modern Capitalism*, Oxford: Oxford University Press.

Widmalm, S. (2008), *Decentralisation, Corruption and Social Capital: From India to the West*, Thousand Oaks: SAGE Publications.

Wright, E.O. (2006), 'Compass points: Towards a socialist alternative', *New Left Review*, **41**, 93–124.

11. Reflections: leaving Flatland? Planar discourses and the search for the g-axis

David A. Westbrook[1]

This chapter has a few purposes. First, I intend to use mathematical metaphors to play with the structure of familiar ways of thinking about society. Second, I suggest that such ways of thinking are somewhat impoverished; we commonly address a complex fabric with a very simple normative vocabulary, often called liberalism, itself an admittedly confusing word. Third, impoverishment of political discourse may be unwise, even dangerous (examples will be provided). Fourth, I'd like to suggest that the social sciences, and anthropology in particular can help to foster a more institutional, and more responsible, political imagination, which would be a comfort. This allows me to conclude in traditional fashion, by calling for more research.

***

The terrain of social life is very traditionally described vis-à-vis government and the market, public and private, as in the title of this book. From this perspective, so ubiquitous as to be inescapable, familiar questions arise: How do the actions of market actors affect presumptively or at least ideally democratic government? Or, working in the other direction, how does government shape and affect the market?

In such questions both 'government' and 'market' are ontologically interesting. The government is not, for example, the administrative apparatus of the state of Colorado, where I write these lines, peopled by the usual collection of elected and unelected officials, with the usual panoply of authorities and obligations, more or less established by law, to say nothing of virtues and foibles reflecting the human condition, easy to remember on an early winter day. 'Government' here is not a phenomenon, located in time and space, but an idea – the state, the sovereign, *Leviathan*, the monopolist of legitimate force and so forth. Similarly, 'the market' does not mean the place where I buy wine or the price I might receive for a real property, but *the market*, that special context where the invisible hand pushes things forward, where alienation causes modernity to happen, and all destruction is creative in this best of all possible worlds – if you get my drift. That is, simple questions, familiar from everyday appropriations of the social that we might call journalistic (one may no longer blithely refer to newspapers) require a veritable mythology of political life, are indeed only comprehensible with such a mythology populating one's mind.

Actual institutions, including institutions studied in this book, typically participate both in 'markets' and in 'governments'. For a simple example, a 'private' corporation in the United States might be thought to be the quintessential marketplace actor. But even such corporations are chartered by states; the broad outlines of their governance structures are provided by statute as elaborated by courts; they are regulated by state and federal law, and sometimes by foreign jurisdiction and international laws (the *lex mercatoria*); may participate in quintessentially political processes; and in some cases, their existence is guaranteed by the federal government, using taxpayer money. One can of course work the other way, and find 'marketplace' behavior by governments. Agencies of the government may participate across the range of economic activities; hire and fire individuals; think of those they serve as consumers, for which they may compete with other institutions and so forth. In short, discussing an institution, for instance a foundation, it seems natural to discuss whether it is more like 'the government' or like a 'private' actor who participates (in self-interested and rational fashion, classical microeconomics tells us) in 'the market'.

Note that 'the government' is almost always thought of as a person; at least in parlance, the imagination of the sovereign seems indispensible. So we speak, in international law, of the state's ability to bind itself. We morally judge the actions of governments – did (the king) do the right thing? Conversely, 'the market' tends to be imagined as a place, for example a marketplace, an often-heartless environment, ruled by Darwinian principles of survival of the fittest. Businesses often deny that they had choices; they were forced to ______ by conditions in 'the market'. Thus it makes sense, on a certain poetic (mythological and historical) level, to think of the government in opposition to individuals, conceived as marketplace actors who act in their own self-interest, and who may even unite to form the state. This is, of course, the state of nature story.

As you perhaps remember from school geometry, two points determine a line. 'The government' and 'the individual' thus establish a spectrum, along which we can locate various institutions. We can ask whether a given institution is functioning more like a government or like a private actor. Indeed, I wrote a book, *Between Citizen and State*, that explicitly did just that – considered many different forms of business organization, and organized the lot of them along this spectrum determined by the citizen and her sovereign (Westbrook 2007). This 'political spectrum' is useful for an introduction to corporate law in part because it is beyond familiar – it has become intuitive. The imagination, at least the duality between the individual and the king, is very old, going back at least to Hobbes, and has been more than useful over the centuries; it is embedded in how we think about politics writ large. It is the way we talk about rights, about the proper role of government, and allegiance, for example we describe political interests and aspirations in terms of 'left' (tending toward the 'government') and 'right' (preferring to journey towards 'the market').[2]

The political spectrum is also, quite literally, a one-dimensional image. Surely public life cannot be described in one dimension, along a single line? Surely there are many institutions, organizations, which are neither individual (though they comprise individuals) nor fairly can be called 'the state' (though they certainly have public aspects and social consequences). Consider corporations, or foundations or churches. Consider, in short, the subjects treated by this book.

Indeed, a more complex geometry that provides a way to articulate social actors that are neither natural persons nor sovereign is almost as ubiquitous. When we consider public affairs, we tend to think of government and individual as distinct, with their own interests. So, for recent example, it is taken as given that government has an interest in monitoring the activities of its enemies, terrorists, other governments, maybe your neighbors, maybe you . . . that is, the interest of government (in surveillance) is understood to be at odds with the individual's interest in not being watched. This brings us to the language of balancing, so ubiquitous in the law, in which 'government' and 'individuals' are thought to have interests, that is, are considered to be holders of quantities (for example, Greenberg 1973).

Quantities, one might ask, of what? But that is not the point. Individuals and states are holders of quantities of interest in whatever it is in which they are interested. So, in the foregoing example, the government claims to have an interest in surveillance. We may speculate as to the reasons. Surveillance may aid in self-defense. It may help to control a population. It may be just what a certain kind of professional, or a certain kind of agency, does – gather information about other people, institutions and even government, that may prove valuable for some reason in the future. Conversely, an individual may have an interest in not being watched because it is illicit, or because she fears the government, or because she just likes to be left alone. In short, the holder specifies the substance of the interest.

Not only is the substance of an interest specified by its holder (what are you interested in?); so is the quantity (how important is this to you?). So the government's interest in a matter may be small; perhaps the government has no (zero) interest. Or perhaps the government's interest is unbounded (infinite), as is often said in wartime? One might say similar things about individual interests, for instance that they range from zero to infinite. In short, interest, a quantity of infinite divisibility and unspecified content, may be figured as a real number.[3]

The interests of the individual in a given social matter, *S*, are distinct from, indeed sometimes opposed to, those of the state. What interest does the individual have in *S*? As noted earlier, the answer is thought of quantitatively, for instance, as a real number, which we may traditionally enough call x. What interest does the state have in *S*? So long as we understand the state in terms of its interests,[4] we may equally traditionally call the state's answer y. We might even write our answers pairwise (Interest of the Individual, Interest of the State), or more traditionally, (x, y).[5]

These quantities can be graphed vis-à-vis one another in Cartesian fashion, that is, along the x and y axes, establishing what might be called the liberal plane, in which government action is always understood vis-à-vis individual interests, and vice versa. If we graph the state's interest along the y-axis, then we might get a 'map' of social life. National elections, in which both individuals and governments have a high level of interest, would appear on the upper right; military secrets would appear on the upper left; sexual proclivities (between consenting adults – this is the liberal plane, founded on autonomy) would be in the lower right corner. Things neither government nor individuals have much interest in, academic articles perhaps, would appear in the lower left corner, if at all.

But while it describes a great deal of contemporary political discourse, and is not wrong, the liberal plane is still a plane, and as such, two dimensional, flat and truth be told, rather boring.[6] And on that plane, everything must be, as a matter of logic, describable in terms of either government or individual interest. This creates a certain awkwardness around the term 'social'. Rephrased, have we really understood *S* by describing it in terms of what 'quantity of interest' two abstractions 'the individual' and 'the state' have? This is a rather elaborate mythology. Our example of the social, *S*, is by definition, *social*, comprising numerous people, and therefore S is not individual. At the same time, the social is not exactly the will of the king. Most (but not all) of what we understand as social is done by groups smaller than states, and certainly differently constituted. A great deal of life that begs to be understood 'socially' does not map well onto governments. Consider the audience for a painter, or for a scientific publication. None of this really makes sense in terms of an individual's, or the state's, interest. So the description is awkward, the Cartesian graph clunky and the political discourse skewed.

In Europe and to generalize, the discourse is skewed towards the interest of the state, that is, the social has tended to be understood under the rubric of the state. In the United States, in contrast, the social has been treated as if it were essentially private. So we speak of 'private enterprise', and the fact that much of society's needs, for education, health care and the like, are provided by non-state enterprises is presented as if merely the happy working of the invisible hand. In both Europe and the United States, it seems clear that the dominant political language only awkwardly addresses key elements of society's life together, and in that broad sense, politics.

One might have thought that the emergence of the social sciences in the nineteenth century would have fostered a richer political imaginary. For whatever reason (I have elsewhere blamed the exigencies of doing business across vast spaces, Westbrook 2004, pp. 213–33), the social sciences have not yet succeeded in creating a political imaginary of anything like the influence and power of the social contract or the liberal plane. I think this is more than an academic failing; it means that important aspects of political life not only escape whatever democratic contestation may survive, but also preclude even the solace of understanding.

In *Flatland*, the Victorian author Edwin Abbott told the story of a square, prosperously living in a society located (and understood) in a two dimensional plane (Abbott 1884[1998]). One day 'A. Square' is visited by a sphere, which he perceives as a point that gradually grows into a large circle.[7] Circles are royalty in Flatland, so A. Square is suitably impressed, but he cannot understand what the sphere has come to say, namely, that there are other dimensions. The sphere has come to Flatland as an emissary from his 'higher' world; the government of Spaceland undertakes such missionary expeditions every 1,000 years. After fruitless efforts to demonstrate the mathematical possibility of three dimensions, the sphere lifts A. Square out of Flatland, and shows him the world of three dimensions, and also Lineland, land of one dimension, and even 'Pointland, the Abyss of No dimensions' (Abbott 1884 [1998], p. 108). From his travels, A. Square gradually comes to understand the concept of spaces of n dimensions, where n is some non-negative integer.

Crucially for our purposes, A. Square comes to see that social life itself can be understood through fewer, or more, dimensions. The life of a point is not the same as life in Lineland, which itself seems pretty limited from the perspective of Flatland – much of *Flatland* is devoted to articulating how a society operates under different 'geometrical' constraints. In particular, A. Square is at pains to explain to his readers, inhabitants of three dimensions, how life is possible without a perception of three dimensions, volume and other aspects of our – but not necessarily all – realities. *Flatland* is also, critically, about culture.

Perhaps worryingly, Flatland is not a very nice place, rather totalitarian in fact. Speech is limited, as are opportunities. When A. Square attempts to share his knowledge of the three-dimensional world, he is thrown into prison. Had he been a less important citizen, he would simply have been executed. (Arts majors may be unsurprised to learn that Euclidean society is draconian.) But Abbott's point here is quite serious. Limitations on the imagination, insofar as they are seen to be constitutive on the state, are likely to be enforced by the state, violently if need be. I will bracket the questions of whether the current administration's insistence on 'progressive policies', so long as control of information is maintained, should be understood in Huxleyan terms (Huxley 1932). For my purposes, it is enough to point out that the effort to articulate the social, on the liberal plane, leads to distortion. So, for example, 'culture', as in 'the culture of investment bankers', quickly is translated into a marketplace idiom, 'reputational risk'. In general, trying to articulate our lives together with a very limited vocabulary is, at the very least, intellectually trying.

***

Other mathematical metaphors are available for how we do, and how we might think about, our own culture. Observing my parlor games, my colleague Jack Schlegel urged analytic geometry and calculus. Indeed, the seeds of such an approach are in *Flatland* itself. In Flatland, social status increases with the number of sides. At some point, the number of sides is so large that they cannot be perceived as individual sides, and the shape is regarded as a circle, and so titled.

If we move from the straight edge and compass geometry of Euclid to the still Euclidean, but infinitesimal, geometry of Newton and Leibniz, marvelous things appear – the infinitely variable world of curves, and curved shapes! This geometry looks a lot more like the world we perceive with our eyes, nature. Curves – and more powerfully still, parts of curves, may be defined, to whatever degree of precision one pleases. But thinking along a function, analytically in that sense, is different from thinking in terms of regular polygons and circles. For example, as we move along a sine curve, defined *ex ante*, we travel first upward then downward. The curve is concave, until we reach an inflection point, and it becomes convex . . . for a lawyer and a historian, the message is clear. The same (social) function expresses, and signifies, differently at different points in time.

Or recall the central notion of calculus (why it is called analysis, I presume), the idea that a solid, or a curve, can be described as the sum of an infinite number of infinitely small shapes (infinitesimals), each of which is perhaps better understood. The curve, then, is the limit (summation, hence the '*S*' for integration) approached by the collectivity of infinitesimals. So, by analogy, one might think of the social as the sum of the imaginations of the vast hordes of individuals that make up a mass society.

On further reflection, however, maybe this is not the way to proceed. Perhaps the geometric frame we have assumed (as a sort of Kantian a priori) is not the most apt imaginary, does not frame the best analysis. The history of mathematics offers other possibilities that may be worth considering. For example, perhaps a non-Euclidean space (in which the parallel postulate does not hold) makes more sense? Perhaps tendencies extended infinitely do meet in a point. Would the oft-noted convergence of communism and fascism be an example, that is, the space of our social lives is more akin to the space of our globe, and elliptical geometry is appropriate? Or perhaps the number of ways history can 'rhyme' is infinite, our stories are hyperbolic from the beginning and there is no single parallel?

And while we're playing, does it make sense to think of aspects of the social along dimensions that are presumed to be integers? Wouldn't it make more sense if dimensions were understood to be real numbers? Might we not try to imagine a fractal geometry of social relations? My daughter Sophia (a budding mathematician, already beyond my best) thought there was great potential here, but I am skeptical, not of the elegance of the mathematics, but of their trenchancy as metaphor, beyond this: Playing with any one of these models accomplishes a key task of philosophy, making us aware of the structure of our own thinking.

So, for the purposes of this chapter, I'm going to stick with *Flatland* as metaphor.

***

From this rather dull perspective, the task is rather clear: how might we, from within the liberal plane, conceive of the social, so that we might imagine politics in at least three dimensions? Is there some way to understand the social as a third dimension, orthogonal to the individual and state that determine the plane of ordinary political discourse in liberal societies? It is difficult from Flatland to imagine Spaceland; it is similarly difficult to articulate the social from the perspective of either the interest of the state (in a defensible rational order, or what is often claimed to be the 'neutrality' that characterizes the rule of law, human rights and so forth) or the rational individual of economic discourse. *Flatland* is about limitations on the imagination, and metaphorically, about the difficulties we have in articulating a political economy that accounts for the social, culture.

Intuitively, this should be an ideal task for social science. The social sciences presumably are concerned with the social, and are thus in a position to insist on those aspects of their inquiry that are *not* individual and *not* governmental. That is, our object of social inquiry S can be partially located by its x (individual) and y (governmental) coordinates, but cannot be understood, because what defines S is not x, and not y, but something else, which we loosely and vaguely label 'the social'. The geometer would be inclined to label this the 'z' axis (and would be happy to consider the construction of n-spaces), but we will call it the 'g' axis, for reasons explained further on. The question, now, is how may we come to understand and begin to understand politics outside the liberal plane, in social terms, somewhere along the g-axis? How can we see our lives together in (at least) three dimensions?

Where to start?

We all have social experiences; we participate in organizations that are not reducible to the state. What happens if we think of such organizations from a participatory, internal, perspective? As members of organizations, we do this all the time: we have intensely 'political' discussions that are not reducible to the state or the citizens, but turn on understandings of the institution in question. Consider, in this regard, faculty politics. Academics speak (and hire, deny tenure and so on) on the basis of what they expect from their discipline and their colleagues, and more or less implicitly, based on their understanding of the purpose or end of the faculty. In philosophical terms, academics regularly and unselfconsciously engage in teleological discussions of faculty politics. Much the same can be said about participation in not-for-profits, with their endless retreats, discussions, restatements and refinements (gradually acknowledged to be insufficient until the cycle is begun anew) of 'the mission'. Even business, nominally organized by the profit motive, is in fact organized by teleological discourses, often under the rubric of 'growing the brand' or 'the business model', depending if one emphasizes marketing or finance. 'Profit' is great, but without more, invocations of the profit motive say nothing about what is to be done today, tomorrow, next quarter and by whom, and in lieu of what. Thus to understand a corporation as an operating company (as opposed to an economic or legal abstraction) in terms of the profit motive is a fatal oversimplification because it precludes the key question: What is this social institution about, 'what do we do here?' Or to put it in more comfortably philosophical terms, what is our purpose, our collective *raison d'être*, our *telos*? Such questions are routinely asked, and answered, in corporations, churches, schools, even government agencies.

***

By this point, we are well and truly off the liberal plane. To see why this is so, a short detour may be helpful to some readers. Recall that on the liberal plane, institutions are located in terms of the individual's interest (x) and the government's interest (y). Recall also that the individual's interest is assumed to be self-interest, that is, individual. From this perspective, it is 'rational' for individuals to understand institutions, for example a corporation, in terms of 'what have you done for me'. What is good for the institution is not the issue for *homo economicus*, except insofar as it benefits him.

The view is somewhat more complicated from the perspective of the modern liberal state. As noted earlier, the 'state' at issue here is first and foremost an idea, a pole of discourse. The modern Western state at least publicly legitimates itself on the basis of impartial process (the rule of law) and democratic choice (autonomy) rather than shared notions of identity, the good or the will of God. Leaders are elected rather than born. The state acts 'rationally', in the sense that Weber spoke of the formal rationality of bureaucratic officials, who do their duty rather than impose their will (like nobles). This familiar complex of ideas is what we mean by 'modern' and, in this context, 'liberal'.

The most famous recent statement of these ideas is Fukuyama's argument that liberal ideology occupies the discursive field, and hence, that history understood as ideological contest has come to an end (Fukuyama 1989). This was hotly contested and generally denied. Even in the halcyon days after the fall of communism, many people argued that time had not stopped, and history, therefore, continued. This was not quite fair – Fukuyama never argued that time stopped. But more tellingly, many argued that ideological contest continued – witness not only the discontent over globalization, the suppression of dissent in China and elsewhere, but also 9/11, the US wars in the Middle East and latterly, the Arab Spring.

Part of the difficulty in this controversy was that the topic itself is somewhat amorphous. Even considered philosophically, the idea of the state cannot be completely disentangled from states as experienced in social life or governments. By extension, history understood in Hegelian terms as the evolution of ideas recognized as civilized cannot be completely sundered from actual history, often quite brutal, even in civilized places, as Hegel well knew. But even if we turn from philosophers' history to historians' or journalists' history, there is some reason to consider the triumph of liberalism rather carefully. So, for recent examples in the United States, traditional understandings of marriage have been both transformed in favor of more contractual notions of partnership, and legally, have given way to claims for equal protection. Such conceptual developments seem to many people to be 'modern', and opposition to such developments decidedly unmodern.

Triumphal liberalism is often supported precisely in those instances in which modern states do not live up to their liberal self-image or, sometimes, ideals. Surely relatively homogenous states, many in Europe, in fact do have shared notions of identity and the good, often tacit. Even in such situations, however, the ideology of liberalism reigns. So when, for example, European nations become more Muslim, there may be a nativist backlash – which is immediately branded (from a liberal perspective) as xenophobic, even racist, and hence simply outside the bounds of acceptable discourse. Entire political parties may be banned. Or consider the convoluted ways in which the neutral term 'diversity' is used in the United States as a stand in for, again, not just race, but American-born, black, 'African-Americans'. Or consider the insistence on 'patients' rights' in hospitals. One might continue ad nauseam; liberalism simply is how we speak, even (especially?) when other things are on our minds.

On the other hand, those 'other things on our minds' may raise the suspicion that the anodyne language of liberalism is a rather too polite account of the present. International relations hardly seem governed by the elegantly liberal language of public international law. Technology, and especially destruction more or less creative, does not seem to obey the rules of contract. Dionysus, to say nothing of animal spirits, suffuses our capitalism. Democracy, understood as public reason, is in short supply even where it used to be most common, and has never taken root or been extirpated elsewhere. In short, there is much else to be said about our history, especially under conditions of globalization. To quip, we may be at the end of history, but it is not enlightened liberalism that we have achieved. Or so I have argued. Be that as it may, I think it is hard to dispute Fukuyama's claim that liberalism has triumphed as a matter of ideology, if not for all time, at least for the foreseeable future.

From the perspective of the liberal state, with its rational officials, as from the perspective of the rational individual, 'the social good' is not really an issue. The purpose of the state is to preserve order (requiring the defense of the state itself), and to ensure some level of material well-being, but not to adjudicate transcendent matters (for example, religion) or private matters (such as sex and, in some versions, recreational chemicals). If anything, this is even more true in advanced economies, for instance Germany, which provide substantial material goods but seem drearily purposeless. Or, as law and economics scholars never tire of reminding us, the state is necessary to secure property and contract, so that individuals may pursue their own happiness. All of this is familiar; there are local variations; much is in bad faith – but the general ideological imagination is clear, and has been since Hobbes. Individuals surrender some of their autonomy to Leviathan, in exchange for security. Leviathan, perhaps restrained by a regime of rights and countervailing institutions – first exemplified by the US Constitution, leaves a 'space' in which individuals pursue their own ends. Nowhere in this scheme is the social good articulated as an end in itself.

This imagination of political life has been criticized since it was articulated. To schematize: liberal political life is an order, yes, but the Hobbesian state is formed among strangers who may disagree about everything, who may share nothing – who may have no community, indeed who would otherwise seek to kill one another. How can one love, owe allegiance to, Leviathan? The refinements of Locke and Montesquieu may make the state safer, but hardly make it more loveable. Since Leviathan will act forcefully to defend its hegemony (indeed, this is how Weber defines the state), the individual under liberalism finds himself at best alienated, at worst dominated, by strangers. (This is Rousseau's critique, or, if one reconfigures the argument with attention to property, Marx.) Thus, philosophically speaking, the absence of shared conceptions of 'the good' becomes central to creating states whose members do not feel unduly alienated or even tyrannized.[8]

From this perspective, the nature and importance of the social is clear: it is within social institutions, which are neither state nor individuals, that the good can be fostered, articulated and used to form community. The social provides what liberalism needs but has had to suppress. Or, to put it in terms from *Flatland*, it is social life that gives depth and volume to the otherwise flat schema sketched by the interplay between government and market individuals.

***

The triumph of liberal language may impede political life in contemporary societies in more specific, political in the narrower sense of partisan, ways. Much political contest is inadequately, if at all, expressed by the relationship between 'individual' and 'state' interests. In most cases, the 'interests' at stake turn on notions that may not be articulable within the terms of liberal discourse, or expressed only awkwardly, for instance, as 'preferences'. As a result, contemporary political discourse tends to be superficial, fails to grasp the issue and descends into mere talk and professional ambition. People turn away. At its worse, the polity itself is undermined, falls into paralysis and/or corruption, as we have seen in country after country since the end of the Cold War, and what policies do emerge advance the commonweal little if at all. In short, people may be hurt unnecessarily.

Less dramatically, liberal politics often just does not work that well, or becomes incomprehensible even to its participants. Consider, in this regard, the government shutdowns in the United States, or the quagmire of European financial regulation, to say nothing of immigration policies on both sides of the Atlantic. Many misunderstandings arise from the fact that many political issues turn on their social aspects, on the g-axis, which is largely unspeakable and so barely thought, much less democratically contested. For further examples, the politics of gun control, or headscarves, or health care or even bank regulation cannot be understood as a sensible balance of individual and government interests. Something else is always at stake, the imagination of what might be (whether hoped for or feared), which is framed and constituted on social (and over time, historical) grounds that are barely cognizable in liberal language. Neither the individual nor the state gives meaning to guns, or headscarves, or health care or even bank regulation, and so political contest over such matters, when it does occur, is weighted down by baggage previously acquired someplace else. Formal politics in liberal societies therefore tends to be belated – the real political moments, when hearts are determined and allegiances made, are earlier, and elsewhere, in that vast terra incognita called the social, or, in terms of this chapter, along the g-axis.

In the United States, the belated nature of political process has come to be protected by law. In *Citizens United*, the Supreme Court held that the First Amendment precluded most regulation of corporate involvement in political campaigns, thereby overturning a great deal of federal law regulating campaign finance.[9] In the Court's view, the First Amendment means, among other things, that the government cannot discriminate among participants in political speech. If some participants happen to be corporations, which the Court understands not as institutions, but as people organized in the corporate form, then no matter. (As an aside, the Court attached no significance to the corporate form, the group, as such – leading to rather grievous errors of corporate law, see Westbrook 2011, pp. 65–73.) The Court thus substantially curtailed Congressional influence on the processes through which American society makes its collective decision on the leadership of the United States. Real politics, then, is left to happen in the formation of opinions, not by government action or even in government fora. In a commercial society, it is unsurprising that money talks very loudly.

While the liberal neutrality enforced by the Court is hardly good news for the democratic governance of the republic, it is good news for social scientists. For it is social science, particularly sociologists and anthropologists of the contemporary, and perhaps even thoughtful journalists, who are best positioned to ask how the social is constituted. More precisely, social inquiry can ask after membership, the shared sense of what matters, how 'we' see the world, our values, that is, those things that make us a 'we'. Thus, as I have argued at great length with regard to contemporary anthropology, what political understanding at the present time requires is not so much an analysis of the objective interests of the state (as often asserted by international relations) or the collective objectives of rational individuals (the 'demand' of economics), but an essentially subjective understanding of the world as perceived from within various groups, especially those with power (Westbrook 2008). So, for example, how do central bankers, or populist parties in Greece, see the world? What are the political consequences of acting upon such imaginaries?

Leaving the liberal plane to explore the g-dimension of social life, however illiberal, offers the possibility of a deeper understanding of more than just political allegiance and the exercise of power, as important as such things are. We may also learn much more of the ways in which it is possible for people who find themselves here, now, to be modern. The 'individual' lives, grows and so is formed through participation in and identification with groups, and so acts as a consumer, a voter and otherwise in ways that express that identification. But what constitutes the groups within the individual's imagination? Some groups are easily defined, at least at the first cut, for example, the football club for which a fan cheers, or the church he attends. Other groups, such as implied by 'the security community' or 'hackers' or consumers of 'Aeropostale' may be harder to delineate with any trenchancy, but it is such groups (or the state in a somewhat illicit, illiberal, role – consider the *esprit de corps* of military units) that give lives meaning.

As should perhaps be evident but may be worth saying explicitly, the vast human environment denominated by 'the social' is worth exploring for its own sake.[10] Most of our lives (especially in the United States) are conducted in civil society, the corporations, schools, local governments, synagogues, clubs and even universities – the terrain on which we live is social. A map, or even a coffee table book, describing the place (our home, such as it is) would be of interest.

Let me close by making two perhaps obvious analytical points.

First, while social science may still find itself constrained to present itself as a science, the inquiry at issue here is into collective subjectivity, and thus inherently interpretive, rather than objective. Economics presents the desire of the individual as data, quantified by price – demand. Political science presents the interests of the state in similar fashion. But the inquiry urged here asks why the individual, or the state, wants *this* and not *that*? In what world, to what end, is *this* understood to be good, worth organizing for, demanding sacrifice for? Rephrased, if the new science distinguished itself from its ancestors by abandoning teleology (Galileo), it is precisely the reengagement with teleology that is urged here, not for the study of nature, but for the study of communities, with their constitutive norms. Thus, more deeply, one cannot understand inquiries along the g-axis, the axis of teleology, as science.

Second, the tables have turned: we began confronting the social by mapping it in terms of the individual's interests (x) and the interests of the state (y). Now we are thinking about the social (g) in order to make sense of the interests that the individual and the state claim. From this perspective, the qualitative social sciences in which the authors of this book have built their careers could be seen as almost poetic inquiries into what is prior to, rather than derivative of, our imaginations of Leviathan and *homo economicus*.[11]

NOTES

1. Louis A. Del Cotto Professor of Law, State University of New York (SUNY) at Buffalo Law School. My thanks to Perry Alexander, Jack Schlegel and Sophia Westbrook for indulging my puns on the mathematical tradition. Further thanks to Douglas Holmes and Joseph Westbrook for quick gut checks. I really appreciate the encouragement and patience of Christina Garsten and Adrienne Sörbom, for otherwise I would not have finished this confection. Matthew Zambito provided excellent research assistance. The failings are my responsibility.
2. This present polarity, described in terms of 'left' and 'right', is a legacy of the French Revolution, and so a few centuries younger, see Gauchet 1996.
3. At least as a non-negative real number – the metaphor of balancing interests is quantitative, and quantities are presumed to be zero or positive.
4. As Lord Palmerston famously said: 'England has no eternal friends, and no eternal enemies; only eternal interests' (Kagan 1995, p. 144). Substitute any state for 'England'.
5. Balancing competing interests runs through Constitutional jurisprudence. See, for example, *Roe v. Wade*, 410 U.S. 113 (1973).
6. This harks back to Nietzsche's objection to Hegel's 'universal and homogeneous state' (see Fukuyama 1992, pp. 300–312).
7. By touch and visual acuity, Flatlanders can perceive distance, so A. Square sees the sphere as a circle rather than a line.
8. The life of the nation happens at the borders, or even outside, its ideology. The United States is the most legalistic of countries, literally founded by lawyers, acting through documents. But very little of even the United States can be understood or explained by our social contract; too much happens outside the four corners of the documents. From this perspective, liberalism is a partial, even disingenuous, discourse (Westbrook 2003).
9. *Citizens United v. Federal Election Commission*, 558 U.S. 310 (2010). See also (Westbrook 2011).
10. As an aside, it might be argued that understanding intellectual life, and particularly academic life, in terms of the duality composed by the individual and the state is perhaps a trace of the university understood in essentially national terms (see Readings 1996).
11. See Neil Simon's brilliant meditation on Chekhov, *The Good Doctor* (1973).

REFERENCES

Abbott, E.A. (1884), *Flatland: A Romance of Many Dimensions*, in [1998], London: Penguin Classics.

Fukuyama, F. (1989), 'The end of history?', *The National Interest* 16 (Summer 1989).
Fukuyama, F. (1992), *The End of History and the Last Man*, New York: Macmillan.
Gauchet, M. (1996), 'Right and left', in L.D. Kritzman (ed.), *Realms of Memory: Rethinking the French Past, Vol. 1*, New York: Columbia University Press, pp. 241–98.
Greenberg, P.S. (1973), 'The balance of interests theory and the fourth amendment: A selective analysis of supreme court action since *Camara* and *See*', *California Law Review* **61** (4), 1011–47.
Huxley, A. (1932), *Brave New World*, London: Chatto & Windus.
Kagan, D. (1995), *On the Origins of War and the Preservation of Peace*, New York: Doubleday.
Readings, B. (1996), *The University in Ruins*, Cambridge, MA: Harvard University Press.
Westbrook, D.A. (2003), 'Le "noble mensonge" de l'Amérique après le 11 septembre' ['Constituting a Nation, Making a Home, After September 11th'], *La Revue Nouvelle* **116** (3) 89.
Westbrook, D.A. (2004), *City of Gold*, New York: Routledge.
Westbrook, D.A. (2007), *Between Citizen and State: An Introduction to the Corporation*, Boulder, CO: Paradigm Publishers.
Westbrook, D.A. (2008), *Navigators of the Contemporary: Why Ethnography Matters*, Chicago: University of Chicago Press.
Westbrook, D.A. (2011), 'If not a commercial republic? Political economy in the United States after Citizens United', *University of Louisville Law Review* **50** (35), 35–85.

Index